# THE REINVENTION
# OF RELIGIOUS MUSIC

# THE REINVENTION
# OF RELIGIOUS MUSIC

*Olivier Messiaen's Breakthrough Toward the Beyond*

*Sander van Maas*

Fordham University Press

New York   2009

Library of Congress Cataloging-in-Publication Data

Maas, Sander van, 1968–
The reinvention of religious music : Olivier Messiaen's breakthrough toward the beyond / Sander van Maas.
    p.   cm.
  Includes bibliographical references.
  ISBN 978-0-8232-3057-0 (cloth : alk. paper)
    1. Messiaen, Olivier, 1908–1992—Criticism and interpretation.
2. Music—Religious aspects.—Christianity.   I. Title.
ML410.M595M34   2009
781.70092—dc22

                                                    2008047148


Printed in the United States of America
First paperback printing 2012

*To Jan Dijkstra,*
*Earwitness*

# Contents

Preface                                                     ix

Acknowledgments                                             xi

Introduction                                                 1

1.  It Is a Glistening Music We Seek                        13
2.  Five Times Breakthrough                                 37
3.  Balthasar and the Religion of Music                     61
4.  The Gift of Dazzlement                                  89
5.  The Technics of Breakthrough                           126
6.  The Circumcision of the Ear                            158

Epilogue: On Affirmation                                   179

Notes                                                      181

Bibliography                                               221

# Preface

At a time when culture has increasingly become the field of play where the opposing forces of secularization and religion meet, the question of the position of art is acquiring new meaning. Today, the secular status that art has held since the Enlightenment, and that was almost immediately contested by the adversaries of this revolution, has come increasingly under pressure. A development comes into view, not only in the visual arts but also and especially in music, that actualizes the question of the religious meaning of music or of listening to music. Since the fall of the Berlin Wall, the work of a number of composers with an explicit religious thematics has reached the West, and it seems that, within the canon of Western European and North American traditions, there is less diffidence in publicly touching upon religious and spiritual themes. Such developments once again make clear that involving religious perspectives in the practice of creating and (to a lesser extent) performing music has never fully disappeared; that even those moments in the history of twentieth-century music that were, ostentatiously, among the most antireligious or areligious were accompanied by a certain religious-spiritual discourse all the same.

Academic thought on the relation between music and religion, however, appears to be seriously anemic. Musicology—whether historical, formalist, or "new"—seems to have lost the sense for studying music as a phenomenon with a certain penchant for religion. The social process of secularization and the diminished significance of religious practice and theology entailed by this have created circumstances in which publicly testifying to the possibility of a *musica sacra* has become increasingly less acceptable. Musicography (both inside and outside academia) has followed this dual trend, discarding religious music as the subject for critical and systematic study. As a phenomenon with a relation (frequently either underestimated or overestimated) to the religious, music forms no subject for debate, unless it be either in circles of all too credulous music lovers who, wholly in the spirit of the Enlightenment, are guided by their own individual opinions, or with those who,

steering by the beacon of dogma, adhere to theological and practical orthodoxy—each group, in other words, having particular reasons for shunning
a critical distance in broaching the subject. Such approaches have become
outdated, because of both the return of the religious in the public intellectual debate and far-reaching transformations of orthodox forms of religion
in the contemporary world.

This new momentum, which appeared to have found an ideal vehicle in
the music and discourse of Olivier Messiaen, is precisely the impulse for
writing this book. Many agree that, as a child of the twentieth century and
thoroughly aware of contemporary developments in art, religion, and society, Messiaen paved the way for a new, open form of musical religiosity.
The public has discovered his music by now, and many are attracted by it,
searching in one way or another for more than just the notes and construc-
tive principles that Messiaen so gladly elucidated. Without doubt, his music
is "*bien harmonisée*," but at the same time there is something in listening to
his music that requires an analysis not just in technical terms. As I discovered
in the early stages of research, neither aesthetics nor theology dispose of the
adequate means to this end—and, in this respect, musicology or theory of
music do not appear to be very fruitful, either. An attempt to counter the
risks, in contemporary thought, of a facile rejection of the strange yet famil-
iar talent of music to relate in one way or another to the religious, this book
is most of all concerned with the question of offering a different perspective
on a modern dilemma, by freshly exploring the possibilities for continuing
to think through precisely the disconcerting dream that was fostered by the
lore of ancient, naïve, but possibly so wise philosophy of music: a music that
escapes the constitutive coordinates of the aesthetic object.

*Acknowledgments*

This book would not have been written if I did not have the support of many people. Foremost, I wish to thank Hent de Vries, who over the years has inspired my writing and enriched my mind with his overwhelming erudition and grand-scale approach to matters philosophical and theological. I feel privileged that I could always rely on his warm support and encouragement for this wildly interdisciplinary project. My other supervisor, Rokus de Groot, deserves an equal share of my gratitude for his infinite patience and his preparedness to let me go into any direction I wanted. In our many sessions he showed me how the ear is the organ of curiosity and that, ultimately, to think well is to listen well. Of all the others who have contributed to this book—and there are many more than I can mention here—Kiene Brillenburg Wurth should be mentioned as the true savior of the project. Although we have had more beautiful things to share since the birth of Titus, I cherish the days in Amsterdam and Paris when it seemed that every stone in the pavement hid a crucial insight for the argument of the manuscript. Her love for nineteenth-century theories of art opened my eyes for what was really at stake, and surely I am not alone in this respect. However, all this could have led to the present book only through the support of one incredible person, whose career spans the publication of many books cited in the pages that follow: Fordham University Press editor Helen Tartar. It was she who inspired and supported unwaveringly the translation and reworking of the original Dutch book. I thank Aleid Fokkema for translating the wide-ranging and sometimes technically difficult manuscript so skillfully, and the Dutch Organization for Scientific Research (NWO) for their financial support. I thank Andrew Shenton and the anonymous reviewer for their support for and critical comments on earlier versions of the manuscript and, last but not least, editors Gregory McNamee and Eric Newman for their diligent work in the final stages. Needless to say, all remaining flaws are mine.

And it came to pass, when the minstrel played, that the hand of the Lord came upon him.

—2 Kings 3:15

*Auris prima mortis ianua, prima aperiatur et vitae.*
The ear was death's first gateway; let it be the first to open up to life.

—Bernard of Clairvaux, *Sermons on the Song of Songs* 28:5

# Introduction

Is what is convincing also true? This classic question often preoccupied me when leaving the concert hall or church where, just before, a work by the French composer Olivier Messiaen (Avignon, December 10, 1908–Paris, April 27, 1992) had been performed. The question seems naïve, because the occasion is so evidently about experiencing a work of art that is manufactured, shaped by human hands, not a religious, sacramental ritual. Nonetheless, the great power of some of Messiaen's work still forces this question on the listener—and I am not alone in this respect. The euphoric ovations or reverent testimony of the audience of, for example, performances of Messiaen's oratory *La Transfiguration* in the Amsterdam Concertgebouw in 1991, or the concert performance of his opera *Saint François d'Assise* in 2000 (in the same venue), might point to an experience of something "other," something that cannot simply be ascribed to musical persuasion.[1]

The question, then, is whether the musical experience of the work of Messiaen merely results from ingenious rhetorical techniques, or whether something else—or something more—is the matter, and, if indeed something more is the matter, whether this surplus should be understood in terms of Messiaen's *religious* program (which the audience is presumably aware of, if not through the music then by means of the program notes), or rather in terms of a surplus in the *aesthetic* experience, an excess that can no longer be described in terms of beautiful persuasion. In this respect, the words of the (probably) first-century author Longinus provide food for thought. In his tract on the sublime, *Peri hypsous*, he points to an alternative for persuasion:

> The effect of elevated language is not to persuade the hearers, but to entrance them; and at all times, and in every way, what transports us with wonder is more telling than what merely persuades or gratifies us. The extent to which we can be persuaded is usually under our own control, but these sublime passages exert an irresistible force and mastery, and get the upper hand with every hearer. Inventive skill and the proper order and disposition of material

are not manifested in a good touch here and there, but reveal themselves by slow degrees as they run through the whole composition; on the other hand, a well-timed stroke of sublimity scatters everything before it like a thunderbolt, and in a flash reveals the full power of the speaker.[2]

With this structure of overwhelming, the sublime seems to show the way to describing the intense experience in listening to Messiaen's work. Because it is a phenomenon that has always been closely connected to religion, the question of the truth of this experience is easy to understand. The last words in the quotation, however, yet again point to the problematics of answering the question of truth, and now in a more disconcerting and ambivalent way. The conclusion that the whole spectacle reveals the power *of the speaker*, and perhaps not of (divine) truth, indicates an aporia, because if the force of persuasion still could be reduced to (musical-rhetorical) argumentation, here we have a phenomenon that appears as an enigma, a flash, a thunderbolt. It becomes manifest in the manner of an irrational, (pseudo-) religious revelation; it presents itself as coming "from the beyond," but it is, according to Longinus, also *at once* a sign of the force of genius, the speaker, the deft illusionist. The notion of the sublime, which as such seems to be such an apt concept for the music of Messiaen, entails the question of the boundary between truth and technique, between revelation and construction; and between religion, philosophy, and art. How to decide on the overwhelming of *La Transfiguration* or *Saint François d'Assise* as the event of truth, on the one hand, but on the other as a sublime truth *effect*, the *apparent* event of truth in the manner of *as if*?

The question of this distinction is central to this book. Is what is musically overwhelming also true? The starting point in elaborating this question is formed by a lecture that Messiaen delivered in Paris, in 1977. Here, he states that a "breakthrough toward the beyond" is possible in music, and in his music particularly. This would be related to seeing colors inwardly when hearing certain chords and clusters (synesthesia), and to the experience of an inner "dazzlement" (*éblouissement*) that might be evoked by this. In the eyes of Messiaen, this concerns a *religious* experience, which in a lecture of 1985 he related to meticulously specified passages from *La Transfiguration de Notre-Seigneur Jésus-Christ* (1965–69). This brings, however, the latent contradictions in his Notre-Dame lecture to a head; namely, that the absolute, no matter how tentative, cannot only be experienced, but can moreover be experienced in the context of art and can even—in a paradox that borders on blasphemy—be evoked by art. In his later work, Messiaen emphasizes the idea that truth is connected with manifestation, with a dazzling, over-whelming manifestation. This implies that the question of the relation between rhetorical overwhelming and truth should be phrased more accurately as the question of the relation between manifestation and truth. Is what cannot become more manifest (that is, a music that dazzles its listener) also true?[3]

Messiaen's critics signaled and named the paradox early on. Peter Hill and Nigel Simeone reconstruct the history of the so-called Case of Messiaen in their recent biography of the composer.[4] The phrase refers to the critical debate on the work of the composer that arose early in 1945. The cause lay in the premiere of the piano cycle *Vingt regards sur l'Enfant-Jésus* (Twenty Adorations of the Child Jesus) in Paris in March 1945. In response to this premiere, Bernard Gavoty, the reviewer of the *Figaro* who probably can be credited with launching the debate, makes short shrift of the music and commentaries of Messiaen. He mocks the "abysmal" language used by the composer in commenting for this occasion on the music—in person and before each of the twenty parts. The music itself did not meet with his approval, either. Gavoty describes Messiaen as an "erudite composer who is a prisoner of his own system, attempting to translate the sublime utterances of the Apocalypse through muddled literature and music, smelling of the hair shirt, in which it is impossible to detect either any usefulness or any pleasure." Such trenchant criticism prepares for the paradox that is at the center of Gavoty's objections against Messiaen: "There is a persistent contradiction here: like a lunatic curator of a vanished museum, the composer announces marvels when he speaks, but which the piano immediately refutes."

Despite colorful language and keen observations, however, the result of the debate between supporters and critics of Messiaen was disappointing. His critics can be granted with a fine sense of the scandal in Messiaen's music: the fact that, in the eyes of some, his music breathes "a whiff of sulfur," signals that apparently a line has been crossed. Such a transgression, however, might also have been read in light of Messiaen's entering a new territory, and a closer examination of the alleged incongruences in his work would have been more fitting. But this did not happen. At the close of the debate a year later (although Messiaen felt that the denouncement lasted for at least a decade), it was clear that the majority of Messiaen's critics saw the composer as "a very great musician of our time," and that "the majority are also in agreement about rejecting all the literature and commentaries which the composer or certain bumbling exegetes place around his works, and concur that these do the music a disservice." Keeping notes and commentary apart, separating religion from music: this has largely been the state of affairs ever since. The new territory broached by Messiaen has disappeared from view. All we know is that, yes, Messiaen is an excellent composer, a craftsman, a musical genius perhaps, and whatever else he appended to his musical music notes is secondary and in essence a private matter.

With respect to aesthetics, something comparable occurs. The notion of *musica sacra*, pertinent to Messiaen in this respect and particularly in his discourse on "breakthrough toward the beyond," is highly problematic in our modern age, and so is, by extension, the radical possibility in music that he points out. The phenomenon of a musicosacral blinding or overwhelming (*éblouissement* or dazzlement) has become—both in Messiaen's discourse and outside it—stuck between, on one hand, the modern view on art, which is mainly determined by its humanist, aesthetic, and technological coordinates; and, on the other hand, a theology of the glory of God, which seeks to understand beauty in art as a reflection of nonmanufactured (that is, nonhumanistic, nonaesthetical, and nontechnological) divine splendor. This book ventures to overcome the split between these respective musicological and theological approaches to Messiaen's music, and, in the wake of this, to give an impulse to the thought on the musicosacral or the sacromusical. To this end, the question of the interface between the musical and the religious is at the core of this study, and in particular the issue of criteria for distinguishing *éblouissement* as a religious experience with the paradigmatic trope of "breakthrough toward the beyond," and *éblouissement* as a nonreligious experience.[5] Because this latter experience would imply, theologically speaking, an adoration of music *as such*, which means that it is removed from all theological transcendence, I will use the notion of musicolatry—a term coined by Philippe Lacoue-Labarthe—to refer to the logical reverse of breakthrough. If the split outlined here is not to remain the false fundamental for thinking about the relation between religion and music, then this relation will have to be thought all over again from the start—in other words, the whole idea of what *musica sacra* is needs to be reconsidered, with no prior guarantee, by the way, of (re)discovering a simple, healing harmony between the constitutive parts of this term.

The question of the distinction, in musical experience, between breakthrough and musical idolatry, first calls for a debate on the notion of orthodoxy, which traditionally hovers over the background of Messiaen discussions. The pretence, however, that there is a priori clarity about what does or does not belong to the domain of faith, a distinction that subsequently enables determining what is Christian, let alone Catholic, about Messiaen's music, must be abandoned. In order to be able to attain a reflection on the Christian in Messiaen's music, the *singularity* of his music needs to be considered. A theology that is restricted to the aim of reaffirming doctrines that have already been confirmed will never be able to think about religious *music* as such. It is not the interpretation of music as a *representation* of faith that will lead us to the musically Christian, but the interpretation of the structure of the *actual* experience of music. As I will further clarify, therefore, my approach is removed from the hermeneutical reflexes in theology. Conversely, art scholarship that intends to think only in secular terms about its object will never be able to approach the singularity of *religious* music as such. Thinking on music and its musicological representations therefore needs to be pried open, too. As will become clear in the following chapters, the distance between musicology and theology is much less wide than is usually assumed, and the difference between the two is, in some respects, undecidable.

Thinking about the boundary between music and religion and considering the relation between them inevitably brings, apart from the concept of religious music, its possible reversal to the fore in the form of a (pseudo-) religious cult of music. An exemplary historical expression of such a move is found in nineteenth-century *Kunstreligion*, religion of art, in which music not only surpassed all other art forms but also eventually vied with religion itself in revealing mystery. In this book, the concept of musicolatry does not so much concern this historical attempt at substituting religion by music as the systematic problem of this reversal and the structural possibilities it entails.[6] My question about *criteria* for the distinction between breakthrough and musicolatry can thus be reformulated as a question of the distinction between theological aesthetics and aesthetical theology, that is to say, between a discourse on beauty as an element of a more encompassing theology on one hand and the absorption of theology by the discourse on beauty on the other.[7] Ludwig Tieck's famous remark that music is "the ultimate mystery of faith, the mystique, the completely revealed religion" constitutes an example of the latter.[8] It is tempting but dangerous to discard such a substitution of religion as sheer idolatry, because the assumption of knowing what idolatry is, or musicolatry for that matter, implicitly involves the presumption of knowing mystery. Therefore, this book is not oriented toward observing the work of Messiaen within the pure limits of orthodox theological aesthetics, as has so frequently been done, or toward portraying it as a twentieth-century variant on heterodox religion of music. Instead, it intends to explore precisely what constitutes the quiddity of demarcating religious music. What does it mean to draw a line between "inside" and "outside," between orthodoxy on one hand and heterodoxy or idolatry (or musicolatry) on the other? In its tow, the question arises what Messiaen, *homme de foi*, may have meant when he asserted that there is no such thing as sacred or profane music. This book is driven by the conviction that one can aspire to come close to the (possible) phenomenon of the musicosacral or the sacromusical only by positing this demarcation question continuously and persistently.

In elaborating on this question, it is foremost important to resist the temptation of reducing Messiaen's testimony regarding the "breakthrough toward the beyond" to little more than a certain desire on the part of the composer, or to a symbolic, metaphorical, or perhaps allegorical representation of the content of faith. The latter is truly tempting, because the Thomistic conception of music, namely that religious music is subservient to the Word and to the liturgy, invites such a move in interpreting the self-declared Thomist, Messiaen.[9] It is the route of escape for music, however, inasmuch as the focus is no longer on what or how music *is*, but only on what it *means* in a religious context. The majority of theological interpretations of Messiaen rely on the skeptical attitude with respect to the religious *force* of music. The composer's remarks about a breakthrough cannot easily be accommodated to this framework; they testify to an uncommon faith in music that usually is not found in these circles. The Platonic (or Neoplatonic) character of the images that Messiaen uses in his discourse, together with the description of dazzlement (*éblouissement*) and the great sensitivity to the theological possibilities of beauty, rather appear to require an Augustinian reading of breakthrough with Messiaen, who equally was a self-declared Franciscan as well.[10] This reading, which is examined in the present study, involves an important reorientation: away from the contents of his music (so generously suggested and commented upon by Messiaen himself) and toward the *structure* of musical experience. The formal approach that this move requires is not characterized by its focus on formal musical structure (departing from the available and all too privileged formal representations such as scores) for describing the source of this experience, but on the manifestation of music in the phenomenal sense. The ritual character of Messiaen's music has often been signaled, but in this book I will argue that the

Christianness of his music is not about understanding musical-religious *content*, let alone about the event or sense of religion, but instead about the structure of musical-religious experience as such. An orientation to this structure is necessary for clarifying "breakthrough" and, more generally, Christianness (in Heidegger's terms) in Messiaen's music.[11] As will become clear, especially in Chapter 2 and Chapter 4, musical forms of *kenosis* play an important part in this.

The method used for this study is syncretistic, for reasons born of both practical necessity and strategy. Although the literature on Messiaen is extensive, it is limited with respect to the problematic outlined here. I have cherished the most important examples of critical and theological approaches to Messiaen, and they are given ample attention here. The lack of specifically relevant literature might have been compensated for by a plethora of literature on music and religion in general, but the field is rather barren here, too. In 2000 Jeremy Begbie, who has done much since to fill the gaps, arrived at the same conclusion in his study on the theology of musical time. The list of mostly English-language references that he supplies is modest. The most remarkable title in the field is Jon Michael Spencer's *Theomusicology*, which has named a new discipline to be developed further.[12] The collection of essays edited by Joyce Irwin, *Sacred Sound*, remains somewhat of an early classic.[13] Of great importance but often overlooked is Albert Blackwell's *The Sacred in Music*.[14] Outside the English language, it is most of all German publications that call for attention. These include the impressive but now slightly outdated compendium of Oskar Söhngen, *Theologie der Musik*, and the important volume edited by Helga de la Motte-Haber, *Musik und Religion*.[15] I have attempted to draw as much as I could from these and other sources, but the phenomenological character of my question required roaming the fields of more remote literatures.[16]

The strategic motive for maintaining a certain distance with respect to the methods used, and for admitting a certain methodological heterogeneity, is contained in the role of the deconstructive logic of *iterability* in this study. This logic controls to a large extent—although often only in the background—the argument in the second half of this book. It paves the way for thinking together singularity and repetition, two tropes that guide the argument in the twin forms of miracle and technique, or breakthrough and musicolatry. The argument in this book throughout will continuously work toward effectuating this logic of iterability, in respect to which the more traditional analytical methods used will be treated with some reservation. This methodical disbelief has prompted a certain aloofness from a strictly formalist analytical tradition in discussing Messiaen's music in Chapter 2, but also from the phenomenological approach in Chapter 4. My uses of phenomenological methods or perspectives deviates, in this respect, from the way Thomas Clifton (*Music as Heard*) famously applied phenomenology to the purpose of musical analysis, or from the work of Mikel Dufrenne, where phenomenological premises as such are less the subject of debate.[17] Apart from that, the logic of iterability bridges the gap between Augustinian thought on musical experience and contemporary critical thinking, especially in the French tradition.[18] As I will attempt to show, this logic offers the possibility of discussing formally marginalized problems in the actual context that concerns the relation between music and religion. Finally, methodic disbelief also suits the methodic atheism that acts as an underlying principle for the possibility of addressing the question of religious music (or musical religion—that will be the persistent question) again. An ironical or critical distance, an *epochè*, is maintained with regard to theological problematics, in order to create room for thinking through the arguments and practices of composers and thinkers regarding the sacrality of music. In this respect, the present study takes part of a wider interdisciplinary discussion about the boundaries of philosophy and theology—a discussion that, as far as I am concerned, will be extended to, and will have consequences for exploring the relation between music and relation, or musicology and theology.[19]

My starting point in Chapter 1 is the question of what Messiaen exactly had in mind with his compositions. Messiaen here appears to be a musician who presumes of an orthodox, unshakeable faith, emphatically marked by hope, that has always, directly or indirectly, been oriented to the Revelation of John. As I will demonstrate, there was a gradual shift with Messiaen in the musical localization of religion. Where, in his earlier works, he emphasizes the sincerity of feelings, his later sayings on the objective in composing create the impression that this subjective dimension has faded into the background or indeed has disappeared from view. This is especially true for the 1960s, the period of composing *La Transfiguration*. The second part of this chapter is devoted to the question of Messiaen's conception of the relation between music and religion—a relation that has been decisive for a composer who believed that it was his primary and most important mission to illuminate the truths of faith. It will become apparent that Messiaen was ambivalent both about the idea of pure music, whose formalistic core he wished to retain, and about the idea of expression. The rejection of programmatic music here leads to the question whether there is a case of musical mysticism in Messiaen. The chapter ends with an inventory of the theoretical figures that provided Messiaen with the possibility, in his view, for realizing his project. It turns out that for Messiaen, music can approach, beyond the level of liturgy and religion, the proximity of the beyond when synesthetic means are employed. It is here that the key passage of this study, on the thematics of dazzlement, makes an entry.

The compositional side of the music of dazzlement will receive closer attention in Chapter 2, inasmuch as the idea of aiming for theological music and the search for theoretical openings represent only part of the story. Messiaen gave concrete examples of the music of dazzlement in one of his lectures. These concern five passages from *La Transfiguration* (and besides a part from the final act of *Saint François d'Assise*, Messiaen's opera and magnum opus) that he describes in detail. In the concise consecutive analysis of these passages, it becomes apparent that there are great mutual differences between them, but also a number of tendencies that they have in common. It can be established, for instance, that, at the site of the spectacle of breakthrough and dazzlement, Messiaen is doing a great deal more than evoking synesthetic effects in his music. There are aspects of narrativity and mise-en-scène in play that suggest a step beyond musical content in the direction of form. Form is not really to be understood in the sense of a formalist theory of music, but in the sense of presentation and manifestation; or the motion of revelation as such (instead of presenting some kind of content, message, symbolism, and the like). This conclusion is related to the observation that there is, after 1950 or so, a turn in the music of Messiaen toward the exterior, away from religion as a felt content. The exterior here is quite different from—and subtler than—the alleged objectivity that is often ascribed to Messiaen's music.

Chapter 3 then turns to the theological issue of how music can relate to the Christian in general, and specifically here with respect to Messiaen. In examining this question, I will show that in important aspects, the music of Messiaen appears to fall beyond the theological schemes that it alleges to suit, and that these theological schemes have the greatest difficulty in maintaining what they actually assert. The reference point here is formed by the theology of Hans Urs von Balthasar, the theologian whom Messiaen truly discovered only in his later years. Messiaen considered him to be of particular importance in understanding his work. Balthasar appears to be designated for answering the question of this chapter, because he explicitly addresses, in his theology, the theological interest of beauty and the arts. Form is especially significant to Balthasar; in this, his theology and the practice of Messiaen's music appear to converge. In closely examining one of his first works, which is, as is often the case with the early works of modern philosophers and theologians, about music, it results that the formulation of a theology of music is a risky business. Balthasar bases his musical theology on the notions of Gestalt and on the thought of an "in-formation" of the total Idea in the arts, in the form of a flowing rhythm, theatrical plot development, and evolving melody. As I will attempt to make clear in this chapter, the Gestalt of melody comes as a welcome connective for construing a formal analogy between music and the image of Christ. But, at the same time, this seat of the musical-Christian remains indeterminate. What is more important: it is systematically entwined with the possibility to deteriorate into the musical-demonic. The history of *Kunstreligion* makes it clear that Balthasar can safeguard music for religion only by departing from the Word and subjecting thought about music and religion to the Word.

Because neither a musicology based on theories of music (Chapter 2) nor a theology based on the Word (Chapter 3) appears to be suited for tracking down the particularity of Messiaen's breakthrough, Chapter 4 will embark on a new journey. The phenomenology of Jean-Luc Marion offers an interesting opening, in the perspective of the possibility of studying dazzlement as a phenomenon. Although Marion bases some aspects of his thought on the theology of Balthasar, it is his ambition to come to an analysis of (the possibility of) religious phenomena in sheer philosophical terms, without any appeal on theology. He rejects the Kantian postulates of phenomenology in his works and attempts to show that it is not up to the subject to determine the conditions that are favorable for the manifestation of a given phenomenon, but that, conversely, it is always an excess in the givenness of the world that constitutes the subject. Marion then contrasts everyday experience to two exceptional phenomena that constitute a frame in this chapter for further interpreting the phenomenon of breakthrough. The first is the idol, whose staggering luster is closely related to the thematics of overwhelming in *La Transfiguration*; the second is the icon, which Marion relates to a different sort of excess than the one found in the idol. The icon is not about a blinding reflection that secretly originates in myself, but about a givenness coming from the Other to me, giving me (to myself) in every respect. This chapter is concerned with the question whether the phenomenology of idol and icon provide a key, from "objective evidence," that is, from a quality within music (or from a given excess in music) to thinking the relation between religion and music. I will argue that the position of Messiaen is poised between idolatry and iconicity. The melodic contour that might save, as it were, the iconic countenance of music, appears to converge in Messiaen's work with the intensity of the idol. Although Marion's phenomenology is helpful in clarifying much of what is the matter in Messiaen, it is yet again fundamentally impossible to decide whether dazzlement occurs with respect to breakthrough or whether it is connected, in the end, to musicolatry.

The theme of undecidability returns the discussion to Augustine and the aporetic relation between music and faith that he had noticed already. The music of Messiaen, far from offering an exemplary musical illustration of conventional theological doctrine, looks the undecidable structure of *musica sacra* straight in the eye. This is where the power and challenge of his music lies, and for this reason it is necessary not only to reopen the "Case of Messiaen" but also to keep it open. Chapter 5 sheds a new and different light on the ostentatious conflict (that had already filled the romantics with stupor) between, on the one hand, Messiaen's testimony on the hyperreligious qualities of his music, and, on the other hand, the technicity of the same. In discussion with Paul Griffiths, who proposes in his book on Messiaen that we avoid considering theology in analyzing his music, I will look into the possibilities of evading the break this would cause in the work of Messiaen. It appears that the breaking point can be identified by the use of the concept of technics. It turns out that Griffiths adheres to the view on Messiaen that construes his music, including the composer's ideas on breakthrough and the like, as a representation for which a formal-technical structure provides the scaffolding. Because this would involve an erasure of the actual experience of breakthrough (yielding to the mere representation of breakthrough), I will advance here a concept of technics that can be used for thinking the singularity of breakthrough together with both the structural possibility and empirical cases of the repetitions of it. If, in other words, the artificial character of music constitutes for many a stumbling block for seeing this music as more than a representation of something that was not actually held possible in music, I will postulate here that the technical is a constitutive part of what Messiaen calls breakthrough. Again, the motive of undecidability comes to the fore: the singularity of religious experience is always—whether in music or elsewhere—contaminated with the artificiality and repeatability of technics. As I will show with reference to Kierkegaard, this emerges in Messiaen in the element of kitsch and in the entwinement of breakthrough with the economic, the erotic, and the demonic.

I will abandon phenomenology and the postphenomenological reflection on technique in Chapter 6 in order to focus on what is perhaps the most crucial aspect of breakthrough. Messiaen indicates that this is not so much concerned with seeing (a content being revealed) but with faith and with the *passage* from listening "here" and listening (in the) "beyond," which would involve a different type of listening. Referring to Griffiths once again, what is at stake is not a quality in the object or in the phenomenon proper (as examined in Chapters 3 and 4), but the quality of listening: *how* one listens, or rather: what it means to listen. In inspecting this idea, I will explore, in this chapter, two directions that the Judeo-Christian tradition yields. The first is the circumcision of the ear, which in Jeremiah refers to the difference between the ear that can hear the divine and the ear that cannot. By confronting this concept of listening to the quasi-totalizing manners of listening that are connected to musical formalism (Schoenberg, Adorno), it will become clear that breakthrough cannot be conceived from the act of listening to musical structures. A different relation of listening is required, one that is opening, rather than one that will find what is already given. I will map this other listening by means of the second direction, the notion derived from the patristic tradition of the spiritual ear. The theory of spiritual senses implies an economy of two levels for the senses—the physical senses and the spiritual senses—that are both considered essential for Christianity. Caught in the double entendre of spiritual listening, the ear belongs, as it were, to both sides of the dividing line. As I will demonstrate, Messiaen stands in this tradition of the aporetics of the senses: in a certain fashion, breakthrough has always occurred already and is always, nonetheless, on the verge of taking place. This means that breakthrough toward the beyond, which Messiaen presents as a musical possibility envisaged and realized by him that surpasses religious music, situates the listener at once inside and outside faith. This constitutes the necessity of faith in music, but also its lurking danger.

# 1. *It Is a Glistening Music We Seek*

## Composition: To What End?

Olivier Messiaen is mentioned in many a twentieth-century survey in relation to the role he had in serialism. Around 1950 he was seen as a forerunner in the field of conceptual and technical innovations in music. During this brief period he produced works with often purely technical titles that to all appearances did not refer to religion. But although these works may possess an implicit religious meaning, as some authors have pointed out, Messiaen's overall oeuvre—on paper, in any case—is emphatically determined by the many works with explicit religious titles, themes, and mottos.[1]

In the historical period in which his work came about, religion had already lost an important part of its undisputedness and communal basis in society. In a number of places, Messiaen records that he feels that he is not understood as a composer because he is speaking of religious affairs before "people who don't believe in it or have little knowledge of religion and theology."[2] His preference for the "surreal" in faith, which is expressed in the eccentricity of some of his titles and mottos, reinforces the impression that religious intentions and programs predominantly determine Messiaen's oeuvre. But he was also working in a compositional environment that was rapidly becoming more and more science-driven; the alterity of his faith is squared, as it were, by the enigmatic character of his musical avant-gardism.

For some time, Messiaen was considered to be a "mystical" composer, and to a certain extent this is still the case. Insofar as this is correct—and this needs to be considered more fully—it is also an effect of his excessive clarity. Messiaen has spoken and written remarkably much about his work, and his music, too, shows a penchant for the unequivocal. This may be a fortuitous circumstance if one desires to learn more about the relation between music and religion today. What, according to Messiaen, was his concern in composing? How did he perceive this relation himself? These are the questions that form the springboard for an exploration, in this chapter, of the *why*, *what*, and *how* of his composing. In addressing the last, the emphasis shall be on the theoretical, that is, on the *structural possibilities* that the composer saw for realizing his project.

Messiaen's lament that he was not understood—a theme that emerges frequently in his career—appears to indicate a desire for communication. It must first be established, however, that this is not necessarily the case. An anecdote recorded by Messiaen in his *Traité de rythme, de couleur, et d'ornithologie* shows that the sharing of meaning is, to him, secondary to the experience that precedes it, namely, the pure pleasure of inner listening.

> One day one of my students asked me why I compose music. That's the type of question one oughtn't ask. One could also say: Why do you live in a city? Why do you prefer the mountains to the city, or the sea to the mountains? Why are you married? Why aren't you? Why do you have enemies? Why are you alive rather than dead? etc. I have tried to answer my student through successive elimination. I do not compose for a broad audience—neither do I compose for a few initiated. So, the student said, you compose for the single listener that you are yourself? Then, I found myself very embarrassed. I compose for the pleasure of inner listening at the moment itself of composing.[3]

Although Messiaen here appears to be indifferent to other listeners in such joyful composing and to have no intention whatever of communicating anything to others, he is emphatically clear in other places about his aim to compose in order to express, indeed to express something very specific. The following passage, dating from the 1960s, indicates perhaps most concisely the background against which his work is usually perceived, and it contains in addition a number of commonplaces characteristic for Messiaen, such as the notion that he was "born a believer."

> Personally, I compose to champion, express, and define something. . . . The first idea I wanted to express, the most important, is the existence of the truths of the Catholic faith. I have the good fortune to be a Catholic. I was born a believer, and the Scriptures impressed me even as a child. The illumination of the theological truths of the Catholic faith is the first aspect of my work, the noblest, and no doubt the most useful and most valuable—perhaps the only one I won't regret at the hour of my death.[4]

Messiaen's core interest then appears to lie in "the illumination of the theological truths of the Catholic faith." This is not surprising, given the mostly religious titles and mottos in his scores. One of Messiaen's earliest declarations of intent can be found in the manifesto of a group of four musicians who called themselves La Jeune France (Young France). They were opposed to the musical zeitgeist that was, in their eyes, either too frivolous (music-hall, Jean Cocteau's *Le coq et l'arlequin*, and the like) or too revolutionary (Schoenberg and company). A manifesto, which Messiaen signed, was distributed at the group's first concert in 1936, advocating, with some overtones of culture criticism and nationalism, a humanist-spiritual commitment. It was well received in right-wing Catholic circles. The opening paragraph begins to outline the manifesto's mission statement.

> As the conditions of life become more and more hard, mechanical, and impersonal, music must always bring to those who love it, its spiritual violence and its courageous reactions. La Jeune France, reaffirming the title once used by Berlioz, pursues the road upon which the master once took his obdurate course. This is a group of four young French Composers who are friends: Olivier Messiaen, Daniel-Lesur, Yves Baudrier, and André Joliviet. La Jeune France proposes the dissemination of works [that are] youthful, free, [and] as far removed from revolutionary formulas as from academic formulas.[5]

Later, Messiaen would play down his association with this group, which existed for only a few years.[6] His statements become weightier around the time of his tract *Technique de mon langage musical* (1944), in which Messiaen, thirty-five years old at the time, explains the language and technique of his music. The first chapter gives an indication of what he concretely sought to achieve: "It is a glistening music (*musique chatoyante*) we seek, giving to the aural sense voluptuously refined pleasures. At the same time, this music should be able to express some noble sentiments (and especially the most noble of all, the religious sentiments exalted by the theology and the truths of our Catholic faith)."[7]

Elsewhere in the treatise, this brief program is expressed in rather more messianistic terms. Not only his remarks on the distinction between technique and feeling but also his description of the content of that feeling are of interest here. It should be remarked in passing that the slightly self-congratulatory implication of this programmatic passage is a long-standing aspect of Messiaen's way of expressing himself.[8]

> Although I have written a good number of religious works—religious in a mystical, Christian, Catholic sense—I shall further leave aside this preference; we treat technique and not sentiment. I shall content myself, on this

last point, with citing an article in which I formerly glorified sacred music. After having asked for "a *true* music, that is to say, spiritual, a music which may be an act of faith; a music which may touch upon all subjects without ceasing to touch upon God; an original music, in short, whose language may open a few doors, take down some yet distant stars," I stated that "there is still a place, plainchant itself not having told all." And I concluded: "To express with a lasting power our darkness struggling with the Holy Spirit, to raise upon the mountain the doors of our prison of flesh, to give our century the spring water for which it thirsts, there shall have to be a great artist who will be both a great artisan and a great Christian." Let us hasten by our prayers the coming of the liberator. And beforehand, let us offer him two thoughts. First, that of [Pierre] Reverdy: "May he draw in the whole sky in one breath!" And then that of [Ernest] Hello: "There is no one great except him to whom God speaks, and in the moment in which God speaks to him."⁹

The surrealistic language Messiaen uses here—the name of Reverdy indicates Messiaen's intense interest in surrealism at the time—alternates in the same period of time with the expression of his intentions that is sometimes equally poetic as formal and precise. It was sometimes but decades later, however, that the meaning of these terms would become apparent.¹⁰ In 1946, Messiaen formulates his mission in response to an enquiry. Answering the question as to what the "canon" is on which his aesthetics and technique are based, Messiaen says,

> I have tried to be a Christian musician and to sing my faith, without ever succeeding. No doubt because I am not worthy of it (this said without false modesty!). Pure music, profane music and above all theological music (and not mystical, as the majority of my audience think) alternate in my production. I truly do not know whether I have an "aesthetic," but I can say that my preferences are toward a glistening (*chatoyante*) music, refined, even voluptuous (but not sensual, of course!). A tender or violent music full of love and vehemence. A music that rolls and sings (praised be melody, the melodic phrase!). A music which could be new blood, unknown perfume, a singular gesture, a bird without sleep. Stained-glass music: a swirling of complementary colors. A music which expresses the end of time, ubiquity, the glorified bodies, the divine and supernatural mysteries. A "theological rainbow."¹¹

These words express in a nutshell the grand themes in Messiaen's oeuvre, such as the emphasis on the theological, religious synesthesia, and the thematics of time. In summary, it seems that for Messiaen the point in composing music is, apart from the joy in hearing music inwardly at the moment of the act of composition, about a religious, and in particular a theological-compositional program. Until the late 1940s, this program would continue to bear the signature of a musical experience of religious sentiments and remain connected to the spiritualized joy in the senses ("voluptuously refined pleasures" that "of course" are "not sensual"). By the 1960s, this subjective-romantic determinacy of the musical-religious would occupy a much less prominent position and possibly disappear altogether.[12] In this period, Messiaen appears to be focused on a more abstract illumination of theological ideas, although, as will become clear below, the idea of the senses will not lose its privileged position.[13]

### Faith—and Music

Messiaen's conception of faith remains implicit in these declarations of intent, which is also the case for the "theological truths" he refers to. In order to form a better picture of the kind of faith he sought to express in his music, the question needs to be addressed of what specific form of religion he adhered to, and what elements made up his musical program. It is not easy to answer this question, because Messiaen does not much show his hand, despite the suggestion of the contrary in all his explanatory notes. A first tentative exploration, then, is necessarily restricted to the way Messiaen presented his own faith.

To begin with the widest perspective, Messiaen has said in conversation with Almut Rössler what to him is the essence of religion and the reason for his faith. The inclusive yet open nature of Messiaen's Christianity becomes apparent in these words, in conjunction with his capacity to put his personal religious convictions into perspective. As such, the combination of both aspects is characteristic for Messiaen's faith, and will return in the analysis of his music in the next chapter.

> We foster a great admiration for [the] cosmos, but we all, even the unbelievers, have an obscure feeling that there's something else which is beyond time, space and stars and everything we know,—something which isn't before or after them, but is completely outside them, which supports and

contains what everyone who isn't entirely insensitive can feel—and which one can call God. Basically, religion is above all this: a relationship with the extraordinary spirit which is outside everything, which is totally different. Throughout the history of our planet, there have been founders of religion, religious geniuses, prophets, outstanding popular leaders, like Mohammed, Buddha, and Moses, too; but there's something unique, that's even more unusual than the totally other deity: namely, that God—as different, as distant, as terrible, as motionless, as eternal, and as infinite as He appears to us—came to us and tried to make Himself comprehensible in our language, in our sensations, in our attitudes of mind. That's the most beautiful aspect of the Godhead: the Mystery of the Incarnation, and that's why I'm a Christian. In saying this, I'm not thinking about differences between Orthodox Christians, Protestants, Catholics—and a Christian is a person who understands that God came.[14]

Messiaen maintains that such faith did no evolve gradually, nor was it received in dramatic conversion (as, for example, with Blaise Pascal or Paul Claudel, who act as a foil to him).[15] He repetitively asserts that he was simply born a believer and never doubted his faith.[16]

Apart from the theological interpretation of his faith, however, Messiaen also offers a genealogical explanation: his faith was awakened by an affinity with fairytales and tales of the fantastic, which he relates to his mother, the poet Cécile Sauvage. Various biographies quote Messiaen's professed love for, for instance, *Les Aventures du dernier Abencérage* by Chateaubriand; Shakespeare's tragedies, which he performed with his brother in home theatrical productions (his father, Pierre Messiaen, translated Shakespeare's complete works); and the tales of Anderson, Perrault, and, above all, Marie-Catherine d'Aulnoy.[17] The affinity with the marvelous was, however, truly fed ("*a trouvé sa vraie pâture*") by tales from the Bible, where the marvelous is entwined with the Truth ("*le conte de fées réel des Vérités, avec un grand 'V,' de la foi catholique*").[18] Messiaen describes this transition from literature to Christian faith through the marvelous:

> I really believe it is because of fairy-tales that I have become a believer. The Marvelous is my natural climate; it is where I feel comfortable. I have the need to live a Marvelous, but a Marvelous that would be real! In general the Marvelous is inscribed in myths, in tales of fantasy and imagination, whereas in the Catholic faith the Marvelous that is given is real. It is a Marvelous that one can lean on. In this way I have gradually, and almost without realizing

it, entered the state of being a believer. One could say that I unwittingly passed over from the surreal of fairy-tales to the supernatural of faith.[19]

The particular conviction that this surreal, which resembles the supernatural and forms the transition to it, should be taken as a feature of the beyond, is preceded by the thought that things are different from here, in the beyond: "If everything were 'normal' in the visible world, what would be the difference between Infinity and the finite, between God and human beings, and what would remain for us to learn in eternity? 'Blessed are they that have not seen, and yet have believed!': it is written in the Gospel."[20] Messiaen's conception of faith conduces to a "poetics of the marvelous" (*poétique du merveilleux*, Massin), more on which will come in the next chapter.

Because of the emphasis on the marvelous, Messiaen's conception of the Christian faith acquires the aspect of a somewhat one-sided *theologia gloriae*, as critics have not failed to point out with some frequency.[21] These are the questions that Hans Urs von Balthasar once raised about Mozart's music: "Where is the Confession of Sin? . . . And where the fear of Judgment?"[22] It seems as if Messiaen does not speak at all of suffering and sin. His much-quoted statement, which he often repeats, that he has no talent for suffering (a condition, moreover, that "isn't interesting, dirt isn't interesting")[23] drowns the sparse mentions of the same. Regarding the works, there is a modest list, put together by Harry Halbreich, of compositions that thematize suffering.[24] Rössler recalls the "way of the Cross" Messiaen personally went in composing and instrumentalizing his monumental opera *Saint François d'Assise*.[25] And Messiaen himself occasionally sketches the difficulties in believing and maintaining one's faith—apparently from his own experience. His statement constitutes a unique moment in the literature on Messiaen, in highlighting an aspect of faith that will guide our discussion as from Chapter 3.

> Do you think it's easy to constantly convince oneself of [the glory and majesty of God]? I'd like to give an example to illustrate my thoughts: When the Apostle Peter saw Christ walking on the water, he asked Him to give him his hand, so that he could walk on the water along with him. Christ gave him his hand, Peter looked at him and was able to walk on water in the same way. Suddenly he became aware of this, began to stumble and was in danger of drowning. He had doubted Christ who then said to Peter: 'Oh, man of little faith!' That's how it is for all of us every day. We must constantly strive afresh not to doubt and not to drown.[26]

Such words, then, are atypical for Messiaen, who normally emphasizes the glory of life in the beyond—a life that can be attained, for the believer, only through death—and the reflections of that life in the mundane. Messiaen therefore praises the Revelation of John as "the loveliest Book and the one which dominates all others."[27] Its faith is oriented on light, and therefore on the events in the New Testament (and corresponding liturgical moments) where such light has a main part both literally and in the figurative sense: the dazzling light in the scene of Transfiguration; the inner light of Easter; the radiant light of Ascension; the manifold lights of those who have risen from the dead; the colorful light in the book of Revelation.[28] Insofar as there is a case of violence, it is always the terror of the sacred that cannot be borne by finite humankind. In this respect, Messiaen appears to join Rilke, whose lines in his *Duino Elegies* assert that "For beauty is nothing but / the beginning of terror, that we are still able to bear."

The "theological truths" Messiaen spoke of do not just concern these crucial moments, but other main elements from the catholic creed as well: ranging from the mystery of the triune, omnipresent God, via the birth of Christ and the *triduum sacrum* of Easter, to the descent of the Holy Spirit and the expectation of Celestial Jerusalem. In *Conférence de Kyoto*, Messiaen supplies a long list of theological truths that are illustrated in his works, specifying these works as well. The "spirit of the catalogue" (Massin) of this enumeration is not only characteristic for the way he speaks, but for the manner of composing as well.

A major part of my work is devoted to the meditation on the mysteries of the Christian and Catholic Faith. The *Méditations sur le Mystère de la Sainte Trinité* for organ (1969) deal with the first and the greatest mystery of the Faith. The *Trois petites Liturgies* for female choir, piano solo, Onde Martenot, vibraphone, celesta, percussion, and string orchestra (1944), speak of the Presence of God: in us ("Antienne de la Conversation intérieure")—in Himself ("Séquence du Verbe," "Cantique Divin")—in all things ("Psalmodie de l'Ubiquité de l'amour"). Also various mysteries of the life of Christ, Man-God, are evoked. The birth of Christ in *La Nativité du Seigneur* for organ (1935), in *Vingt regards sur l'Enfant Jésus* for piano solo (1944), his Transfiguration in *La Transfiguration de Notre Seigneur Jésus Christ* for seven instrumental soloists, choir and very large orchestra (1965–1969), his passion in "l'Amen de l'agonie de Jésus" (third piece from *Vision de l'Amen* for two pianos [1943]), his death in "Puissance des ténèbres" from *Livre du Saint Sacrement* for organ (1984), his Resurrection in "Résurrection" from the

*Chants de terre et de ciel* for soprano and piano (1938), in "Combat de la mort et de la vie" from *Les Corps glorieux* for organ (1939), in "Apparition du Christ ressuscité à Marie-Madeleine" from *Livre du Saint Sacrement* for organ (1984), his Ascension in *l'Ascension* for orchestra (1933). Since the Resurrection of Christ is the pledge for ours, two works are especially devoted to our own resurrection: they are *Les Corps glorieux* for organ (1939), and *Et exspecto resurrectionem mortuorum* for an orchestra of woodwinds and brass, chimes, gongs, and tam-tams (1964). And finally a work is dedicated to the Holy Ghost: *Messe de la Pentecôte* for organ (1950).[29]

Apparently, Messiaen feels the need to defend his position, as the tone of this catalogue suggests.[30] Elsewhere, he says that there were other cases, too, of having to counter the criticism that he lacked the knowledge of Christian dogmas. From his response in those occasions it can be inferred that such criticism was prompted by the sometimes eccentric nature of his music and of the religious themes he had chosen. He enjoys pointing out the violent imagery and texts that are (also) at the source of the Catholic faith, and which some of his critics appear to have forgotten.[31] Messiaen's conception of faith steers a middle course between the two extremes. On one hand, it testifies to a great affinity with the eccentric or surreal in faith, on the other hand his faith testifies to an enormous longing for rationality. This is perhaps best symbolized by the name of Messiaen's favorite theologian, the scholastic Thomas Aquinas. Messiaen proudly asserts that he has read, in the course of this life, Aquinas's main work, *Summa Theologiae*, almost entirely. Messiaen frequently uses it as a referential text—and a few times even as a lyric for his vocal parts, or a source to be musically codified.[32]

Although Messiaen is uncharacteristically explicit in saying what he wishes to express with his music (the preference for the unequivocal appears only to grow in the course of this life), he is reticent when asked whether he wants to convey a message. "Perhaps," he answers, "but not intentionally."[33] He wants clarity without evangelism, which is the key, perhaps, to his formal rejection of mysticism. Clarity may be threatened by evangelism on the hand, but likewise it may be breached by "mystical" elusiveness. Note, however, that various parties (including himself, as became clear above) associate Messiaen's music with the mystical, but that it remains unclear what is meant by this designation.[34] When asked what he meant with this term, Messiaen said in the late 1970s,

> Personally, I deeply distrust this word. It doesn't suit me at all, and I'd like to say why not. As soon as one starts talking about mysticism, people think

of a diseased state, of a neurotic who has vague sentiments and ecstasies. I don't like that; I'm a devout man and I love the sound, solid gifts of faith. There were real mystics with real visions and ecstasies, like St. John of the Cross, for instance; and even in the Bible, such things already existed, Moses, for example, had visions. But no one is a mystic by power of his own will; a person who is one isn't conscious of it and doesn't have the right to say he is one; and in my opinion, nobody has the right to say of another that he is one, as long as he isn't dead. It's a too personal and too poorly understood thing.[35]

In other words, it seems that Messiaen feared in particular the negative connotations of the notion of the mystical, such as elusiveness, sentimental intuitions, and irrationality (for which he himself was often criticized in the 1940s).[36] He also associates this notion with a type of religious music, "a sweetish music, vaguely mystical and above all soporific" that does not merit its name, or that he anyway does not want to compose.[37] Perhaps this connotation bears not so much on the mystical as on its derivative, mystique, which is rather more oriented on sentimentality and intuition. The discussion in Chapter 3 will be concerned with Messiaen's rejection of this derivative, with respect to the romantic cult of musical experience. It will also explore the meaning of the preference Messiaen manifests for concrete form in both thought and music.

It will be evident that Messiaen's intentions are oriented toward "the illumination of the theological truths of the Catholic faith" and that he is especially concerned with the truths contained by the notion of resurrection. How, then, does he think to realize such a program in his music? Is it at all possible to express anything in music, let alone such truths? The theoretical possibilities that Messiaen discerned will be discussed here. Starting with his thoughts on the possibility in general of programmatic music and then moving on to his subsequent awareness of the impossibilities contained in his projected program, the discussion will end with the three privileged figures that, in the view of Messiaen, do eventually enable such a program. The tour of this chapter comes to a halt at Messiaen's extraordinary claim that in his music there is, due to the effect of synesthetic overwhelming, the possibility of a "breakthrough toward the beyond" (*percée vers l'au-delà*). This thesis will provide the focus for thought in the coming chapters.

*Expression in Music*

The debate on pure versus programmatic music is pertinent in the case of Messiaen because of the largely instrumental nature of his music. Although

Messiaen did not overtly participate in the debate, his relative position is known. The aesthetics of "pure music" were propagated, among others, by Stravinsky, who stated that "music is, by its very nature, essentially power-less to *express* anything at all, whether a feeling, an attitude of mind, a psy-chological mood, a phenomenon of nature, etc. . . . *Expression* has never been an inherent property of music. That is by no means the purpose of its existence."[38] Against this fundamentally romantic vision of the essence of music, Stravinsky posits the view that music is, in essence, a form of order, especially the order of the relation between time and humankind. To a cer-tain extent, Messiaen goes along with this. He rejects criticism that his music is mere idle play, a purely intramusical affair. For instance, the critique that the subtle duration differences that constitute movement of "Soixante-quatre durées" in *Livre d'orgue* are inaudible to the ordinary listener and hence musically irrelevant causes Messiaen to protest vehemently against the idea of music for music's sake. He asserts that even in these most "pure" moments, music still is connected in a significant way to what is outside music: "These nasty people are in truth the victim of a terrible conceit. They turn music into an end in itself and forget that, in the universe, music is but a tiny manifestation of rhythm, which would not exist without mo-tion and change, in itself the manifestations of time."[39] Thus, in insisting on the relation between humankind and time, Messiaen joins Stravinsky, but the implication of the idea of music for music's sake contained in that posi-tion is forcefully discarded.[40]

This raises the question whether Messiaen's music is, in the last instance, programmatic after all. He appears to subscribe to the idea of expression by means of music, as when he talks about illuminating theological truths.[41] The content of the relation between humankind and time might constitute an element of such a program. Indeed, Harry Halbreich endorses the idea that Messiaen's music is programmatic in nature, although he considers the term inappropriate because it would degrade music too much to a childish narrative or a form of excessive naturalism (a description, nevertheless, that appears to suit much of Messiaen's music). Thus, he praises in his book from 1980 the "symbiosis" of Messiaen's music and its program:

> In at least the last ten or fifteen years, poetic titles have flourished again in the youngest music, which seems to have distanced itself definitively from the abstract forms upon which the West has relied for centuries. But beware: the commentaries that accompany these pages bearing names that so much suggest the promise of escape, are generally repulsively technical, and their

authors seem to excuse themselves beforehand that they did not entitle their work *Etude*, or *Composition No. 1*. In contrast, read the notes that accompany a work by Messiaen: there, inextricably mixed with technical explanations of the most rigid kind, and furthermore of the most perfect clarity ("*ce qui ce conçoit bien . . . [s'énonce clairement*, a French saying meaning that what is well conceived is clearly expressed]), you will find a world of feelings and sensations, a dazzlement of poetry and color that normally would have to remain exterior, or at least parallel, to the music. Hence, what we have here is a perfect coexistence between musical thinking and "program," a wholly natural symbiosis. The truths of faith, or birdsong, colors, and landscapes can only become incarnate by virtue of the modes, rhythms, and timbres which are so patiently elaborated by the composer.[42]

Messiaen, however, is deaf to such compliments and persists in rejecting the notion of programmatic music, even when bracketed in scare quotes. Yet, his resistance against the concept of program is differently inspired. It is not the possibility of childish or naturalist connotations that worry Halbreich that trouble him. Rather, Messiaen is concerned with the blasphemous implications of reducing an overwhelming religious content to a mere "program." This becomes apparent in the following passage from an interview with Antoine Goléa (the work Goléa refers to is Messiaen's work for piano *Vingt Regards sur l'Enfant-Jésus*):

> GOLÉA: After the essential clarifications, let us return to the work itself. You just uttered the word "subject" with respect to the work. Given its title and the titles of the twenty pieces it consists of, does that mean that it concerns a programmatic work?

> MESSIAEN: Programmatic, what an abject term! In reality, it concerns the contemplation of the Child-God in the crib, and the gaze that rest upon him, from the unspeakable adoration of God the Father to the adoration of the Church, passing through the inaudible adoration of the Holy Spirit and the Spirit of Joy, through the so tender adoration of the Virgin, through the adorations of the angels and wise men, and the immaterial and symbolic creatures: Time, the Heights, Silence, the Star, the Cross.[43]

The alternatives envisaged by Messiaen when engaging musically with such massive religious truths will be addressed later in this chapter. First however, in preparing the ground for the second chapter, a preview on Messiaen's way of composing. His music may not be called programmatic just like that, but at a pragmatic level, Messiaen does wield a distinction between form and content; or music and subject. Elsewhere, they appear to be unified once again, as if it concerns the Chalcedonian view on the nature of Christ. Music and subject are neither mixed nor strictly separate.[44]

This shows in the practice of composing. When embarking on a new work, Messiaen begins with searching a theme. He reads extensively on this theme and undertakes a few journeys to develop a sense of landscape and atmosphere before beginning with the actual composition.[45] The latter activity is an occupation that excludes all others, including contemplation, meditation, or any other form of reflection. When asked if he has ever felt the "joy of mysticism" (a moment of epiphany, of certainty) during the act of composing, the response is a resolute, "No, not at all. When I am working, there are so many things that require immediacy, so many details to manage, that all I can do is be attentive to what I am doing. I do not experience what you mean. I do not contemplate but act."[46] The strict separation between technique and program is reflected in the commentary on his work, *pace* Halbreich. Paradoxically, the distinction is confirmed by Messiaen's remark that the thematically oriented reading that precedes composing is indispensable. Regarding the mottos in his works for organ, he comments,

> These quotations are of the greatest significance; I'd go so far as to say that, if that were not the case, I might just as well pack up; I wouldn't compose any more music. These quotations are inseparable from the origins of my organ pieces and of most of the works I've written which have a religious content. Generally speaking, I've allowed my thoughts to revolve around a specific subject—a mystery of the Christian faith, such as the birth of our Lord or his Resurrection, or else a mystery of the Holy Spirit such as the Feast of Pentecost; and in the Bible, in writings of the fathers of the Early Church or in other religious texts, but above all in the Holy Scriptures, I've tried to find everything which has to do with the subject I've chosen and then have tried to translate it into music—not just into notes, not just into sounds and rhythms, but into sound-colors as well, into colors.[47]

Elsewhere, the distinction between form and content returns as a distinction between technique and feeling, as in the remark cited earlier: "Although I have written a good number of works—religious in a mystical, Christian, Catholic sense—I shall further leave aside this preference; we treat technique and not sentiment,"[48] or in the statement that "music is to a certain extent a specialty, a technique, whereas faith, piety, is a need."[49] Halbreich and Messiaen may both insist on the inseparability of form and content, but they do not achieve true unity, not in their theoretical conception of the relation between the two, in the practice of composing, or, as a glance at the score learns, in the texts that are the result. Commentary, mottos, and other clues bearing on content remain strictly separate from the music, as two distinct worlds. The question remains, then, whether one world grazes against the other (which would enable expression). If the answer is positive, then in what manner can it be conceived?

*Religious Expression in Music*

The unspeakable cannot, as the term suggests, be expressed. Messiaen's intention—illuminating theological truths that are in essence unspeakable—clearly stumbles on a problem. How can something that escapes all form of reference, description, or explanation be illuminated? Messiaen is conscious of this problem, and of the apparent or real impossibility of his objectives.

> Christ incarnated in order to lead us from the visible to love of the invisible. Christ the man can be represented, not Christ the God. God is not representable. He is not even expressible. When we say, "God is eternal," do we think about the significance of these words? "God is eternal" signifies not only that he will never end, but that he never had any beginning. Here is where temporal notions of "before" and "after" encumber us. To conceive of something without a beginning absolutely overwhelms us, we who have begun, first, in our mother's womb, then in our earthly life. The same goes for other divine attributes. Perhaps the ancient Israelites were right when they forbade the name of Yahweh to be spoken.[50]

Messiaen's awareness in this general observation determines to a certain extent his attitude with regard to his musical project. Thus, in explaining the subject of his quartet *Quatuor pour la fin du Temps* (namely, the awe-inspiring angel announcing the End of Time), he exclaims twice even that "this is mere trying and stammering, when imagining the devastating grandeur of the subject!" Elsewhere he declares only to have made some tentative approaches: "How to express all this with ondes Martenot? I am completely unworthy of all this."[51] Yet, Messiaen sees a shimmer of (relative) possibility through his awareness of impossibility, inadequacy and unworthiness: "I wished to express the marvelous aspects of the Faith. I'm not saying that I've succeeded, for in the final analysis they're unspeakable. . . . I would add that most of the arts are unsuited to the expression of religious truths. Only music, the most immaterial of all, comes close to it."[52]

The background to this moderate optimism takes us, symbolically speaking, from the Sinai to Bethlehem. Messiaen is willing to admit that the divine is "in the final analysis" unspeakable. But on the other hand, as he had already pointed out briefly, Christ is born. God is, moreover, the creator of heaven and earth to Messiaen. In discussing the notions of the Swiss theologian Hans Urs von Balthasar, for whom the idea of beauty (with the arts and especially music in tow) occupied a central position in theology, Messiaen tells Claude Samuel that people are not justified in being shocked by this notion:

> Which shocks iconoclasts above all, the people who reject stained-glass windows, paintings, music. But these people are mistaken, for God is the creator, and whatever he has created is beautiful. Look at the stars, the landscape on our little planet, our mountains and oceans: their beauty is the work of God. This was Saint Francis's opinion, and in this sense, I'm very Franciscan.[53]

The importance of the beautiful, especially beauty in music, in connecting to the world beyond (of death, creation), is confirmed in the following quotation, where Messiaen speaks of the ecstatic violin solo for the angel in *Saint François d'Assise*.

> No one can see God without dying; it's not possible until after resurrection. To hear the sounds of the invisible on this earth is an extraordinary joy, a kind of knowledge of the beyond through music—And what a marvelous opportunity for a composer! But a dangerous opportunity, for the music definitely must be quite beautiful.[54]

Messiaen uses various descriptions for depicting the positive relation between music and the heavens. In the preceding quotation, it is about the appearance of elements from the heavens ("the sounds of the invisible"), descended unto earth like angels. Elsewhere, he describes how music "may adapt itself to the sacred," apparently presupposing a more or less compelling presence of this sacred.[55] He also speaks of "music which approaches with reverence the Divine, the Sacred, the Ineffable,"[56] which implies a certain liberty for humankind in searching God. And, as we have seen above, he speaks of the "attempts to express the divine Mystery" which appears to imply the experience of the divine.[57]

According to Messiaen, music works in a manner that is related to the dream, which gives it, within his surrealistic orientation on faith, an extraordinary religious force: "In a certain sense, music possesses a power that is superior to the image and the word because it is immaterial and appeals more to the intellect and to thought than the other arts. It even verges on fantasy and belongs to the world of dreams."[58] Or, in the preface to his organ cycle *Méditations sur le Mystère de la Sainte Trinité*: "Music . . . does not express anything directly. It can suggest or evoke a certain sentiment, a state of the soul, touch the subconscious, expand dream-related faculties, and there are its immense powers. It cannot at all 'tell' or inform with precision." This is not the dreamworld of Freudian obscurity and twistedness, the realm of the soul's reverse side.[59] It is a world of the surreal, of light and the marvelous, predominantly under the sign of hopeful religious promises—related to the dream in which God reveals himself unto man in the Old Testament, and to the imagery used by the prophets and John of the Revelation to depict the divine and the heavens.

## Privileged Figures

The combination of dreamworld and rationality that Messiaen favors offers him a number of possibilities to connect the musical and the religious to each other. Three of these possibilities—three figures for thinking about religious music—have a preferred status: (1) a certain "lack of truth" in music (which implies that it refers, beyond itself, to something more essential), (2) the analogy of the marvelous, and (3) the experience of dazzlement by an "excess of truth." A brief elucidation shall clarify the significance of these figures.

### ABSENCE: "LACK OF TRUTH"

According to Messiaen, music leads to God "through lack of truth" (*par défaut de vérité*). These words are uttered by the angel making music in the fifth tableau of Messiaen's opera *Saint François d'Assise*. The entire statement is, "God blinds us through an excess of Truth. Music leads us to God through lack of Truth."[60] Messiaen explains the origin and significance of these words:

> It's from Saint Thomas [Aquinas], but a little bit arranged or rather gathered up à la Messiaen! But what I try to express in *Saint François*, following saint Thomas, is this: music may carry us towards God by means of symbol and image, hence, by lack of truth, but at the same time God is like the sun, one cannot look straight into it. The high point of contemplation is a dazzlement, therefore an excess of truth.[61]

The notion of "lack of truth" looks like a variation on another of Aquinas's sayings, when he discusses the question of the metaphorical nature of religious precepts: "Just as human reason fails to grasp the import of poetical utterance on account of its deficiency in truth (*defectum veritatis*), neither can it grasp divine things perfectly on account of their superabundance of truth; and therefore in both cases there is need of representation by sensible figures."[62] In *Music and Color*, Messiaen explains this variation on the thought of Aquinas:

> The arts, especially music but also literature and painting, allow us to penetrate domains that are not unreal, but beyond reality. For the surrealists, it was a hallucinatory domain; for Christians, it is the domain of faith. "Blessed are those who have not seen and who have believed." They haven't seen, but they have a secret intuition about what they don't see. Now, I think music, even more than literature and painting, is capable of expressing this dreamlike, fairy-tale aspect of the beyond, this "surreal" aspect of the truths of faith. It's in that sense that music expresses the beyond with its absence of truth, because it isn't inside the actual framework of reality. God alone is the single true reality, a reality so true that is surpasses all truth. . . . "Absence of truth" doesn't signify falsehood. It's the symbolic representation of an event that isn't really visible, whereas celestial meditation is no longer symbolic: it's a reality.[63]

The relation between music and truth described here by Messiaen is much like a Platonic duality of the world of appearances versus the world of Ideas, translated into a Christian terminology. Music is rooted in a terrestrial reality and is, if only because of this, as a finite entity dependent on a higher truth, that of its Creator. What has been created refers in (and through) its transience to eternity or the uncreated. In other words, to the everlasting, true reality of God (in the theological sense, then, music functions as a *signum*). This referential aspect of music is caused by the fact that it is created and therefore has a negativity, a (relative) lack of truth, in what is created. According to Messiaen, this is true for music, but one might add that it is true, within the same Platonic-Christian conception, for any other phenomenon or creature. A more specific and consequently more positive determination of the relation between music and the divine comes to the fore in the other two privileged figures.

## ANALOGY: "THE MARVELOUS"

The first figure was concerned with lack in the phenomenal world. Here, in the second figure, the (positive) traces of the divine that Messiaen encounters in the world are central, or in other words, the analogies with the divine that one may find in the world. According to Jean-Rodolphe Kars, there are, in Messiaen, two manners for expressing the divine: "vertical," as a direct experience of the divine in music, and "horizontal," as an indirect, comparative approach to the divine.[64] With the latter we should think of metaphor, allegory, and especially analogy. A number of attributes related to the divine, in Messiaen's eyes, have already been mentioned: the unspeakable, the everlasting, and eternity.

Apart from these "absolute" qualities, however, Messiaen mentions a number of qualities that occur in a more general sense in the world, by means of which the divine in music can be evoked. Examples are the beautiful, the marvelous (*le merveilleux*, with connotations of splendor, luster, or the majestic, or more generally the supernatural),[65] the illustrious, the immutable, the glorious, the terrible, the mysterious, the immaterial, the abstract, the detached (not to be confused, given its etymology, with the absolute), the anonymous, the majestic, the dreamlike, and the loving.[66] Messiaen uses most of these qualifications to indicate the divine in (human) nature. In music, too, he recognizes these qualifications and uses them in support of qualifying certain music as religious. Thus, he speaks of the "purity, the joy, the lightness" of Gregorian chant and especially of its neumes, in particular their "rhythmic suppleness" and "quickness."[67] He also speaks of its "majesty" and "dreamlike quality," and praises its "purity" and "anonymity."[68] Gregorian chant is the only liturgical music, and perhaps even the only true religious music, "because it's detached from all external effect."[69] As for his own music, he meant to express, as we have seen, "the marvelous aspects of the Faith." Apart from this privileged quality there are many other qualities, comparable to divine attributes, which Messiaen employs in his music. This entire list returns in his work.[70]

The role of the analogy of the marvelous (closely related to the surreal) in his texts deserves to be considered here, too. There are, to begin with, the poems he wrote for the songs and choral works he composed. Thus, he describes in the poem of *Trois Petites Liturgies de la Présence Divine*, part 3, how "From the depths a ripple rises, / The mountain skips like a ram, / And becomes a great ocean. / Present, / You are present. / Imprint your name in my blood" (*De la profondeur une ride surgit, / La montagne saute comme une brebis, / Et devient un grand océan. / Présent, / Vous êtes présent. / Imprimez votre nom dans mon sang*).[71] Such imagery is reminiscent of the cosmic catastrophes and bizarre scenes sketched by John in the book of Revelation. The titles and mottos of Messiaen's work refer to similar marvelous images and events. The evocation of the descending, gemstone city in *Couleurs de la*

*Cité céleste* provides an example, or titles such as "Joy of the blood of the stars" (*Joie du sang des étoiles*), "The Lyre-bird and the Bride-City" (*L'oiseau-lyre et la Ville-Fiancée*), "The angel of the perfumes" (*L'ange aux parfums*), and "The eyes in the wheels" (*Les yeux dans les roues*). With the latter, the title from the sixth part of his organ cycle *Livre d'orgue*, Messiaen supplies a motto from Ezekiel: "And their rings were full of eyes round about them four. For the spirit of the living creature was in the wheels" (*Et les jantes des quatre roues étaient remplies d'yeux tout autour. Car l'Esprit de l'être vivant était dans les roues*) (Ez 1:18, 20).[72] A similar use of the marvelous, the extraordinary, unimaginable and wholly other, recurs in Messiaen's theoretical work, where he does not hesitate to juxtapose H. G. Wells's *Time Machine* to modern physics and the Angels of the Apocalypse.[73]

Messiaen is not very explicit in addressing the question of how the transition from the marvelous in faith to the marvelous in the world (and back) can be made in a theoretical, rather than imaginative or rhetorical sense. His view on this can be inferred from the explanatory notes in the twelfth part of *La Transfiguration de Notre-Seigneur Jésus-Christ*:

> It was while looking, on a bright day, at the Mont Blanc, the Jungfrau, and the three glaciers of the Meije in the Oisans, that I understood the difference between the minor splendor of snow and the great splendor of the sun. There I could also imagine in what sense the site of the Transfiguration had been terrible![74]

Perhaps he acquired this insight after reading Aquinas's commentary in the *Summa* on the Transfiguration.[75] The image of reflection is used elsewhere with respect to indicating the divine quality of love: "A great love is a reflection—a pale reflection, but nevertheless a reflection—of the only genuine love, divine love," in which love, when expressed in music, can establish a (be it indirect, because relative and weak) connection between this art and the heavens.[76]

The principle that is implicitly wielded here is that of the *via eminentiae*, which, together with the *via causalitatis* (the Aristotelian notion that everything in the world must have a cause that does not have the transience of this world) and the *via negationis* (the notion that no positive assertion can be made about this cause-without-cause), form the nucleus of Aquinas's thought on the analogy. The *via eminentiae* is founded on the thought that any quality that is attributed to God is applicable to Him, not in a worldly sense but in the sense of supremacy or eminence. Apart from these analogous, indirect connections between music and the heavens, however, Messiaen distinguishes a third possibility: the immediate experience of a "breakthrough" in music, due to the experience of an excess in sound and color. Messiaen asserts that he has experienced such a breakthrough himself, and he affirms that he would like his audience to share in this experience of, in his words, a religious vertigo or dazzlement.[77]

## PRESENCE: "DAZZLEMENT (*ÉBLOUISSEMENT*)"

*Je ne suis pas théoricien . . . seulement croyant.*
*Un croyant ébloui par l'infinité de Dieu!*[78]

Dazzlement (*éblouissement*) is thematized for the first time in the preface to *Couleurs de la Cité céleste*. Here, Messiaen refers to the use of dazzlement in the Revelation of John to indicate the Holy of Holies:

> The sound-colors are in turn the symbol of the "Heavenly City" and of the "Him" who inhabits it. Outside all time, outside all place, in a light without light, in a night without night. . . . That which the Apocalypse, even more terrifying in its modesty than in its glorious visions, only designates with a dazzlement of colors.[79]

*Éblouissement* always involves an overwhelming, either of the senses (especially the eye and the ear, including the inner eye and ear, which then implies a form of blinding) or of thought (which implies a form of vertigo) but in most cases both meanings are implied.[80] Even before he began to use this term, Messiaen described the experience. The quotation is from *Quatuor pour la fin du Temps*:

> In my dreams I hear and see classified chords and melodies, known colors and forms; subsequently, after that transient phase, I pass into the unreal and undergo a swirling, a gyrating copenetration of superhuman sounds and colors. These swords of fire, streams of blue-orange lava, these sudden stars: behold the confusion, behold the rainbows![81]

To Messiaen, the archetypical experience of dazzlement is represented by the overwhelming impression of stained-glass windows, first experienced when he was about ten years old, on a visit to Sainte-Chapelle in Paris.[82] There is a shot in a documentary film of Messiaen as he looks at these windows, standing in the chapel, saying, "When one sees a stained-glass window, one does not immediately see all the figures. One has a sensation of color, and one is dazzled [*ébloui*]. One has to close one's eyes."[83] The experience was repeated in Notre-Dame and the cathedrals of Chartres and

Bourges. In 1977, when he is almost sixty-nine, he speaks again about these windows in his *Lecture at Notre-Dame*:

> What happens in the stained-glass windows of Bourges, in the great windows of Chartres, in the rose-windows of Notre-Dame in Paris and in the marvelous, incomparable glasswork of the Sainte-Chapelle? First of all there is a crowd of characters, great and small, which tell us of the life of Christ, of the Holy Virgin, of the Prophets, and of the Saints: it is a sort of catechism by image. This catechism is enclosed in circles, medallions, trefoils, it obeys the symbolism of colors, it opposes, it superimposes, it decorates, it instructs, with a thousand intentions and a thousand details. Now, from a distance, without binoculars, without ladders, without any object to come to the aid of our failing eye, we see nothing; nothing but a stained-glass window all blue, all green, all violet. We do not comprehend, we are *dazzled* [*éblouis*]![84]

Messiaen attempts to reproduce these experiences, which "certainly exerted an influence on my career," in his music.[85] His synesthetic capacities offered him the possibility to do so—Messiaen claimed to see certain colors inwardly with certain tone combinations (though not the reverse): "When I hear a score or read it, hearing it in my mind (*intellectuellement*), I visualize corresponding colors which turn, shift, and combine, just as the sounds turn, shift, and combine, simultaneously."[86] This is not a case of physiopathological dysesthetics, but a visual type of synesthesia, also called "photism" and in particular its auditive counterpart (that is, an extraordinary relation between hearing and seeing).[87] Messiaen always knew whether he was effectively hearing something or not: "I see them inwardly; this is not imagination, nor is it a physical phenomenon."[88] The simultaneous effect on the inner eye is partly involuntary, partly due to "literary and artistic influences," and had such a constancy that he was able to draw up tables of the correspondences between specific clusters of sound and color.[89]

He did not see any colors when doors screeched, nor when hearing individual tones, nor even did he recognize something in the connections drawn by Scriabin between tone and color.[90] He saw them especially in chromatic sound clusters, such as chords from the self-designed "modes of limited transposition" but also in simple triads. Thus, the major triad on G was yellow, the one on E was red, the one on C was white, the one on A was blue, and the one on F sharp was "a sparkling of all possible colors."[91] In the course of his career he became more an more convinced of these correspondences and used them ever more consciously, which shows, among others, in the fact that from the 1960s he began to add annotations of the corresponding colors to musical notes.[92]

His synesthesia opened the possibility for Messiaen to translate the intense experiences that in various churches and chapels had occurred to him into music. Or rather, into sound-color or *son-couleur*, as he called it: the intermedial connection of sound and color.[93] It is not just that he *imitates* the colors of stained glass in his music, but, by means of the violent contrasts in color (as the red and blue of Chartres), he aspires to achieve a musically mediated *experience* of dazzlement.[94] The reason for this objective was already announced in the preceding: dazzlement is, to him, the mystagogical and transformative experience, regardless whether it takes place in chapels and cathedrals, or in music.

> The more the sounds strike and knock the inner ear, and the more these multicolored things move and irritate our inner eye, the more a contact is established, a rapport (as Rainer Maria Rilke said) with another reality: a rapport so powerful that it can transform our most hidden "I," the deepest, the most intimate, and dissolve us in a most high Truth which we could never hope to attain.[95]

This experience escapes the limitations of time and space, which brings Messiaen to setting up a hierarchy, in *Conférence de Notre-Dame*, of different sorts of religious music. Gregorian chant, much praised by Messiaen, is assigned the lowest position because it is tied up with the rhythm and situation of the liturgy. Above this position comes what he here calls "religious music," that is, "all music approaching the Divine, the Holy, the Unspeakable with respect." Examples of such music are to be found in a wide range of different works by Mozart, Debussy, Penderecki, Japanese gagaku, Tibetan horns, and the works for organ by, among others, Frescobaldi and Tournemire. The highest position is taken by his own invention: sound-color.[96]

> It is . . . true that I put colored music above liturgical music and religious music: liturgical music celebrates God in His dwelling-place, in His Church, in his own Sacrifice; religious music discovers Him at every hour and everywhere, on our planet Earth, in our mountains, in our oceans, among the birds, the flowers, the trees, and also in the visible universe of stars which circle around us; but colored music does that which the stained-glass windows and rose-windows of the Middle Ages did: they give us dazzlement (*éblouissement*). Touching at once our noblest senses: hearing and vision, it

shakes our sensibilities into motion, pushes us to go beyond concepts, to approach that which is higher than reason and intuition, that is, FAITH.[97]

According to Messiaen, this faith is perpetuated in life after the resurrection, where the believers will undergo, as glorified bodies, a "perpetual dazzlement" in which they will know Christ. Messiaen expresses this truth by means of what he describes as a variation on the Psalms and Revelation: "In Thy Music, we will SEE the Music, / In Thy Light, we will HEAR the Light."[98] He further endorses his interpretation, not so much argumentatively as through the juxtaposition of quotations, by comparing his own descriptions to statements ascribed to Aquinas ("God dazzles us [*nous éblouit*] by excess of Truth") and the mystic Jan van Ruusbroec ("Contemplation sees something, but what does it see? An excellence above all, which is not one thing, nor another"). He concludes,

> All these dazzlements (*éblouissements*) are a great lesson. They show us that God is beyond words, thoughts, concepts, beyond our earth and our sun, beyond the thousands of stars which circle around us, above and beyond time and space, beyond all these things which are somehow linked to him. He alone knows Himself by His Word, incarnate in Jesus Christ. And when musical painting, colored music, sound-color magnify it by dazzlement (*l'éblouissement*), they participate in this fine praise of the *Gloria* which speaks to God and to Christ: "*Only Thou art Holy, Thou alone art the Most-High!*" In inaccessible heights. Doing this, they help us to live better, to better prepare for our death, to better prepare for our resurrection from the dead and the new life that awaits us. They are an excellent "passage," an excellent "prelude" to the unspeakable and to the invisible.[99]

This prelude is more than mere preparation, as becomes clear when Messiaen sums up his lecture: "Finally, there is that breakthrough toward the beyond (*la percée vers l'au-delà*), toward the invisible and unspeakable, which may be made by means of *sound-color*, and is summed up in the sensation of dazzlement (*éblouissement*)."[100]

Remarkably enough, Messiaen does not use this term when describing the mystic breakthrough experienced by Saint Francis in the fifth tableau of *Saint François d'Assise*, a breakthrough that Messiaen compares to the appearance of Christ to Saul on the way to Damascus (Acts 9:3–9). Saul is not dazzled (*ébloui*) but becomes temporarily blind (*aveugle*).[101] When, however, later in the opera, Francis is definitively received in heaven, Messiaen makes him call out "Lord! enlighten me with thy presence. Deliver me, enrapture me, dazzle me [*éblouis-moi*] forever with thy excess of truth."[102] The score indicates that the stage then should be flooded in a dazzling, white light: "All disappears and fades away. The choir takes up a front-stage position. There is only an intense single light illuminating the spot where the body was of Francis. Gradually, this light should augment till the end of the act. When it has become blinding (*aveuglante*) and unbearable, the curtain drops."[103] Compare his words elsewhere: "The summit of contemplation is a dazzlement, therefore an excess of truth."[104]

In fact, the connective "therefore" (*donc*) points at a creative misreading on the part of Messiaen. Aquinas uses the image of blinding in the metaphor of the bat that cannot see the sun because it shines too brightly (*excessum luminus*; blinding is not a word used here).[105] Aquinas uses this metaphor, however, to express a thought that he subsequently *rejects*. He contests the notion that the human spirit cannot "see" (that is, understand) God, that there would be an essential and insurmountable disproportion between the human spirit and God, as expressed in the bat metaphor. Therefore, Aquinas believes that a purely negative approach to God (as advanced by Dionysius the Areopagite, whom he quotes) does not suffice, and he indicates various positive relations between the spirit and God. Thus, Messiaen appears to contradict Aquinas in the matter of dazzlement, when he claims that dazzlement is in itself an expression of our positive relation to God. What we see here is an example of the implicit debate that the "Franciscan" Messiaen, in the Augustinian tradition of the Franciscans (Bonaventure in particular), is having with the thought of Aquinas. This lead will be taken up in the subsequent chapters.

## 2. Five Times Breakthrough

### La Transfiguration: *A Privileged Example*

The first chapter mapped the "program" of Messiaen and exploring the theoretical possibilities that he discerned for putting it to practice. Now it is time to turn to the question of how he endeavored to realize these possibilities. What does it look like in practice, this "glistening music" of sound-color, dazzlement, and breakthrough? How does Messiaen actually compose this music of *éblouissement*? What is it that makes music and religion relate so intimately to one another? Several levels come into view. What chords and colors exactly come into play? How does Messiaen use them? Are there perhaps any other musical factors that play a part in dazzlement?

Messiaen furnished an answer for these and related questions, although these answers do not immediately settle the matter and give rise to a number of additional, even more pertinent questions. In November 1985 Messiaen visited Japan and gave a lecture in Kyoto.[1] In this lecture, published as the *Conférence de Kyoto*, Messiaen again addressed the issue of *éblouissement*. This time, however, he made a remarkable reference to two specific works that, according to Messiaen, are "directly related" to the experience.[2] One of these is *La Transfiguration de Notre-Seigneur Jésus-Christ*. He specifies and describes five particular passages in relation to *éblouissement*: "Several passages of *La Transfiguration* are directly related to what I call dazzlement (*éblouissement*), that is to say an inner color sensation that is analogous to the visual sensations that are produced by the stained-glass rosettes and windows of the grand Gothic cathedrals, something of the terrible and the sacred, whose details cannot be understood, that transports us to a world of light that is too strong for our reason." The following brief analysis of these passages will offer some insight into the form Messiaen actually gave to his music of *éblouissement*.[3]

Messiaen composed *La Transfiguration* between 1965 and 1969.[4] The work is written for seven instrumental soloists, choir, and orchestra. Its form is reminiscent of Bach's passions or the eighteenth-century oratorio, consisting as it does of a number of vocal "recitatives," "commentary" movements, and two closing chorales. Its fourteen movements are grouped into two *septénaires* (septenaries), the second running at twice the length of the first. The text of the work is a patchwork of scriptural and theological fragments, all addressing some aspect of the transfiguration of Christ as related in the gospel of Matthew (Mt 17:1–9).

> [1] And after six days Jesus taketh Peter, James, and John his brother, and bringeth them up into an high mountain apart, [2] And was transfigured before them: and his face did shine as the sun, and his raiment was white as the light. [3] And, behold, there appeared unto them Moses and Elias talking with him. [4] Then answered Peter, and said unto Jesus, Lord, it is good for us to be here: if thou wilt, let us make here three tabernacles; one for thee, and one for Moses, and one for Elias. [5] While he yet spake, behold, a bright cloud overshadowed them: and behold a voice out of the cloud, which said, This is my beloved Son, in whom I am well pleased; hear ye him. [6] And when the disciples heard it, they fell on their face, and were sore afraid. [7] And Jesus came and touched them, and said, Arise, and be not afraid. [8] And when they had lifted up their eyes, they saw no man, save Jesus only. [9] And as they came down from the mountain, Jesus charged them, saying, Tell the vision to no man, until the Son of man be risen again from the dead.

Messiaen spread this text over four "evangelical recitatives" (*récits évangeliques*), each followed by two "meditations" (*méditations*), in which texts that relate to the thematics of transfiguration are set to music. These include passages from Psalms, Genesis, the Book of Wisdom of Solomon, and the letters of Paul, extracts from the liturgy of Transfiguration (August 6), and remarkably long excerpts from Aquinas's commentary on the transfiguration of Christ, among other writings.[5] All texts are sung in Latin.

*First Passage: Part VIII, "Et ecce vox de nube . . ."*

The third recitative of *La Transfiguration* narrates how Peter, Jacob, and John, standing on top of the mountain and witnessing Christ's transfiguration, are overshadowed by a luminous cloud: "While he yet spake, behold, a bright cloud overshadowed them: and behold a voice out of the cloud, which said, This is my beloved Son, in whom I am well pleased; hear ye him" (5). In *Conférence de Kyoto*, Messiaen elucidates the first example of *éblouissement* in practice:

The first of these passages is located in the eighth piece, at the moment when the Voice from the cloud says: "This is my beloved Son." The Voice is entrusted to the choir. It is accompanied by multicolored, tremulating chords in the strings, whose colors move at different speeds. They are "turning chords" (*accords tournants*), played in two superimposed transpositions, to which are added the shivering of harmonic sounds and the trills of triangle and cymbals. The movement is very slow, the dynamic shade is pianissimo. Gradually, the crescendo and the "turning chords" introduce a light which is amplified by the victorious major third.[6]

Messiaen's musical setting of this scene reveals a number of details that are important for a deeper understanding of the music of *éblouissement*. In the same way as in the other three recitatives, this third recitative is introduced by a strongly syncopated percussion phrase featuring the temple block, leading into an enormous explosion of tam-tams and gongs and a long-held trill on the chimes. The instrumentation and, above all, the unusual timing of this percussion play are reminiscent of Southeast Asian musical traditions. It is an illustration of Messiaen's great love of metallophones with long and rich resonances (vibraphone, bells, gongs), which, according to the composer, "add a certain mystery" to the music and evoke an "unreal quality."

> These instruments offer us power, poetry, and an unreal quality: the vibraphones with their quivering resonance, the gongs, the tam-tams, bells, with their halo of harmonics and false fundamentals (*fausses fondamentales*), and other very complex sound phenomena that actually bring us close to some of the enormous and strange noises in nature like waterfalls and mountain streams.[7]

After this introductory gesture, the choir of tenors starts singing the biblical texts. Its musical setting strongly evokes the Gregorian antiphon, followed by an equally liturgical piece of recitative *recto tono* (that is, on one pitch only). This pseudomonastic passage is followed by eleven measures of uneven ascending and descending clusters in the strings, some of which are played in harmonics (representing, according to Messiaen, the moving cloud). These alienating elements lead up to the passage he quotes in *Conférence de Kyoto* as being related to *éblouissement*.

The passage proper starts at fig. 5 and extends into the tenor recitative: "*Et ecce vox de nube, dicens: Hic est Filius meus dilectus*" (And behold the cloud, saying: This is my beloved Son). At this point in the score, there is a remarkable footnote referring to the figurative character of the music.[8] In fact, the note adds technical instructions to the general idea of the piece, which Messiaen had already described in the short analyses that preface the score:

> Rhythmical introduction (varied). Continuation of the evangelical text in the recitative. The luminous cloud is represented by groups of glissandi in the strings, glissandi of various lengths and tempi. The "Voice" from the cloud is accompanied by the multicolored, tremulating chords, the colors of which move at different speeds. The trills of the triangle and chimes join the harmonics of the strings, emphasizing the quivering light.[9]

Messiaen wants his music to represent a number of things, to begin with the presence of God. Messiaen depicts this in a thoroughly apocalyptic way, deriving the images of quivering light (cloud and Son) and color (Father) from Revelation 4:2–6. Second, he wishes to convey the Voice of God coming from the cloud. According to the instructions in the score, it should sound as if coming from very high up and far away and remaining so. And third, his textures are to represent the triumph and glory of the present Trinity: the crescendo and the "victorious third" (as Messiaen refers to it) render the triumph of the Trinitarian God.[10]

Before this musical depiction comes to life, Messiaen orders a "moment of silent expectation": a short pause, which he prepared for two measures earlier by using a two-beat rest. After that, the music gradually builds up with a foreboding recitative and expectant rests, until at fig. 6 a sudden clarity appears. The instrumentation of this *éblouissement* passage consists of sopranos and tenors, first and second violins, violas, double basses, and percussion. The richness of timbre as well as the verticality of structure contrast sharply with the sober, unison singing of the tenors that precedes the sudden change. Messiaen fills the vertical space of this sound image with materials that originate in the tradition of religious music, such as a drone (the B in the lowest and highest strings, also as harmonic), organlike clusters (reminiscent of the voix céleste's effect of arid transparence and harmonic saturation), the fairy tale sound of the triangle, and the "mystery" of the chimes. In the high and middle registers the strings produce chromatic chords that can be identified as belonging to Messiaen's paradigmatic *accords tournants* (turning chords).[11] The heterogeneous sound image that results from these trills, clusters, resonances, and harmonics is stabilized by the continuity of the drone and the revolving turning chords that saturate the sound spectrum.

The passage, which is only six measures long, is played in a mesmerizing slow and perfectly constant beat of 20 mpm, so that its timing and form contrast sharply with its context. As we shall see, the creation of this sort of window is typical of most musical passages that Messiaen mentions as examples of *son-couleurs* and *éblouissement*. A situation is created in which a sudden change in the musical context occurs, which leads into a completely different (contrasting, opposing) musical situation.[12] Immediately after this breakthrough, the music returns to its previous style, which in general is less complex and more homophonic. It could well be argued that besides any consideration of synesthetic color, this very window form itself produces the effect of breakthrough. In Part VIII, after the sudden introduction of the music of *éblouissement*, the music reverts to a soprano-and-tenor recitative, and loses all luminosity, complexity, and heterogeneity. And, it should be added, it loses all reference to religious breakthrough, too, for Messiaen does not even mention setting to music the remainder of God's own sentence, "*in quo mihi bene complacui: ipsum audite*" (in whom I am well pleased; hear ye him).

### Second Passage: Part IX ". . . quia solus est"

The second passage is located at the end of the ninth piece. In a grand combination of rhythms, the rhythm of the choir is superimposed on three different rhythmic groups, using Greek meters in short and long notes of different duration, and deçi-tâlas from India in retrograde movement. Each rhythmic group has its own harmonies: "chords with contracted resonance," "turning chords," [and] "chords with transposed inversions." The small cymbals, the chimes, and the gongs double the rhythm of the woodwinds and strings; the trumpets and trombones reinforce the rhythm of the choir. The sonority is very powerful; it consists of enormous colors, each evolving in a massive way from the other.

The above-discussed recitative that opens the second septenary is followed by two "meditations," the first of which, Part IX, is designated by Messiaen in relation to *éblouissement* and breakthrough. A quotation from a commentary on transfiguration by Aquinas is set to music in this meditation. The translation of this remarkably (given its musical application) prosaic and theological-technical text is given below. The passage addresses Aquinas's question "whether the testimony of the Father's voice, saying, This is my beloved Son, was fittingly heard."

Men become adopted sons of God by a certain conformity of image to the natural Son of God. [Now this is accomplished in two ways.] First of all, by the grace of the wayfarer, which is an imperfect conformity; secondly, by glory, which is a perfect conformity. . . . Baptism we acquire by grace, while the splendor of our future glory was foreshadowed in the transfiguration. Therefore it was fitting that at the time both of his baptism and transfiguration the natural filiation of Christ be made known by the testimony of the Father: since he alone together with the Son and the Holy Spirit is perfectly conscious of that perfect begetting.[13]

Messiaen ingeniously divided the text into two halves for Part IX, with the second half a condensed form of the first, as a repeat and with largely the same musical content.[14] As Aloyse Michaely shows, Messiaen made deft use of the structure of Latin. In the first part the phrases of the text are arranged in such a way that the word *est* is accentuated, thus creating a certain emphasis on the presence or Being of God: "*Quia solus est / Quia solus est, simul cum Filio / Et Spiritu Sancto*" (Since he alone is / Since he alone is, together with the Son / And the Holy Spirit).[15] In the second part the emphasis shifts to what Aquinas means to say with this, namely that only the Trinity—which is not overtly named as such—is perfectly aware of perfect descent: "*Perfecte conscius illius / Quia solus est perfecte conscius / Perfectae generationis*" (Perfectly conscious of that / Since he alone is perfectly conscious / Of that perfect begetting).

As for the music, Messiaen opted for a mosaic structure, just as in the other parts of *La Transfiguration*. It is a succession of contrastive, autonomous entities: sections with "Hindu rhythms" played by the complete orchestra ("powerful and chaotic, as the musics of Sikkim" according to the score), birdsong cadenzas for piano and cello solo, 'volières' for wind instruments and percussion, solos for baritone and tenor to which a chorus of choir and orchestra sweetly responds, sections with gong and tam-tam strokes, massive *tutti* for choir and orchestra, and finally, "at the close of the ninth piece," the section with the "grand combination of rhythms" that Messiaen relates to *éblouissement*.[16] A number of these elements should be taken as a symbol, according to the composer. The "Sikkim" section represents, by means of confronting the high chords for wind instruments with deep pedal notes for trombones, "the heights and depths of the mystery."[17] The thematic of filiation and the promise of resurrection is symbolically expressed by the many birds that make an entry in this part (most of them referred to in the score by name and country of origin). In Messiaen, birds symbolically stand for, among other things, the joy, power, agility (*agilitas*), and clarity (*claritas*) of the resurrected (*corpora gloriosa*).[18]

## PREFATORY EVENTS

The section Messiaen refers to is introduced at fig. 49 by seven measures whose structure is reminiscent of the introduction to the passage from Part VIII: again an announcement interrupted by intermittent silences. Now, however, there are a number of accompanying elements, framed in such a scheme that the passage is rather suggestive of certain announcements prescribed by Stravinsky in *The Rite of Spring*.[19] In the case of Messiaen, we have a "ringing" alternation of two chords, played by the piano and percussion (temple block, cymbals, and gongs) and accompanied by cello, mallets, and woodwinds.[20] The ringing (Messiaen actually refers here to the song of the Mexican mockingbird, but that will elude most listeners without access to the score) gradually lasts longer, from two to five times. There are two pauses that interrupt the ringing. Although with each retake of the ringing the color of chords is a fraction different, the general impression of growth and accomplishment that this passage yields seems to be most of all due to the gradual buildup of an integrating harmony.

To this end, the passage deploys a pattern known from the so-called adding song. After each interruption, the play of piano and percussion becomes somewhat longer and, in the vertical direction, the chord of the accompanying instruments becomes more complete. This pattern keeps the listener at tenterhooks about what will be added to the whole after the next interruption. The logic of the pattern admittedly entails a certain predictability about what is to come, but it fulfills at the same time with the predictable the most important condition for surprises (such as the opening of the passage). The ringing of piano and percussion redoubles the tension that is evoked by the passage, as if a marvelous bell is keeping the listener in thrall. At fig. 49 the scheme consists of three phases; in the analogous passage from the first part of Part IX, at fig. 22, it consists of two phases. There, the described prefatory and tension-laden effect is less strong. Messiaen uses a similar buildup in the passages that come after the introductions, in the respective halves. Here, too, the second appearance of the passage is more complex and has a stronger effect than the first. This can be the reason why Messiaen, with respect to *éblouissement*, does not refer to the first instance of the passage but to the second.

## BREAKTHROUGH

While the gongs are still reverberating in the pause after the third phase of ringing, the passage specified by Messiaen begins. This transition has certain aspects in common with the one that introduces the passage of Part VIII. There, we had a large contrast between the monody of the introductory vocal parts, and the orchestral mass and abundance of the passage proper, divided by a pregnant silence; here the relative uniformity of the ringing, followed by a similar silence, leads to a simultaneity that affects the entire range of the orchestra; a superimposition of individually moving musical layers. There is then a total of three orchestral layers, in addition to the melody of the choir singing the words *"quia solus est perfecte conscius illius."*[21]

It is a vast contrast with the preceding, as the part largely consists of birdsong that has the character of a multipartite signal. The structure of the part can be pictured as a consecutive string of such signals and other autonomous entities (refrain, tutti, cadenza). However, in the *éblouissement* passage there is no linear discontinuity, but rather a superimposition of layers that are individually continuous. If there be a case here of discontinuity, this rather affects the verticality of the passage, between the different layers. The overall effect of these simultaneously appearing layers is stasis—not the stasis of the aforementioned consecutive string with no directional development or the static verticality of the passage from Part VIII, but the stasis of totality that comes about because of the simultaneous appearance of so many heterogeneous elements. This stasis is further redoubled by the languid tempo (*presque lent* with quarter-note = 46 mpm).

Each of the three orchestral layers features the color chords (sound colors) that Messiaen associates with *éblouissement*. It concerns five different chords that together form a cycle or ostinato: two turning chords, a few "chords with contracted resonance," and a "chord on the dominant with appoggiaturas."[22] The divergent rhythms on which the five chords are positioned perpetually create new combinations for these already rather complex, for the most part eight-note chords. This copious variation is compensated by the uninterrupted presence of the major triad on B-flat. This calls to mind the turning chords in Part VIII, whose movement took place against the background of an uninterruptedly resounding tone B. The first chord of each layer is slightly altered with respect to its stereotypical form, in such a manner that the upper voices of all three chord layers produce a constant major triad on B-flat. The intervals that constitute this triad (B-flat$^1$–F$^2$–D$^3$) correspond to the distances between the individual layers. These consist, as was mentioned earlier, of transpositions of one and the same series of chords.[23]

There is something special about the arrangement of the chords, as Michaely points out. The four eight-note chords are separated by a seven-note appoggiatura chord, which causes a symmetrical division of density: 8-8-7-8-8. Symmetrical patterns like these have a special religious significance for Messiaen and deserve therefore to be briefly clarified here. In the case of a pattern that, when read from back to front, yields the same as when read from front to back, Messiaen speaks of a "nonretrogradable rhythm" (*rythme non-rétrogradable*). It is a term he introduces to indicate that, from the compositional perspective, the retrograde yields nothing new. Messiaen favors these rhythms for their special, occult "charm."

> This is the charm of impossibilities (*le charme des impossibilités*)—they possess an occult power, a calculated ascendancy, in time and sound. It's been said that some of my works had a spellbinding power over the public. There's nothing of the magician in me, and this spellbinding power isn't achieved crudely through repetition, as has been claimed, but perhaps results from those impossibilities enclosed within such and such a formula.[24]

Messiaen deployed the "charm of impossibilities" in several compositional means, a number of which were applied to the passages concerned.[25] The most important is a system of modes he had developed, the so-called modes of limited transposition (*modes à transpositions limitées*). It is a system that consists of seven modes, each constructed from small, repetitious cells. After a number of transpositions of such a structure, the initial form is automatically reached again. In other words, these modes are *limitedly* transposable, which marks their occult "charm," according to Messiaen.[26]

These modes occur in all the mentioned passages, but in their most natural shape they occur in Part XII. In Messiaen's mind's eye, each mode had an individual color or combination of colors. For many of these colors he identified a certain morphology—he saw spiral colors, bands of colors, flames, stars, and so on. The color *chords* used by Messiaen in the five passages can to a certain extent be described in terms of color *modes*. Because each of these modes possesses an individual symmetrical construction (the first mode, identical to the whole-tone scale, is even pansymmetrical), it is natural to think that many of the chords that are derived from these modes (or can be reduced to them) will possess the "charm" of a nonretrogradable rhythm. Insofar that the effect of these chords is related to symmetry, however, this turns out to be arranged by context (such as the symmetrical order mentioned above) rather than by the internal structure of the chords proper.

As for the purely rhythmical application of "charm," Messiaen had developed other instruments too. Thus, he deploys, especially from the 1960s on, "symmetrical permutations" that consist of a successive rereading of a fixed rhythmical series, which always returns to its starting-point. In the passage of Part IX, the charm of such rhythmical "impossibilities" recurs in particular in the rhythm of the three orchestral layers. While the harmonic structure of these layers is mutually equal (all are based on the succession of five color chords), each layer disposes of its proper rhythm. Such a separate, "isorhythmic" treatment of pitch and duration results in a continuous shift between the harmonic and the rhythmical pattern, with the effect, in theory, that after a number of cycles the initial situation returns. The passage from Part IX, however, ends before this unusual event occurs. The sheer possibility of this return (and so of testifying to the "magic" restriction or "impossibility" of this music, that is, the moment of self-identity) should, however, be counted among the structure and effectiveness of this passage. The "eschatological" fulfillment of such coinciding can, however, can be discerned within the *individual* layers of this passage.[27]

## Framing

The passage in Part IX and its parallel appearance in the first half of the part (fig. 23) should be perceived in line with each other, as far as the rhythmical structure is concerned. All layers, both in their first and second occurrence, can be reduced to a sequence of three *deçî-tâlas* (deshitalas, that is, Hindu folk rhythms): *râgavardhana*, *candrakalâ*, and *lakskmîça*. Messiaen began to use these rhythms frequently from the 1940s. He first learned about them in an article on Indian music theory, which he had accidentally discovered in an encyclopedia.[28] The bottom layer is formed by the succession of these *tâlas*, in retrograde and in rhythmic augmentation. The duration of the parallel to this passage (at fig. 23) determines that after twenty beats (i.e. quarter notes) the pattern is stopped. This moment occurs just after the start of the repeat of the pattern, in *lakskmîça*. In the passage proper (at fig. 50), the pattern is retaken where it was stopped, and so we have the remainder of the *lakskmîça*, followed by *candrakalâ* and *râgavardhana*. A loose quarter note follows before the passage is stopped again (before fig. 52).[29]

Likewise, the middle and upper layers that these can only be understood when the passage and its parallel are observed in relation to one another. Messiaen asserts in his commentary that these consist of "Greek verse feet of short and long notes of varying duration," but in fact they are constructed as permutations of those elements that form the basic structure of *lakskmîça*, *candrakalâ*, and *râgavardhana* in their original form. When taking this passage and its parallel together, a thrice-repeated pattern emerges in both the upper and the middle level. As Michaely shows, the makeup and total length equal that of these three *deçî-tâlas*; and in the middle layer these elements form four nonretrogradable rhythms. The upper layer can subsequently be understood as the retrograde of the middle, of which the elements are exchanged, in pairs, in chiasmus.[30]

In the midst of this astonishing complexity of mutually shifting cyclic and symmetrical patterns that are taking place at very different levels, there is the choir, divided into six vocal groupings, that sings the text of *"quia solus est"* while supported by three trumpets and three trombones. The melody can be seen as a variation in three parts on the theme in the first measures of the passage and its parallel. This theme ambulates around the note $C^2$ with a tritone above and below (G-flat$^1$ and F-sharp$^2$) as supporting notes. Together the melody notes form an almost complete whole-tone scale (the pansymmetric first mode of limited transposition).

Within the oceanic totality of heterophonous and mutually heteromobile orchestral layers, Messiaen thus manages to create melodic structures that—in ambulating around a single tone and through a far-reaching symmetry—form a stable horizon. This horizon joins the horizon of the uninterrupted major triad on B-flat resulting in the five color chords. Together, these two horizons form the skeleton for the structure that frames this passage. Just as in Part VIII, the moment stops with the transition to a strongly contrastive music. Here, the transition is still cruder. Apart from the theoretical moment in which they all coincide, the cycles do not have a natural end, and Messiaen does not bring them to a halt one after the other, either. He opts instead for an ending *ex abrupto*. After ten measures, the passage suddenly ends and transmutes after an eighth note rest into its opposite: a perfectly homophonic declamation, supported by low brass instruments filling in, of the "terrible words" (Messiaen in his commentary) *"perfectae generationis."* This abrupt transition mirrors the same suddenness that marked the opening of this passage and joins, in this aspect, the passage from Part VIII. The two horizons form, together with the vertical beginning and ditto ending, a square frame, as it were, for the passage's music.

Part VI does not occur in Messiaen's list of *éblouissement* passages, but a comparison to this part renders the eminent importance of this frame. The music of Part VI, from the first septenary, "Candor est lucis aeterna," consists of an ostinato of repeated chords, just as in the passage from Part IX, and even the same types of chords. The rhythm is equally adapted from *deçî-tâlas.*[31] In Part VI too, a choir sings in brief even phrases. The music of Part

VI is similarly of little duration. It gives the same heterogeneous and yet enclosed and systematic impression as the music of Part IX. There is, however, apart from the appearance of birdsong in Part VI, one major difference: the music of Part VI is no component part of a larger whole to which it is contrasted. There is, in other words, no dramatizing context and therefore no effect of breakthrough such as in Part IX.

Thus, it appears in every respect that *éblouissement* is not the effect of certain color chords alone, but equally, and perhaps more strongly, of the theatrical context these chords are subsumed in. Next to the means of a sudden transition, Messiaen uses techniques that produce a unity in plurality (or, reversely, a plurality in unity). His objective in this appeared to be stasis, joined by the "charm" of limitation and the overwhelming of the massive. Note that these features alone are, independently from the synesthetic effect of sound-colors, features of the experience of *éblouissement*.

### *Third Passage: Part XII "Gloria in excelsis Deo!"*

> The third passage is in the twelfth piece, on the Latin words "*Gloria in excelsis Deo!*" (Glory to God in the highest). The beginning of the phrase is stated with force by the woodwinds, the brass instruments, and the choir. Brusquely, on the word "Deo," one falls into an abyss of tenderness (*abîme de douceur*), the choir and the strings *subito pianissimo* producing a great change in clarity, the counterpoints of pizzicato cellos, the piano playing chords in the "second mode of limited transposition," and "chords with transposed inversions" and "with contracted resonance."

Many elements from the preceding analyses recur in the relevant passage from Part XII. Yet it is less striking than the other ones. Rather, there is a different moment in this part that, regarding vertigo and overwhelming, calls for attention. At its close (fig. 29), Messiaen writes a twenty-part vocalise on the vowel "a." Each voice is supported by a stringed instrument and accompanied by glissandi and other strings (including double basses) and by percussion (gongs, temple block, chimes, and bells). The moment is introduced, according to the directive at fig. 27, by the peregrine falcon (*faucon pèlerin*) and a whir of riffs and accents of the winds, piano, and mallets, tremulating clusters in the strings and agitated percussion (toms, cymbals, maracas). After a tutti crescendo, two *fff* percussive chords and an indeterminate rest, the multilayered vocalise bursts into the open. Abruptly it ends only five measures later, followed by a fermata and then a typical abysmal, rigidly vertical setting of the word *terribilis*.[32] Remarkably enough, Messiaen does not designate this outspokenly terrifying, awesome, and dazzling passage as an example of *éblouissement* and breakthrough, but instead a much friendlier passage earlier in the part, when the words *"Gloria in excelsis Deo!"* are sung.

Messiaen's passage occurs twice (figs. 9–10 and figs. 22–23, respectively), although he does not mention this. The repeat of the passage is a component of the integral repeat of the first part of this Part (figs. 1–13, repeated in figs. 14–25), followed by the closing part described above (figs. 27–30). The repeat only concerns the form (A–A'–B), just as in Part IX. Different texts are sung in the repeat and the musical material is altered, without however obscuring the analogy to the first part. Six fragments form the text: apart from the Gloria (Lk 2:14), a few sentences are borrowed from, respectively, Psalm 104, the *Summa* of Aquinas, and the book of Wisdom of Solomon. For all the theme is luminosity and, in the last fragment, also the terror of the location of transfiguration, high on the mountain, (although Jacob's words derive from a wholly different context): *"Terribilis est locus iste: hic domus Dei est, et porta caeli* (How dreadful is this place! this is none other but the house of God, and this is the gate of heaven)" (Gn 28:17). The text in both occurrences of the passage concerned is of the Gloria, and there are not any noteworthy musical differences either. Perhaps the most remarkable difference is in the fact that the second appearance is set a major third higher, resulting in a significant higher tension in the singing.

It can be inferred from his commentary in *Conférence de Kyoto* that Messiaen is referring to the passage's second occurrence. He mentions a white light: "The light of the 'heights' appears in the chords of the woodwinds and brass instruments, changing suddenly in the pianissimo of the violin's flageolet tones. In that supernatural white light, the pizzicati of the cellos and the color chords of the piano, chimes, and crotales are trembling."[33] Because white is the color that, to Messiaen, corresponds to C major, it will have to be the second passage, because there the major triad on C dominates the "abyss of sweetness" (*abîme de douceur*). At the passage's first appearance, the abyss is in A-flat major, and so a blue light is to be expected, as is indeed confirmed by Messiaen in *Traité de rythme*.[34]

This second passage (figs. 22–23), henceforward assigned as the passage Messiaen had in mind, looks as follows. After a long birdsong cadenza for solo piano (fig. 21), the choir sets in with the text from the Gloria, homophonically accompanied by woodwinds and brass instruments. After the preceding strident sections of percussive chords and austere monophony, this moment stands out for its choral warmth and calm. The chorale melody at fig. 22 is in A-flat major, and from an environment of chords from the third mode (first transposition), it is connected to the predominant "tonality" of *La Transfiguration* in its entirety, E major.[35] The "light of the 'heights'" that Messiaen refers to should be imagined—going by the color tables of Messiaen—as a chiefly blue light, possibly set in the context of gold-orange and milky white.[36] The word "*in*," from the phrase "*Gloria in excelsis*," is set in such a manner that it is emphasized in a special way. Positioned on a C, the third of A-flat major, it is a component of a third-mode chord that destabilizes this third (in particular because of the presence of a B and a G-flat). This instability dissolves only after the transition to fig. 23, when the same tone C takes over as the fundamental for C major. All the time, the powerful third of C major is avoided and only appears after the transition. The two strategies thrust the phrase, as it were, toward the transition. Just as with the transitions for the passages in Part VIII and IX, the transition here has no pause.

The word *Deo* then marks the fall into the "abyss of sweetness," a metaphor that, for Messiaen, suggests the sensation of feeling the earth—which was initially formed by the solid homophony at the beginning of the phrase—slip from under one's feet. Now the woodwinds and brass instruments are silent and the divided strings take over ("in great contrast to the preceding mass of brass instruments"), while the choir sings a pianississimo C-major triad in close middle position.[37] Flageolets in the strings create a luminous sound for the chord, which is further emphasized by the trills on the cymbal and especially on the triangle (see Part VIII).

Somewhat retarded, the three different layers then get under way to fill, color and frame the triad. The first layer is formed by chimes, crotales, and mallets, with a pattern in Messiaen's second mode (first transposition) that sounds as if it is becoming a varied ostinato. It comes to a halt, though, before this can be determined. The second layer is formed by the double basses, divided cellos, and cello. As solo instruments they play much-differentiated pizzicato patterns in septuplets, quintuplets, and triplets. Their pitch complements the second mode, so that a chromatically saturated overall picture ensues. The third layer, finally, consists of the piano solo, playing in equal sixteenth notes the color chords mentioned by Messiaen. These should be understood as chords from the second mode (first transposition), chords from the third mode (third transposition,) "chords on the dominant with appoggiaturas," and "chords with contracted resonance."[38] These chords are doubled and supported by the chords in the first layer, albeit in another rhythmical pattern.

Further analysis brings to light that some of the chords consist of a super-imposition of two chords, including in a number of cases the major triad on C. As for the total effect of colors after the transition, Messiaen writes in his comment to the parallel passage (at fig. 10) that the color chords of the piano form multicolored accents against a background that is determined by the chords of the choir: "just as multicolored birds fly away in a blue rose-window, as the scintillating clarity of dawn when a new day takes position on the points of rock and ice."[39] Mutatis mutandis, the passage at fig. 23 then would have a clear blue background with multicolored color contrasts in the foreground. In Messiaen's mind, the contrast to the music that precedes the sudden transition on *"Deo"* must have been large. The music changes, at the transition, from a clear blue (A-flat major), possibly in a gold–orange environment (third mode, first transposition), via a "supernatural white" (C major) to a sparkling of all sorts of color against this white background.[40]

Just as in the other passages mentioned by Messiaen, the passage from Part XII comes to a sudden end. The richly variegated tapestry of Part VIII led into homophonic *a cappella* singing with the interruption of a pause; the superimposition of heterogeneous layers in Part IX passed into a homo-phonic setting for choir and orchestra after an eighth note rest; and here the inked in space of the C major chord changes without a pause into the terri-ble signal of the peregrine falcon, spelled out for wind ensemble, percussion, and percussion soloists (see the description of the music at fig. 27). The pas-sage, luminous and of differential content, is thus framed by vertical-homophonic musics, with a prominent role for the contrastive "mass" of brass instruments. In the view of Messiaen, the passage depicts the mercy (*douceur*) of God, but it can also be taken to express the marvelous (*merveil-leux*). In particular, the chorale singing coming to a stop on an extended C major chord, the bell-like sounds of evenly spaced piano chords, and the wonderful xylorimba chimes as if from a music box create an atmosphere of expectation, of being spellbound by the miraculous, in naïve amazement.

The role of color chords appears to be remarkably small here. The color effects described earlier are to be ascribed to the modality and colors of tri-ads. The piano chords indisputably add a special sparkle to the total impres-sion, but they are no more than a component of a composite whole. If the passage indeed has the effect that is suggested by Messiaen, then again this must be ascribed to a sudden change in clarity, texture, sonority, and temporality.

### Fourth Passage: Part VII "Chorale of the Holy Mountain"

> And finally, the sensation of dazzlement can be found in the two chorales that conclude each septenary. The first chorale is pianissimo, the second chorale is fortissimo, but the one and the other are only analyzable in terms of colors. These colors are at once sweet and terrifying and they link up with the interpretation of the Psalms addressed to God that conclude my Lecture at Notre-Dame: "In Thy Music, we will SEE the Music—In Thy Light, we will HEAR the Light."

Of the five moments that Messiaen mentions, the closing chorales with each septenary are most like an exhibition of sound-colors. In these parts, therefore, the most direct relation between sound-colors and *éblouissement* is to be expected. Messiaen's comment on the two chorales is rather gnomic: the one ends in pianissimo, the other in fortissimo ("total fortissimo for choir and orchestra").[41] He further mentions the chorales' coloring that is "at once sweet and terrifying." As the score indicates, both chorales are in an extraordinary slow tempo (quarter-note = 30 mpm) and both feature a text from Psalms: Part VII a verse from Psalm 48:2, "*Magnus Dominus, et laudabilis nimis: in civitate Dei nostri, in monte sancto ejus*" (Great is the Lord, and greatly to be praised in the city of our God, in the mountain of his holiness), Part XIV a verse from Psalm 26:8, "*Domine, dilexi decorem domus tuae, et locum habitationis gloriae tuae*" (Lord, I have loved the habitation of thy house, and the place where thine honour dwelleth).

Part VII is the shorter of the two (31 beats, an estimated performance time of four and a half minutes). The chorale evolves in eight phrases, each ending in an extended chord closed by an eighth-note rest. The first phrase introduces an ascending melodic motive that returns at the beginning of the second, third, and fifth phrase. The ascension of this motive continues up till measure 24, where, on the word *monte*, the top of the melodic curve is reached, together with a dynamic peak (fortissimo). Some of the Psalm's words are repeated in the course of this movement: "*in civitate*," "*Dei*" (thrice), and "*in monte.*" The piece ends in pianissimo with a major triad on E. The rest of the melody's harmonization is full of striking contrasts. Chords with a very dense chromatics alternate with major triads on E (mostly in second inversion), once on A (subdominant) and thrice on B-flat (the tritone often has the function of the dominant with Messiaen).[42] In

conversation with Claude Samuel, Messiaen spells out the colors of this chorale measure by measure.

> Here the colors are very distinct because of the very slow tempo. I'll try to
> enumerate them. The first two chords are superimpositions of green-black
> tint. The third chord belongs to the category of turning chords; it contains,
> from high to low, blue-green, pinkish mauve, and green. The fourth chord
> (fourth and sixth of E major) is red. Measures 4 and 5 take up approximately
> the same colors as the opening. Measures 6, 7, and 8 are in both E major
> (red) and in Mode 2 (second transposition), containing gold and brown and
> also red. Measures 9, 10, and 11 return to the colors of the opening. Measures
> 12 and 13 are in Mode 3 (second transposition), which is gray and mauve,
> and they end (at measure 14) on a neutral-blue seventh. Measure 15 takes up
> the turning chords, from high to low: blue-green, pinkish mauve, green,
> then yellowish green, silver, grayish black. Measure 16 (fourth and sixth of
> E major, *pianissimo*) is red. Measures 17 and 18 are in Mode 3 (first transposi-
> tion), containing orange and gold. Their crescendo brings on in force the
> sixth chord of E major in measures 19 and 20: this chord is red, the two
> piccolos heightening its light. Measures 21, 22, and 23 go back to the open-
> ing sonorities in ascending steps, ending (measure 24) on the fourth and sixth
> of E major, *fortissimo*, which is red. Measures 25 and 26 are at once in E major
> (red) and in Mode 2 (second transposition), containing gold and brown and
> also red. Measure 27 is a neutral-blue seventh; there's a great contrast in color
> between the red of measures 25 and 26 and the blue of measure 27. (Further-
> more, measure 27 brings an A-natural and an F-sharp that didn't exist in the
> previous mode.) Measure 28 has two turning chords, from high to low: the
> first one is blue-green, pinkish mauve, green; the second is yellowish green,
> silver, grayish black. Measure 29 is the fourth and sixth of E major, red; in
> measure 30, a cluster on Mode 3 (first transposition), all the notes together
> (except for the B, which is reserved for the last measure), all give, because of
> their close position and low register, a gold and brown that is almost black.
> The last measure is a perfect E-major chord, deep red, very *pianissimo*, mys-
> terious, with the fifth (B) made conspicuous in the upper part (sopranos,
> trumpet).[43]

The overwhelming list of colors here certainly appears to affirm Messiaen's
statements on *éblouissement*, if only because the reader is blinded on the spot
simply by taking in these words, let alone when undergoing this dazzlement
of colors in actuality. At closer inspection, however, it turns out that Messiaen is not just offering a tangle of colors, but is composing a logically constructed story with these colors as actors and protagonists; deploying, in

short, the dramatic means that are normally reserved for tonal, functional-harmonic music.[44] The protagonist is the major triad on E, which, depending on register and chord position, emanates various shades of red; with the antagonist consisting of a number of chords that produce the contrast to red, that is, the color blue.[45] The latter especially concern the chords of measure 14 and 27, which both partake of the third mode (third transposition) and have a "neutral-blue" coloring, according to Messiaen. Then there are also shades of blue in the turning chord number "4-C" (according to Messiaen's categorization), which appears as the first chord of measure 2 (and further also in mm. 4, 5, 9, 10, and 15), and in the chords that resemble this turning chord, in measures 22 and 23.[46] The story that Part VII appears to be telling with these chords is like a drama with a red E major crying victory in the end. The story is told purely at a formal level and as such has an equivalent in tonal music, where it is usually told by means of the antagonism of tonic and dominant, in which the latter mostly, despite of its name, is not dominant at all in the end. As a preliminary remark to this story, it has to be said that all phrases of Part VII end in E major, except the sixth phrase just before the end (mm. 25–27).

At the start of the story, there is a dark green-black, followed by a brief appearance of the first bluish turning chord (m. 2), which melodically leads up to the red major triad on E in the middle register. It is the first confrontation of blue and red, still calm, because the clarity and intensity of the red is not very great, due to the middle register and pianissimo, and because the blue is subsumed in the color pillar of the turning chord which also features the color mauve which is related to red. In terms of musical notes, the contrast is also mediated. On the one hand, the E and B are suppressed in the chromatic chords, but the core of E major (E–G-sharp) is part of their modal structure (modus 3, third transposition). The contrastive effect of the elimination then is partly suspended by the modal inclusion of the target chord.

The rest of the chorale elaborates on the thematics of these first three measures. The second phrase (mm. 4–8) is a slightly varied repetition of the first. The coloring that comes about because of the chord in measure 7 is remarkable, because it is as if the E major red is gathered up here in a sort of gold and brown tinted icon, as if it is receiving its nimbus already right here. The third phrase (mm. 9–16) is a further elaboration of the first two phrases. It has an impressive melodic curve and introduces, subsequently, the antagonist in the appearance of a "neutral-blue" chord. This antagonist does not immediately meet the E major protagonist, inasmuch as the two are at first kept separate by two mediating turning chords. The fourth phrase (mm. 17–20) reaffirms the E major after this indirect confrontation, by means of a series of four chords from the third mode (first transposition), which offer resistance to the antagonist's blue with their orange and gold complementary colors. The E major red is, moreover, in the view of Messiaen, extra clear because of the play of the piccolos.

One and the other are conducive to the glorious display of E major in the fifth phrase (mm. 21–24), the climax of the part. This phrase can be seen as a blow up of the first. Just as the first, this one has chords from the third mode (third transposition) with a shade of blue at the start. The ascension of the first phrase is extended with chords from the fourth and second transposition and a chromatically almost saturated chord from the second mode (third transposition). According to Messiaen's color table, this latter chord would be green, the complementary of red. The transition from m. 23 to m. 24 then concerns not just the almost total chromatics changing into a consonant major triad, but also the shift from blue to red, via the contrastive green.[47] The red here is clear and intense, due to its high position and the fortissimo.

The sixth phrase (mm. 25–27) then presents the long-awaited confrontation. As noted, it is the only phrase that does not close on E major. The phrase duplicates almost exactly the victorious chord of the preceding phrase, but frames it now in "iconic" gold and brown and leads it to the "neutral-blue" chord in m. 27, while going from forte to mezzo forte. In his description, Messiaen emphasizes the contrast formed by this chord to the preceding second mode (red, gold, and brown). The phrase's closing on the dominant requires a stabilizing response, which arrives in the seventh phrase (mm. 28–29) with a compressed form of the passage that responded to the presence of the blue chord in m. 14 at the close of the third phrase. It is a return to E major. The eighth phrase, finally, reaffirms this triad, now from a "holy" obscurity or, as Messiaen has it, a "gold and brown that is almost black," with a "mysterious" deep red. Blue is nowhere to be seen, and thus the close of the chorale conveys the impression of victory, redemption, and breakthrough.[48]

The structure of this chorale allows for a reading, along these lines, of a narrative about the confrontation between two symbolical powers that results in the victory of one. The logic of this narrative, in other words, dictates to a certain extent the experience of breakthrough and redemption. It is not the individual chords that account for such an experience, nor the color effect as such, but the game of opposing powers that results in the dénouement described above. The chords are included in the game and depend on it for their shock effect. Taken away from the game, they would not easily cause the effect of éblouissement, nor give reason for a specifically religious interpretation of this effect. This is made possible only within the musical drama that unfolds as the narrative of protagonist and antagonist.[49]

A number of other elements contribute to the drama, apart from the dualism of colors: the slow tempo; the ritual repeats of the first phrase and of words such as *"Dei"*; the contrast between the stepwise chord connections and the leaps in the melody (not discussed here); dynamic shades and outbursts; rhythmic unity; and instrumental grandeur. These elements frame the color chords or form their background scenery, thus creating the apt conditions for the unique effect (*éblouissement*, breakthrough): they are like the darkness in a church, or the nontransparent lead in stained-glass windows that frame and support the individual pieces of colored glass, thus enabling them to produce the dazzling effect they have as a whole.

### Fifth Passage: Part XIV "Chorale of the Light of Glory"

The chorale that closes the second septenary and so *La Transfiguration* as a whole shows in what manner the mise-en-scène of breakthrough can be reinforced. Unfortunately, Messiaen has left no specification of the exact colors that occur in this chorale. A reconstruction based on the description of the first chorale would be too speculative.[50] The other parameters, however, provide sufficient directions for describing the main lines of Messiaen's musical strategy.

Part XIV consists of two or three components, depending on the criterion used for dividing the form. In terms of musical structure, this part has a tripartite structure (A–A'–B).[51] But when departing from the text, a binary structure is revealed, which ranges from mm. 1 to 46 and from mm. 47 to 76. As a whole, this part is notably longer and more complex than Part VII, if only because of the repeats of its components. Up to a certain extent, the piece can be considered in the tonality of E major. The first musical part ends on a pedal point and a dominant seventh chord on the dominant B (m. 19). The second part ends on the tonic, although in second inversion (m. 45). The third and last part ends on E major in root position (m. 76). The subdominant to E major, the six-five chord of A major, also appears in the third part, in measures 48 and 54.

This tonal base structure is inked in with a large assortment of "special chords" in a larger variety than found in Part VII. Most chords are represented: "chords on the dominant with appoggiaturas," "chords with contracted resonance," and "turning chords." Only the "chords with transposed inversions" do not appear here.[52] In nearly all cases, additional tones are supplemented to these chords, which are on average placed in a higher register than in Part VII. A chromatically saturated sonic totality that gradually increases in the course of this Part (especially from m. 57) is the result.[53] The role played by the two piccolos, which had announced themselves already in measure 5, is emphatically foregrounded in this passage. They soar high above the sonorous sound of choir and orchestra, playing "above ear level" parts that emphasize the superimposition of modes and the layered construction of the special chords.[54] A vertical layering for the ear ensues, as if in listening the ear is climbing a steep rock formation that recalls the spatiality of the colors that Messiaen ascribes to these chords.[55]

Due in part to this layering, a certain stasis arises in this part. The chorale is pinned on an alternation of major triads on E and chords functioning as dominant. The alternation propels the chorale in a certain sense, but this propulsion is annihilated in many places by an excess of chromatics. This happens in two different ways. First, the chromatically saturated music is static with regard to harmony and melody, because all possibilities are exhausted at a single stroke.[56] Secondly, the result of this chromatic saturation is that the two most important propelling forces of the chorale are neutralized. On one hand, then, the distinction between triads and chromatic chords (that guaranteed some sort of motion) begins to fade. The chromatic chords present themselves in the course of the chorale as harmonics of their juxtaposed triads, while these triads in turn appear in the resonances of the chromatic chords. The fountain of harmonics that is induced by both the diatonic and the chromatic chords (each in a different way), assisted by the dynamics of forte and fortissimo, frustrates the propulsion even more. It forms a resonant curtain of color that does not partake at all of the harmonic functionality and ongoing movement that the succession of chords seems to suggest.

On the other hand, the other force behind this propulsion, melody, experiences a similar hindrance from saturation. The motion of melody is smothered in the mire of chromatics (mm. 28–29, 41–43) or impeded in such a way that the ear is drawn rather towards the vertical relations (mm. 57–59). At times, there hardly seems to be question of melody tone (mm.

10, 15, 37–38) or the melody disappears into the chromatic universe of middle voices (mm. 17–18).[57] Despite this, the melody perseveres and realizes the impossible. It is this, compounded by the massive power of the orchestra and its "abysmal" texture (trombones and bass trombones versus high woodwinds), that gives the part a sublime character.[58] Apart from that, the chromatics of Part VII and XIV can also be thought as the strange, lustrous, or marvelous (*merveilleux*), in contrast to the homecoming or return to the major triad. Taken together, they represent (and may cause the listener to experience such a thing) the religious topos of a homecoming in the marvelous, or at least the promise thereof.

## Windows and Expositions

In summary, the passages indicated by Messiaen fall into two groups, which I will respectively call, for the sake of convenience, windows and expositions. The first three passages (Part VIII, IX, and XII) each reveal a careful mise-en-scène of a big sudden change in the music. The change is announced (as the unexpected must be expected if it is to appear as unexpected), and once it has taken place, it is in turn signed off.[59] I call these passages windows because they form a framed opening to a plane that differs strongly from the surrounding context. As we have seen, *what* precisely makes this unexpected appearance in these passages seems to be less important, in a certain respect, than *that* something appears. In other words, the formal aspect carries more weight than the aspect of content. Still, with respect to content these three passages also have a number of things in common. There is always a heterogeneity and massiveness that cannot be captured by a single aural "gaze," and especially not in the way the music before and after these passages can be surveyed. Diversity is stabilized because it appears against the background of elements that are remaining constant, such as a drone or a cycle of chords or durations. The result is, on one hand, a simultaneity of excessive diversity, plurality and motion; and on the other hand an apparent unity, simplicity, and timelessness. For the effect of breakthrough as such, this "content" seems to matter less.

   The second group of passages (Part VII and XIV), which I refer to as expositions, with an eye on the chorale, majestic setting of the color chords, likewise feature both simultaneity and diachrony. Here, diachrony does not appear in the shape of sudden transitions, but in the perpetual linear alternation of complex color chords and simple triads. Furthermore, there seems to be a case of a linear, narrative context, which once again suggests the suitability of thinking about the alleged breakthrough in terms of dramatizing and mise-en-scène. The first brief chorale could be interpreted, as it turned out, as the story of a dramatic confrontation between two contrastive chord colors or color groups, with one of these crying victory in the end. Apart from these diachronic elements, there is a certain entwining of consonance and dissonance that molds the components into a single simultaneity of tension and relief. The effect is most momentous in the second chorale, where, moreover, the conflict between harmony and melody is stronger than in the first. Messiaen speculates on a simultaneity here that I shall attempt to link to the aesthetics of the sublime in the chapters to follow. In those discussions too, it will come to the fore that the *manner in which* music presents itself matters more than *what* is presented.

What is to be concluded from this brief, music theoretically informed exploration of the five *éblouissement* passages? In the first place, it should be kept in mind that according to Messiaen, dazzlement has little to do with the *representation* of religious ideas by visual or musical means. The music of dazzlement certainly possesses many pictorial features, but its most important religious moment lies in the very *erasure* of these figurative elements (the apparent content of the passage), in a way similar to the erasure of the figures in the stained-glass windows. On a musical and technical level, second, it has already been noted that the musics of dazzlement involve strategies that foreground the formal element in music. In the previous chapter, it was argued that there exists a gradual shift, in Messiaen's oeuvre, from subjectivity and "emotional sincerity" to more formal approaches.[60] The passages from *La Transfiguration* quoted by Messiaen highlight this tendency in that they make no attempt to establish a link between subjective "insides" and musical-formal "outsides." Here, the notion of form comes to mean something other than merely formalistic or abstract form. It appears to be much more related to the theatrical and self-referential gestures of manifestation. Messiaen's music encourages an interpretation in terms of *kenosis*, rather than fulfillment by means of symbolic or representational content. In the third place, from Messiaen's references to it in *Lecture at Notre-Dame*, it seems that *éblouissement* depends strongly on notions of grace and the miraculous even—notions that depend on *singularity*. But it is actually the effect of *repeatable* musical-technical structures, of a theatrical strategy of sorts, thereby seemingly reducing *éblouissement* to the trick of a musical illusionist.

Now, should all this, in the final analysis, lead to the conclusion that Messiaen's testimony with regard to *éblouissement* is in fact little more than musical theatricality? Or should his testimony be understood as a contemporary reference to a musico-religious possibility that Enlightenment aesthetics and certain theologies taught us to forget? What is there to be said about *éblouissement* as a phenomenological or musico-religious figure outside the confines of musicological (that is, music theoretically based) interpretation? And ultimately, how can the formal emptiness of the music of éblouissement be understood as an "illumination of the theological truths of the Catholic faith"? In the next chapter, we will examine the concepts contemporary theology has to offer with respect to understanding the unique way in which Messiaen conceptualized as well as shaped the relation between music and faith.

## 3.    Balthasar and the Religion of Music

> And is not the word just the most profound misunderstanding in music?
>
> —Hans Urs von Balthasar

### Messiaen and Balthasar

The connection between Messiaen and the Swiss theologian Hans Urs von Balthasar is barely noticeable. Yet it is much stronger than can be inferred from the occasional reference to the latter (in comparison, Saint Thomas Aquinas figures much more prominently in the composer's writings and scores).[1] When he does refer to Balthasar, it is without exception in admiring terms; he calls him "the greatest contemporary theologian" and claims to have read Balthasar's theological magnum opus, *The Glory of the Lord* (*Herrlichkeit*), in its entirety.[2]

Messiaen probably came across the work of Balthasar during his preparations for the libretto of *Saint François d'Assise* in the early 1970s. As was discussed in Chapter 1, one of the sources for the words of the Angel in the fifth scene—inspired by Aquinas—was supplied by the short book on Saint Francis by Louis Antoine; the same book also refers to Balthasar.[3] Although Balthasar, apart from a few brief allusions such as the one here, does not play a large part in Messiaen's oeuvre, the composer was alert to the importance of this theologian for interpreting his music. Thus, he expressed his wish for a wider dissemination of a certain text by Alain Michel, a scholar in Latin and history of ideas at the Sorbonne, in which he interprets Messiaen's *La Transfiguration* in light of the same "admirable work" by Balthasar.[4] This text, which came out originally in 1974, was included in the volume of writings compiled in honor of the composer's seventieth birthday with the recommendation that Messiaen believed that "Mr. Alain Michel had penetrated the message of *La Transfiguration* particularly well and wished to designate this text for further dissemination."[5]

In fact, since the publication of Alain Michel's essay, one can speak of a new interpretative frame for Messiaen's work. Diverting from the more conventional Thomistic approaches, it opened the way for considering this work in a more contemporary theological perspective. Although Michel paved the way for new interpretations, he offers little insight in the precise relation between this music and the theology of Balthasar. It is the aim of this chapter to amend this lack, first, by addressing whether Balthasar has written a theology of music, and if so, its nature. What are, to him, the possible connections between music and the Christian? And subsequently, by determining in what sense exactly Balthasar's thought creates insight in the work of Messiaen. In the course of this chapter, it will appear that in Balthasar's thought the Christian moment is defined at the expense of music. The ensuing contrast with the theology of music of Augustine (*Confessions*) will, in terms of a strategic opposition, guide the description of two diverging approaches to thinking the relation between music and the Christian. It will emerge that in his discourse on sound-color and dazzlement, Messiaen is, remarkably enough, closer to Augustine than to Balthasar.[6]

First, however, a brief outline of what is at stake in the theological aesthetics of Hans Urs von Balthasar. The general drift of these aesthetics is especially relevant for the study of art, because of the way the notion of beauty is brought back into the domain of theology. In the view of Balthasar, this notion has gradually been relegated to the margins of the theological debate, partly due to the influence of Protestant theology (Luther, and especially Kierkegaard). As a result, the aesthetic, in the eyes of some theologians, has become synonymous to mere outer appearance, the pretense of beauty, and an unethical way of life. It is considered only in isolation, Balthasar argues, "as opposed to its total integration within the one, the true, and the good in the Greeks and in earlier theology."[7] In *Seeing the Form*, the first of seven volumes, Balthasar asserts his resistance against "the elimination of aesthetics (*Ent-ästhetisierung*)" from theology and argues for a reinstatement and revaluation of beauty. It is his aim to spell out a theological aesthetics that can conceive of the beautiful as a transcendental.

Balthasar defines theological aesthetics as "the attempt to do aesthetics at the level and with the methods of theology." It should not be confused with aesthetic theology, where theological substance is betrayed and sold out "to the current viewpoint of an inner-worldly theory of beauty."[8] While referring to the tradition of Aquinas, Kant, and Husserl, he distinguishes these two forms by posing the following series of questions:

> Are we objectively justified in restricting the beautiful to the area of inner-worldly relationships between "matter and form," between "that which appears and the appearance itself," justified in restricting it to the psychic states of imagination and empathy [*Gestimmtheit*] which are certainly

required for the perception and production of such expressional relationships? Or: May we not think of the beautiful as one of the transcendental
attributes of Being as such, and thereby ascribe to the beautiful the same
range of application and the same inwardly analogous form that we ascribe
to the one, the true, and the good?[9]

Answering the latter question in the affirmative, then, Balthasar proposes
to think the beautiful in transcendental terms. In elaborating his theological
aesthetics, he appeals to the notion of form (*Gestalt*): "Those words which
attempt to convey the beautiful gravitate, first of all, toward the mystery of
form (*Gestalt*) or of figure (*Gebilde*). *Formosus* ('beautiful') comes from *forma*
('shape') and *speciosus* ('comely') from species ('likeness'). But this is to raise
the question of the 'great radiance [*Glanz*] from within' which transforms
*species* into *speciosa*: the question of *splendor*. We are confronted simultaneously with both the figure and that which shines forth from the figure,
making it into a worthy, a love-worthy thing."[10] The two moments of the
beautiful correspond, according to Balthasar, to the notions of *species* and
*lumen* in Aquinas, and are related to the subjective moments of respectively
perceiving beauty and being enraptured by it. Thus, he argues that "no
one can really behold who has not also already been enraptured, and no
one can be enraptured who has not already perceived [*wahr-genommen*],"
and that this "holds equally for the theological relationship between faith
and grace, since, in giving itself, faith apprehends the form of revelation,
while grace has from the outset transported the believer up into God's
world."[11] The dynamics of kenotic *ecstasis* and beholding or, in German,
*wahrnehmen* (which encapsulates, fortuitously for Balthasar, the notion of
*Wahrheit* or truth) connects beauty indissolubly to truth and the good. Accepting truth as it is manifested is attended by a form of ethical devotion
(*Hingabe*), a form of applying oneself to (serving) this truth. Balthasar understands this experience to be the very core of the Christian faith. "To be
transported [*Hingerissenwerden*]," as he formulates it, "belongs to the very
origin of Christianity."[12]

   The quintessential form in this context is the form of Christ (*die Christusgestalt*), the Son who is his Father's image, or more fittingly, his icon
(*eikon*). It is a concrete form, proportioned in the material and aesthetic
sense, and in the end irreducible to sheer immanent beauty. In Balthasar's
words: "The form as it appears to us is beautiful only because the delight
that it arouses in us is founded upon the fact that, in it, the truth and goodness of the depths of reality itself are manifested and bestowed, and this manifestation and bestowal reveal themselves to us as being something infinitely

and inexhaustibly valuable and fascinating."[13] Thus, Balthasar rejects the idea that, in Christianity, faith is founded on hearing the Word (*fides ex auditu*) that this should take precedence over the beholding of form. Rather, perception literally is "a 'taking to oneself' (*nehmen*) of something true (*Wahres*)" that includes both hearing and believing. In the same reasoning, he is opposed to the purely negative interpretation of the *via negativa* in Dionysius and Saint John of the Cross. In his reading of these two authors, the "vertical" and the "horizontal moment," or apophatic and cataphatic theology, are always interlinked.[14]

In the emphasis on form and concomitant rapture or transport, the theological aesthetics of Balthasar appears to provide a key to interpreting *éblouissement* (dazzlement) and breakthrough in Messiaen, which appear to be analogous to, respectively, Balthasar's notions of transport (*Hingerissenwerden*) and the profound experience of God in his totality. However, there is only an implicit connection to music and sound (sound-color) in the latter's theological aesthetics. Balthasar, reportedly a respectable pianist and a great admirer of Mozart (just as Messiaen), often deploys musical metaphors to illustrate his argument and regularly alludes to composers. Just one or two pieces of his oeuvre, however, are devoted to music.[15] In order to gain a clearer picture of Balthasar's conception of music and of the relation drawn by him between music and the religious, a discussion of his very first publication is called for. *Die Entwicklung der musikalischen Idee (The Development of the Musical Idea)* was first published in 1925. It is a relatively unknown text that remained in obscurity for decades before it was reissued in 1998; as yet there is no English translation. It turns out to be a seminal work for the themes that would guide Balthasar's later thought.

This early work yields some clues about the way Balthasar envisages the relation between music and religion. In summary, Balthasar's argument runs as follows. He departs from the notion that music contributes to the "Information of the Divine" (12). In art, the notions of form and "information" imply that the divine is rendered within temporal-spatial categories, "a condensed projection of the eternal in the country of form" (10, 12). Thus, form is "revelation from above (for what else could it be?)" (48). Such information is better achieved in music than in the other arts, because music penetrates the human subject more directly and profoundly. There is a reverse, however: the information of the divine remains imperfect in music and is impalpable because of its immediacy. Besides, music is only one art form whereas in truth it is all the arts taken together that can be said to express the total Idea (*Gesamtidee*), that is, the divine (9–10, 12). Balthasar asserts that music is rational, like all art (57). But the divine in music (that is, its Form) is not rational. This Form can only become manifest in the immediate metaphysical experience, an experience that is, nonetheless, structured. Balthasar describes this structure in dynamic terms as an analogy (*analogon*) of the divine mystery: it affects our innermost being but remains, at the same time, incomprehensible and veiled (42–43). Because it is in structure analogous to the divine, it cannot be the divine itself—the divine is designated as "truth" and "unmediated truth." This notion of truth should be understood as "an Idea" (42). In line with this, the divine is also referred to as a "spiritual Idea" and more specifically as the "total Idea" (*Gesamtidee*) (10). The aspect of integration implicit in the notion of totality causes Balthasar to remark that the work of art that is most effective in organically integrating the majority of "eternally valid answers" will be closest to the "total form" of the musical Idea (54, 56). He counts Gregorian chant, the folksong, the fugue, and the classic symphony among such "successful" instances of information (50).

At this point, the analytical moment of the text (the discourse on "information") intersects with the historical. Balthasar describes the historical development of music as evolving organically from the Idea. The historical starting point would be in rhythm, supposedly deployed in primitive society to bring some order to the overwhelming noises of nature. At this early stage there was no melody or harmony: music was purely a physical and instinctive affair. According to Balthasar, the next stage was the development of melody with the Greeks, who related this element of music to the Dionysian, irrational-demonic, which they saw as subjected to the Apollonian order of rhythm. The musical Spirit was not free to move at will, therefore, because it "had not met with a congenial form" (30). Such liberty was found in the third stage, which, just like the one before, incorporated the previous stage. Due to the evolution of harmonic relations, melody was free to explore "the space of tones with unclipped and widespread wings" (36).[16]

Balthasar states that the divine is a "total Idea"; it is "Sense" or "primitive light" that is "unintelligible" and that "surpasses reason" (11–12). At the close of Balthasar's discourse, God acquires more concrete contours. God is "eternally elementary, single and manifold" (always in unison with the notion of "total Idea," however) and "flowing dynamically in his own self as well as in the world as Logos" (44, 57). This dynamic element, then, is mirrored, the reasoning goes, by the temporal nature of the medium of music. Balthasar advances a number of characteristics that designate the "pure form and unmediated truth" of music. Apart from the proximity of mystery and the principle of simultaneity, both typical for music, these are "concentration and expansion," in analogy to the way the Spirit evolved in history, and a high degree of "intensity," that is, of information of the divine Idea constituting an "eternally valid answer" (43, 45).

### Form as Musically Christian

For all its succinctness, Balthasar's text leaves a number of questions unanswered. The principal notions of this seminal work suggest an array of influences, but without proper references to sources it is difficult to determine the precise meaning of terms such as "Form" and "information." There are some other problematic issues, too. To what extent should his historical interpretation be understood in Hegelian terms? To what extent does his text have a Christian purport? The first and only comprehensive commentary to date on *Die Entwicklung der musikalischen Idee* was compiled by Mario Saint-Pierre. In *Beauté, bonté, vérité chez Hans Urs von Balthasar*, he succeeds in clarifying Balthasar's text in a number of places, partly by juxtaposing *Die Entwicklung* to some of the author's other works. Apart from that, Saint-Pierre proposes elements of a musical theology of his own by elaborating on certain passages in Balthasar. In view of the *strategies* employed in theology to legitimate music for its own purposes, a twin reading of Balthasar and Saint-Pierre yields interesting results.

Saint-Pierre argues that an implicit polemic against Nietzsche is raised in *Die Entwicklung*. In *The Birth of Tragedy*, Nietzsche had related the Dionysian to the musical element of melody, letting it prevail over the Apollonian that he associated with rhythm. Balthasar opposed the idea of such specific privileging with the Greeks and argued that the subjection of melody to rhythm should be read in more positive terms.[17] He believed that by suppressing the melodic, the Greeks merely attempted to balance the Dionysian with the Apollonian in order to achieve equilibrium between the "demonic" of melody and the rational order of rhythm. The desire for such a positive opinion on the Apollonian (and of balance and proportion) should be related, according to Saint-Pierre, to Balthasar's *theological* stake. In a Christian reading, the equilibrium between both forces involves, on one hand, the vital lust for life (the Dionysian), and on the other hand, the principle of being created after an image (the Apollonian).[18] The latter aspect constitutes, as form, the positive central point for divine revelation in Christ, the living image of the Father. As such, it is defended in *Die Entwicklung* as well as—and more explicitly—in Balthasar's later work.

It seems that Balthasar's taking issue with Nietzsche really involves a covert critique of Schopenhauer's musical metaphysics, which would not leave enough room for Form (figure, shape) and consequently neither for beauty (proportional form), nor for the arts (form made concrete), nor for the Christian (the figure of revelation). Schopenhauer, dragging Nietzsche in his wake, supposedly was intoxicated by musical metaphysics and lost his bearings. Both philosophers then obscured the truth of art, that is, the *Christian* truth of art. Saint-Pierre writes that Nietzsche's

> absolutization of Dionysian music in the realm of Being and metaphysics radically contradicts the principle brought forward by Balthasar from the very beginning of his work regarding the immediacy and elusiveness of musical experience. While these two features of music reveal its divine dimension (which, in the Christian context, is perfectly justifiable by the thesis of *analogia entis*), they become a projection of vital and ontological energy with Nietzsche. Through music humankind should recapture this immanent world of Dionysian forces in order to taste the joy of the eternal intoxication of pure Will. The new metaphysics is a divinization of passion. Music is the perfect expression of a conception of metaphysics that is incapable of accepting the beauty and truth of art (the discovery of form and luminous splendor as defining the Idea of beauty), because it considers these as being too limited to the Apollonian dimension that attempts to hide or repress that vital principle.[19]

This leads to the Apollonian again, to the notion of Form, and to Aquinas. Balthasar's defense of rhythm with the Greeks is a defense of the Apollonian, which bears visual connotations because of its association with figure, shape, and form. As Saint-Pierre argues, Balthasar is searching in essence for "the discovery of form and luminous splendor as defining the Idea of beauty." If there is to be a place for beauty in art, then these two qualities of form and splendor will have to be recognized and acknowledged. The metaphysics of "the trio Wagner-Nietzsche-Schopenhauer" not only lacks Apollonian form, Saint-Pierre maintains, but it is also devoid of Apollonian splendor, especially in the sense of "clairvoyance" and "clairaudience" (*Hellsehen* and *Hellhören*) or "illuminating the heart."[20]

Despite these differences, the musical point of departure is the same for Balthasar and Schopenhauer. For both the *antinomic structure* of musical experience is central. Music, in this structure, is both the most immediate and the most elusive art form and is brought close to divine mystery, according to Saint-Pierre: "Music is like the *analogon* par excellence of the *analogia entis*, because this art form, somewhat in the manner of God, is at once both the most nearby and the most impalpable, immanent and transcendent. It is incessant movement that submerges and surpasses us (Dionysus) in the immediate expression of melodic forms (Apollo)."[21] The two contrastive elements in this antinomy (of proximity and impalpability) are united in Balthasar's concept of form (both in *Form* and *information*), which appears to be derived from Goethe and can be understood in the context of the latter's notion of *Gestalt*.[22]

Form or *Gestalt* structures not only this early work on music, but Balthasar's later explorations of aesthetics as well. In *The Glory of the Lord*, he compares the architecture of the gospel to that of the fugue and uses Goethe's organic model for growth to sustain his comparison, inasmuch as both fugue and gospel consist of components that are each and all related to each other: "Every element calls for the other, and the more penetrating the gaze of the beholder, the more he will discover harmony [*Stimmigkeit*] on all sides. If one element should be broken off (Christ's eternal divine sonship, for instance), all the proportions will be distorted and falsified."[23] Individual parts or *Einzelgestalten* are mutually related both to one another and to the whole of complete form or *Gesamtgestalt*. According to Balthasar, this form ensures that "the perceiver does not gather isolated impressions (the word logos comes from the Greek to "gather"—*legein*) in order to synthesize them. Rather, he grasps totalities beforehand in their appearance from the depths."[24]

The most emblematic example of form in music is melody, which occupies a privileged position with Balthasar. He is in good company: Schopenhauer and Hegel exhibited melomania, and Messiaen too surrendered soon enough to this musical phenomenon. At the age of twenty-five, Messiaen wrote enthusiastically about the joys of melody: "And finally then what melody permits! She has given us Gregorian chant, the grand composers (Bach, Beethoven, Wagner, Moussorgsky, Debussy!), divine melody who alone can introduce us to the sanctuary of melodies of the beyond, making our soul ineffable, prompting Keats to exclaim: 'Heard melodies are sweet, but those unheard are sweeter.' "[25] Balthasar understands such religious preference for melody in the following terms:

> Melody contains a certain flow, which interconnects tones into a unity and which gives them a new and completely unique character. For if one or more tones were added to a melody (which is most clear in case of a short

melodic idea), the flow of the melody will at once be disturbed. It flows into the new part and deviates itself. In it, the whole is greater than the sum of the parts. Today these structures are called "Gestalten." Logically they cannot be further elaborated, but they are immediately and evidently meaningful. Thus, in melody there lies an irrational, dynamic ground, which elevates music to greater heights, but which also distances it further.[26]

The Gestalt of melody is a spiritual contour with Balthasar resulting from (but larger than) the sum total of tones. The Dionysian aspect is the vitality of the melodic "flow," whereas contour is the Apollonian aspect.[27] The element of Goethe here is in the morphological, organic relation between parts and whole. Tones are concentrated in mutual diversity and expand into a new whole, which nevertheless retains the original. This idea can be related to the Aristotelian principle of entelechy.[28]

This ancient principle also has a part in Balthasar's description of the history of music, with the subsequent stages of rhythm, melody, and harmony consecutively assimilating to one another in an organic fashion.[29] This suggests a similarity to the thought of Hegel, which is further emphasized in the threefold historical development Balthasar sketches by explicitly referring to thesis, antithesis, and synthesis.[30] Balthasar's thought furthermore strongly resembles Hegel's concept of beauty in the emphasis on the manifestation of the Idea or Spirit (*Geist*), and it is narrowly related to Hegel's musical aesthetics in his formal approach to music. Saint-Pierre acknowledges these similarities, but he advances a number of reasons why Balthasar would be influenced by Goethe rather than Hegel.[31] First, Balthasar would refuse to form any sort of judgment on cultural periods of the past.[32] Such reticence goes against the grain of subjecting the course of history to the mechanisms of dialectics, and Balthasar, Saint-Pierre writes, is more at home with Goethe's notion of morpho-organic development. Second, as regards music, Hegel's musical aesthetics is almost exclusively concerned with the immediate inner character of music. Not a word on the "total Idea," or on the (Christian) divine in music. His thought, Saint-Pierre argues, does not lead to mystery—as in Balthasar's analysis of melody—but to absolute knowledge. With Hegel the listening subject is enclosed by the calm of his unfettered inwardness, whereas Balthasar reveals how music *opens* the subject toward religious experience (again: because of the supposed analogy between the antinomy of melody, on one hand, and the antinomy of mystery on the other).[33]

## Musica ancilla verbi

But what constitutes the religious aspect in the experience of formal antinomy? The first word of Balthasar's treatise is "music," the final word "Logos." Music is "the eternal memorial to what humankind can imagine about the nature of God: eternal-simple, manifold and dynamically flowing in itself and in the world as Logos."[34] Saint-Pierre repeatedly points out that Balthasar's references to the transcendental are difficult to interpret. The exact meaning of terms such as "total Idea" (*Gesamtidee*), "Sense" (*Sinn*), and "Spirit" (*Geist*) and phrases such as "the divine" (*das Göttliche*), "divine primitive light" (*das göttliche Urlicht*), and "dynamic God" (*der dynamische Gott*) remains rather ambiguous in this text.[35] A comparison with other writings by Balthasar dating from the same period suggests, however, that the term "logos" is used in the theological sense of Georg Bichlmair, where Logos is the divine Word, as in the *logos spermatikos* of the early church fathers.[36] The germ of the Word of God is disseminated; it is like a ray of divine wisdom, the true effect of Christ as Logos. Whatever part of reality he gazes on, the Christian will find Logos where he looks, according to Bichlmair. He will find it within himself as the living image of grace, outside himself in all that is true, good and beautiful in creation, and above all in the Eucharist.[37]

The phrase "living image" recalls the equilibrium Balthasar sought in the relation between Dionysian vitality and Apollonian form. Logos unites these two principles and penetrates experience as what is most proximate and yet a mystery. Balthasar uses the metaphor of the veil to illustrate this: "Music is the form that brings us most near the Spirit; it is the thinnest veil that separates us from it."[38] Saint-Pierre explains that the image of the veil "permits us to understand that what penetrates us profoundly and yet is incomprehensible is divine light. Music is the preeminent *analogon* to express this unsurpassed concurrence."[39] But what certainty about the relation between music and the divine is rendered? Saint-Pierre acknowledges that the theory as outlined so far cannot offer any form of certainty about the degree of the Christian in music. "Who can tell that from an acorn (at once complete and incipient) a tree will really grow? Who can tell that in the musical experience the mystery of beings is located, unfolding through its transcendental determinations? Who can see? Who can listen? Who can harmonize his life with the melodious rhythm of this musical veil?"[40]

Saint-Pierre supplies an answer by turning to religious dogmatics. Although, strictly speaking, dogmatics is not subject of our discussion here, his argument merits some attention here. At the end of his musical theological work, Saint-Pierre postulates the concept of silent music, drawn from Saint John of the Cross's *Canto Espiritual*.[41] This *música callada* can only be heard if one is united, by the Spirit, with Christ. Christianity, including Christian art, is about "configuring" the "inner man" with this "divine communion."[42] The silence of this melody is again related to the word, the *logos sioton* in this case, the mute word that would be neither conceptual knowledge nor discourse, but a "mysterious antinomy rooted in the heart of Being."[43] Saint-Pierre speaks of a supersensible invisible harmony, an inexpressible music that would be at the heart of mystery. In this harmony or music we could see the life of God and partake of "harmonic silence that fills the entire universe."[44]

As is suggested by Saint-Pierre's contextualization and interpretation of *Die Entwicklung*, it seems that in introducing Logos, Balthasar locates the Christian moment eventually in the subjection of the formal antinomy (proximity and mystery) to the Word. This Word appears in the shape of the "total Idea," the Sense or Spirit. The antinomy, then, can be taken to express a theological hesitance with respect to music. Because of its close proximity to the listening subject, music is indispensable for religious belief, but on the other hand, because it is impalpable, it is also a danger to any determined belief. Its intimacy with mystery bestows a religious significance to music, but it remains indeterminate what this is. The decisive moment therefore does not appear to be in the structure of music or of musical experience, but in the way this indeterminacy is (if possible) suspended. The distinction between, for example, Schopenhauer and Balthasar comes down to the former's appropriating this antinomy to crown his metaphysics of the Will, and the latter's appropriating the antinomy (understood as Gestalt) within his theological frame as analogous to divine mystery. This theological appropriation is possible, on one hand, because the indeterminacy of this antinomy admits a verbal interpretation and determination, and on the other hand, interestingly, because Balthasar makes the image of God organic-melodic (at once eternal-simple and manifold, as the form and notes of melody) and endows Logos with the rhythm of "flowing in the world" (which acknowledges one of the etymological roots of rhythm: Greek *rhéo*, to flow).[45] The musicalization of the divine, however, does not stretch to the Logos, which remains unaffected by the musical-indeterminate.

On the face of it, Balthasar seems to wish to respect the distinction between music and language at the level of art. They are still distinguished when they are absorbed in Sense, the "prime material" (*materia prima, Urmaterie*) of all art forms.[46] There is always a remainder, a distinctive feature that colors the possible content (Idea, Sense) of the artistic media. Sense, then, is not entirely independent from the medium it is expressed by. Or, as Balthasar maintains, information is also deformation. Therefore, music is not merely subservient to the Idea that wishes to inform itself or seeks to be informed by the human subject. Music also determines the Idea. This apparent liberty of music with respect to the Word is rather relative, however. The hegemony of Sense never really is an issue, as in Balthasar's eyes art is first and foremost "something meaningful."[47] The interdependency of the arts and their participation in the "total Idea" is never really threatened, as may also be apparent from the historical development of music. Periods of less intense or successful "information" still take part in the general history of becoming-Sense (*Sinnwerdung*). The differences in Form (and with that, in Idea) are a fact, indeed, but the system of valorizing unites all variations. It is such valorization that precisely enables the unification of all art and artworks in the concept of the "total Idea." The value of music depends, for Balthasar, on the success of informing such Sense. In concrete terms, atonal music is "regressive" because, in breaking with a tradition rather than seeking to join it, it withdraws from the totality of the divine Idea.[48]

The far-reaching subjection of music to the "total Idea" becomes most evident in the final passage of *Die Entwicklung*. Here it becomes clear that music is prior to all other arts because it takes up the most proximate position with regard to the Spirit. However, it remains a tentative position characterized by infinite longing (*Sehnsucht*): "Music shares the tragic fate of all art: to remain infinite longing and hence to be something temporary. Precisely because it is most proximate to the Spirit, without being capable of grasping it, in it infinite longing is the most powerful."[49] Music is like a "handmaid" who approximates the Word from behind her veil, in a reference to Mary's expressing her readiness to bear the Son of God (Lk 1:38): "And Mary said, Behold the handmaid of the Lord; be it unto me according to thy word." The Marian role of music (*musica ancilla verbi*) in informing the word (and, given the association of the Spirit with Logos, the Word) has a special significance with Balthasar. In response, she is prepared to relinquish her free will, prompted by the ecstatic adoration that attends, in the eyes of Balthasar, beholding the form of Christ. Thus, Balthasar advances the "theo-dramatics" of call and *kenosis* against the "theo-aesthetics" of this ecstasy. What the human subject sees when surrounded by and enraptured with God's glory and love (*ecstasis*) should be transferred to concrete existence in his willingness to serve God and act to his will (*kenosis, emptying*).[50]

The role Balthasar assigns to music, then, is one of drawing the larger connections of human existence. As could be inferred from his response to Schopenhauer, it is his aim to retain the concreteness of Form. Modeling his example on the Virgin Mary, he proposes that it is the musician's task (and given the imagery, that of music itself too) to confirm his or her seeing and knowing in a moment of obeisant listening. This will lead to concreteness and totality: "Before the beautiful—no, not really *before* but *within* the beautiful—the whole person vibrates."[51] Along these lines, Balthasar's musical theology joins an old tradition of theologies of music. Music is welcomed on the condition that it is subservient to the Word and by force of the Word to the word in general and to verbal significance. In this perspective, the Word appears as *Sense*, which is dominated by the word and also recoverable, interpretable, stable, and (in part because of this) extramusical.[52] As it goes, the musical theology of Balthasar does not really diverge from the more traditional approaches regarding music. He proposes a way to read the Christian in music that does not proceed beyond exterior—and with respect to music exclusive—determinacy.

## Discursive Music

This interim conclusion to this chapter deserves some emphasis before the discussion tackles a further complication, because the theological approach in interpreting Messiaen is largely governed by the hegemony of the word, and more generally speaking by the univocal. Pascal Ide's work can be taken as an example of the striking detail with which Messiaen's work is read theologically. In the perception of Ide, music is "language looking for meaning," it forms a "sign" of infinity.[53] For Messiaen's music this is all the more true; it belongs to the symbolic order. With reference to the lyrics Messiaen compiled for *Trois petits Liturgies*, Ide states that Messiaen's music expresses divine mystery neither less nor more than the words the music accompanies: "The texture of Olivier Messiaen's musical language embraces and expresses, in its own symbolic order, the theological contemplation of the child in wonder that it always was. Music is no less—or more!—capable than words to express the mystery of infinitely holy God."[54]

By means of Messiaen's work (and, indirectly, of his biography too), Ide tries to argue that Messiaen is no less a theologian than those who write treatises. Thus, he argues, "The etymology of theology is deceptive, because only those who form a discourse (*discourir*), in the proper sense of discourse, on God, would be entitled to this epithet. But really the theologian is foremost someone who loves God, because 'every one that loveth . . . knoweth God' (1 Jn 4:7)."[55] Nevertheless, Ide advances a description of what is contained by Messiaen's theology that stresses a verbal, ultimately discursive articulation. Messiaen's theology would be fastened on four theologems.[56] First, his music is *sacrament* (heart): in the experience of Messiaen's music, Christ acts as a mediator. His love ensures that the heavens ring with earthly sounds and colors of music. Second, his music is *analogy* (head): the synesthetic light of Messiaen's compositions has a spiritual meaning at different levels. Without the danger of confusion, one level informs the other.[57] Third, his music is *creation* (birth, beginning): in absorbing elements from the creation (nature, light, and so on), it refers to the creation. These elements in turn are in themselves (namely, the birds) an example of the force of divine creation. And finally, his music is *glory* (end, closure): it pictures the destiny of these created elements by leading the way tot the glory of heavens and by radiating in this glory.

Is it conceivable that Messiaen's music really utters such theological statements? In order to illustrate his sayings, Ide offers a brief musical analysis of part seven of the work for organ *Les corps glorieux*, titled "Le Mystère de la Sainte Trinité." [58] He states that the piece is about the ineffable mystery of the holy trinity and quotes from Messiaen's own introduction to the work to highlight the symbolic number: "The entire work is dedicated to the number 3. It has three voices and a tripartite form. Each part is a triplet. The main melody is constructed exactly like a Kyrie in Gregorian chant, with three times three invocations." Drawing on Messiaen's explanatory note, Ide then proceeds to connect the music, or rather the symbolic significance of the different parts of the composition, to several theological *topoi*. In the closing measures 22, 23, and 24, Ide reads an exposition on the relation between the Persons of the Trinity:

> The finale of this part and of the whole of the *Corps glorieux* seems to suggest the mutual penetration [*circumincession*] of the Persons and furthermore the blowing [*spiration*] of the Spirit. In fact, the voices of the Father and of the Son, the unique co-principle unmixed with the Spirit ("*unum Spirator sed duo Spirantes*"), unite in the *d*, in the octave, and the Holy Spirit joins them, in a unity which is not a confusion, in a long *c sharp*, which, at the last moment, lowers into a *c natural*. Does not this inclination, which is so discrete and almost imperceptible, evoke the *pondus amoris*, the weight of love in which

Aquinas, following in this respect Saint Augustine, saw the specific nature of the procession of the third divine Person?[59]

This interpretation of Ide may look sound and coherent. Not so, however. The Augustinian notion of *pondus amoris* has no significant part in Aquinas's doctrine on the Trinity. It is also rather unclear how this almost anthropological approach should be connected to Messiaen's objectifying representation of the Trinity. It seems that, in situating various theological tropes, Ide is led by the graphic representation of the score.

The first of these tropes, expressed by the phrase *"unum Spirator sed duo Spirantes"* (One Spirator [Blower], but two Spirating [Blowing]), probably refers to the discourse on the Holy Spirit in *Summa Theologiae*.[60] Here Aquinas addresses the classic aporia whether the Father and the Son should be conceived as two separate principles of the Holy Spirit, or together as a single principle (or coprinciple). In the scholastic discussion about this question, Thomas seeks an exit in uniting the two views. To that effect, he finetunes the distinction between the notions of a single Spirator (Blower)—there can only be one—but two Spirating (Blowing). The Spirit then emanates as uniquely Spirating from a unique Spirator, just as the word is issued from the mouth. This Spirator, however, is supported by two Spirating, the Father and the Son. In a mysterious way they are two and separate Persons, yet they speak with a single mouth (The Holy Spirit).

In the relevant passage in Messiaen (mm. 23–24), this idea appears to be embodied because the Father and the Son form, in the lower two voices, an octave that forms the base for the Spirit (the upper voice). With some imagination then it could be postulated that in this octave the same "word" (the tone identity of D) is produced by two different "speakers" (lower and middle voice). Stacked on this musical figure, Ide then constructs the lowering from C-sharp to C-natural (m. 24) as a representation of *pondus amoris* that would be characteristic for the way the Spirit emanates from the Father. In the music, however, no connection can be established between, on one hand, the figures that would represent the Father (the lower voice, the tone D, and maybe the first three invocations of the middle voice in mm. 2–7), and on the other hand the figures that represent the Spirit (the upper voice, and maybe the third three invocations of the middle voice in mm. 14–19). Apart from that, it is more logical that *pondus amoris*, which is the striving of the will and of love to be near God, be represented as an *upward* (rather than a downward) movement. Thus, it is tempting to believe that Ide was somewhat inspired by the graphic representation in the score in forging conflicting notions and perspectives into an incongruent amalgam.[61]

Ide employs the same techniques in his interpretation as used in historic musicology for making a narrative of music notes. The rules of the game are oriented on creating analytical rigor. On one hand, music should be seriously considered, which happens by means of analytical concepts such as dissonance, modality, form, and texture. On the other hand, theology should be respected by assigning its logics and terminology a proper position. The challenge, then, for a hermeneutical approach consists of forming a logically coherent narrative on the basis of elements from the score and from the thematic material (if there are no lyrics, then for instance from the titles, mottos or concepts involved). Such a narrative supplies music with a certain solidity, a sound discourse, as when the piano accompaniment of (especially tonal) songs can often be read as a comment on the words that are sung.[62] So doing, as in the case of Ide, music is turned into an allegory: a musical narrative that refers to a transcendental and hyperlinguistic universe. Such an approach to interpretation, however, completely marginalizes the nonsymbolical, nonnarrative, nonsemantic aspects of music, leaving a husk of rationality and significance. In many respects, this contradicts music as it is experienced in sound, and this seems notably the case in religious music. Music can "form a discourse (*discourir*)" on theological subjects only if its musicality is suppressed.

It is remarkable, then, that Messiaen himself has done everything to feed such interpretations of his music. He composes "to champion, express, and define something," and supports this intention by means of a great number of elucidations to, and comments on, his scores.[63] He scribbles additional information in his scores, such as the colors of certain chords, the names of the birds that are represented, the provenance of the Gregorian melodies or Indian deçi-tâlas, or the theme that is depicted ("*le Souffle de l'Esprit*," "*Dieu est immense*," "*Dieu est éternel*").[64] This linguistic corset is further stiffened with the introduction in the late 1960s, in the work for organ *Méditations sur le Mystère de la Sainte Trinité*, of a musical alphabet that Messiaen had concocted from various sources in order to transmit the texts of Aquinas into musical notes. Messiaen claims to have been inspired by, among others, the Kabala and the Rosetta stone, which had enabled the Egyptologist Jean-François Champollion to decode hieroglyphs. "I have attempted, in play and to renew my thinking, to discover a sort of communicable musical language (*langage communicable*)."[65] The German names for musical notes provided the foundation for this alphabet, ranging from *a* to *h*. Each letter was assigned an individual tone, register, and duration. Messiaen also thought up a system to encode the grammatical structure of the French language in music. The genitive, ablative, locative, accusative, and dative were each coupled to a musical motive that preceded the transliterated verb. Negation, and the verbs "to have" and "to be" were also assigned a musical motive, and the name of God was bestowed a theme of its own, the "thème de Dieu." The slightly more redundant grammatical forms such as articles and particles were left out. Parts of the texts of Aquinas in French translation were then transmitted into musical notes by means of this system. The resulting single-part music is mostly accompanied by one or more voices that are not based on this principle.[66] As was his habit when he was pleased with his own findings, the system was retained by Messiaen and put to later use in *Des canyons aux étoiles . . .* (Parts 3 and 5) and in *Livre du Saint Sacrement* (Parts 7, 11, and 18.).[67]

Language is not only to be found in the words that figure in or surround his scores; it is also present in the music itself. His music often has an episodic structure, a story told in images that may be reminiscent of cartoons. It is as if Messiaen wants to unfold stories that refuse to be told in the aural medium of music. The impossibility of truly telling his tale in music perhaps explains why Messiaen takes recourse to verbal means or is excessively emphatic in the exposition of the thematic content of his works. The result in some places is that his music becomes overly didactic, as if he is instructing nursery children, putting across his message by means of hyperbolic figures, motives, repetition, and emphasis. Occasionally, a free and truly musical unfolding is hindered by this narrative tendency, as can be heard for instance in the fifth scene of *Saint François d'Assise*. There, in harnessing his music to fit unambiguous narrative, he has opted for maximum intelligibility of the lyrics and an excess of frequently repeated leitmotifs with a signaling function that are musically irrelevant but serve a narrative, if not an apologetic objective ("I compose to *champion* something").[68]

In general, Messiaen had little affinity with the idea of ambiguity, whether this concerned the formal attributes of music or its content. In Debussy, he admired the "sense of vagueness" (*sense du flou*) in a "form completely absurd, and formidable"—that of, for instance, his prelude for piano *Feuilles mortes*. He acknowledges, however, that he would not be able to compose in this fashion.[69] For his own *Saint François d'Assise*, for example, he cleared the biography of the saint from all anecdotes and episodes that could lead to the musical plethora of Wagner's musical dramas, which are choked with intrigue and subversive leitmotifs. Thus, there is no mention of Francis's relationship with Clara or of his troubled relation to his father and his unruly youth, not in the least because Messiaen was averse to an

alternative, psychoanalytical interpretation of the life of the saint.[70] His bat-
tle against ambiguity of meaning is perhaps best illustrated by the fact that
even in old age he traveled the world to attend the performance of his work.
One reason was that he enjoyed the great variety of performances, but he
was also bent on giving maximum clarity about his intentions—this he
found "the duty of the contemporary composer."[71]

## Inversion and Idolatry

The tendency to subject music to the word is but one aspect of the theology
of Messiaen's music. One should also take into account a second force that
arose in the late eighteenth century, and that was focused on inverting the
relation between music and the media (numerical principles, the word) that
had come to dominate it in the course of its history. This inversion is
brought about by the inherent metaphysical-religious potential of music. Its
traces can be found in Balthasar and, as will be argued, it is extremely important for considering Messiaen and his music of "breakthrough." Hence, the
second force that is discussed in this section will determine the angle taken
on Messiaen in the chapters to come.

There is a famous passage in the *Confessions* of Augustine that describes
a problem in listening to religious vocal music. The beauty of music is a
"gratification of the flesh" which should be subservient to the significance
of the sacred words, but in reality it continuously tends to escape such subservience, threatening to govern reason:

> I admit that I still find some enjoyment in the music of hymns, which are
> alive with your praises, when I hear them sung by well-trained voices. But
> I do not enjoy it so much that I cannot tear myself away. I can leave it when
> I wish. But if I am not to turn a deaf ear to music, which is the setting of the
> words which give it life, I must allow it a position of some honor in my
> heart, and I find it difficult to assign it to its proper place. For sometimes I
> feel that I treat it with more honor than it deserves. I realize that when they
> are sung these sacred words stir my mind to greater religious fervor and kin-
> dle in me a more ardent flame of piety than they would if they were not
> sung.[72]

Assuming full responsibility for such erroneous wandering, Augustine writes
that "when it happens to me that the song moves me more than the thing
which is sung, I confess that I have sinned blamefully and then prefer not to
hear the singer." As it turns out, however, it is not so easy to restrain the

pride of "the gratification of the flesh" in case of the "delight of the ear." In reaction, he is tempted by "excessive severity" in a desire to banish the "sweet songs" from the church, and then again the insight grows on him that a good, verbal performance is indispensable for the intelligibility of the words sung. He professes to be swaying between "the danger that lies in gratifying the senses and the benefits which, as I know from experience, can accrue from singing," with the result that "by indulging the ears, weaker spirits may be inspired with feelings of devotion." In other words, Augustine is wavering between giving in to the temptation of beauty in music and relinquishing it in favor of the meaning of the "sacred words." In the first case, there is the wonderful but ambivalent experience of musical beauty—ambivalent, because music can induce a pious mood but can also turn out to be temptation personified. In the second case, the sacred words are salvaged and the good and true safeguarded, but the essential affect necessary to assist these words in penetrating the souls of listeners is lacking.[73] In short, as Henry Chadwick succinctly remarked, for Augustine music is "indispensable but dangerous."[74]

The music described by Messiaen as dazzling and humbling can be taken to exemplify the Augustine's aporia. The ambiguity of musical experience has a part in Messiaen's examples of wonderful, beautiful and dizzying music. The very concept of *éblouissement* is ambiguous, in that it does not only refer to grandeur and truth, but to deception as well. Strikingly, synonyms for *éblouir* include, according to the major French dictionary *Le grand Robert*, verbs with a meaning to that effect: *abuser* (to deceive, to mislead) and *tromper* (to trick, to fool).[75] Plato already felt threatened by such plurality of meanings, which called for, as he argued, the restraint of music. With Augustine and Messiaen, the challenge is to reconcile the desire to retain musical beauty or the musical sublime even in its most enrapturing, addictive, mesmerizing form for the Christian life of faith and music, with the awareness that such beauty or sublimity, to keep it from transcending the limits of faith, should conform to the Christian doctrine. As a result of these tugging forces, arguments and criteria have arisen that advance and defend the distinction between what is and is not musically Christian. These arguments yield some insight in the boundaries between theological and (secular) musicological approaches to music in general, and specifically in the case of Messiaen.

Augustine finds no solution for his dilemma and turns to God: "You however, O Lord my God, give ear, look and see, have pity and heal me, in whose sight I have become an enigma unto myself; and this itself is my weakness."[76] The significance of the moment should not be underestimated. Balthasar's suggestion that the passage on music is concerned with the "personal anxiety" of Augustine with respect to the sensuous, fails to address the systematic problematic of musico-religious experience.[77] And yet there is a moment in his musical theology, when Balthasar envisages in all art, at least in theory, the possibility of "perfect finality."[78] By this he means that all art has the possibility of becoming the perfect incarnation of the Idea, that is, of the divine Word. Music too has this capacity, to a greater extent even than the other arts.[79]

> In my opinion, the unique character of music consists in representing concentration and expansion, intensity, or . . . the dynamic God; and this, it should be noted, beyond thoughts, words, visual representations, *as pure form of immediate Truth*. Faithful to its nature as a temporal art, it is so to speak a *graduator of the Absolute*. The inscription of this curve is the first and most eminent task it fulfills as "absolute music."[80]

According to Balthasar, music "registers" the divine. It does not conceptualize or represent the divine but is in essence the "graduator of the Absolute." The paradox of taking the measure of the absolute generates a metaphor that Balthasar appears to use for referring to the idea that the absolute can "inform," more or less intensively, and that music testifies to the *degree* of such intensity.[81] In this fashion it becomes conceivable that the presence of the absolute is measured by music—a thought that is based, again, on the analogy between the antinomy of music and that of the divine.[82]

The capacity of music to "register" the divine is substantial but subject to certain constraints. According to Balthasar, these are both in the objective and in the subjective sphere. Objectively speaking, the information of the divine in music never is perfect. The subjective constraint calls attention to the condition of the listener, who only in exceptional cases—when detached from the moorings of thought and feeling, in Balthasar's view—will be capable of perceiving music for what it is. This is just as well, because the intensity of what music has on offer could blind the listener if the filters of "thoughts, feelings, and other senses," which include "the word and representation," did not shield him.[83] The function of the subjective, then, is to provide a pair of sunglasses, metaphorically speaking, that enables us to behold divine light somewhat longer, which postpones the moment of definitive dazzlement. A pair of sunglasses? Perhaps the metaphor of the veil is more apt. And then the insidious but radical inversion in Balthasar's reasoning suddenly becomes apparent. The hierarchy of word and music is turned upside down. First the Spirit was behind the veil, and music before it, in infinite longing. Now, however, it appears that music resides *behind* the veil, with the word before it. In Balthasar's discourse the word is described as the filter or veil that tones down the blazing light of music, whose radiance is "informed" by the divine. This means that music now occupies the position of mystery; and the verbally tied Spirit no longer. Music then becomes Isis-like, half-hidden by a veil.[84]

## Music as Religion

What can this signify in the context of a *Christian* musical theology? Can music be related to the Christian mystery without being governed by the word? What can Balthasar have had in mind in referring to a nonverbal yet apparently Christian association of music and mystery?

Answering this question involves a brief excursion into romantic musical aesthetics. The inversion of the hierarchy of word and music refers indirectly to early romantic thought on music, not in the least because Balthasar refers en passant to the notion of absolute music. The term is Wagner's, but the notion was developed earlier, around 1800, by Adam Smith, Michaelis, and E. T. A. Hoffmann, among others. Later in that century Eduard Hanslick would also contribute to this idea.[85] The underlying thought is that "instrumental music purely and clearly expresses the true nature of music by its very lack of concept, object, and purpose."[86] Detached, absolved, and without relations with the external world, devoid of ties with the extramusical or nonmusical; in other words, this music is freed from the shackles of nonmusical content. Thus, it communicates the "nature" of music. And what is this nature? Following the thought of Kant, the answer would be that music is but a beautiful game with "pleasant sensations" that never attains the concept and therefore is lacking in any form of reflexive content.[87] Kant is no less skeptical about the capacity of music to produce lasting works that meet the criteria for art.[88] Michaelis formulated a philosophy of music after Kant and in the tracks of Adam Smith and Friedrich Schiller, arguing that music is an organization of interdependent tones that are effectively related to each other and that result in a work that pivots on itself alone.[89] Music, then, is proposed as an autonomous work of art, a whole of "tonally moving forms" (Hanslick) that can be understood only through the inner logics in which (and through which) it develops as an organism.

This purely formal and literally meaningless approach had little to do with the idea of absolute music. On the contrary, absolute music is all about the expression of the intrinsic, endogenous significance of music. Its independence from any exogenous or extrinsic sense (dictated for example by faith or poetical text) would not just liberate it from verbal subjection but would raise it above everything else, would elevate and absolve it. Hanslick thus describes the essence of music in terms of inwardness and Spirit (or Mind), even though he emphasizes the formal aspects of music. Musical forms are not empty, and there is even a suggestion in Hanslick of a significant plenitude that is revealed: "In music the concept of 'form' is materialized in a specifically musical way. The forms which construct themselves out of tones are not empty but filled; they are not mere contours of a vacuum but mind (*Geist*) giving shape to itself from within."[90]

The romantics eagerly exploited the altered status of music. Music becomes the medium of the sublime (*das Erhabene*) and the (metaphysically or religiously) Inexpressible—the divine (Tieck and Wackenroder) or the Will (Schopenhauer). The Kantian emptiness of music is not interpreted as a nothingness but as a sign of plenitude: its capacity to give the listener an awareness (*Ahnung*) of beautiful Infinity.[91] Therefore, music achieves more, rather than less than language because it surpasses the expressive potential of language. These romantic poets and philosophers held that music can reach regions of expression that can only be dreamed of for language. In the romantic view that counters the paradigm of Kant (which reserved such eminent status exclusively for the oratorio), music becomes the highest art form that preeminently expresses what is inexpressible and elevated.[92]

The idea of absolute music was not only attended by a new philosophical-aesthetical appreciation of music, but was for a number of authors also intimately related with Christianity. In a sense, the notions of romanticism, the musical, contemporariness ("modernity"), and Christian values had become synonymous. Thus, E. T. A. Hoffmann adheres to the thesis that music only matured in the ear of Christianity, that is, the "modern, Christian, romantic" age he lived in. The definition of this Christian musical period is spelled out in opposition to antiquity. With the ancients, "sensual embodiment was all," and music still was "crushed by the power of sculpture."[93] Greek music had a purely rhythmical nature and was devoid of the dimensions of melody and harmony that were typical for the "modern" and "Christian" age. Hoffmann situates these historical considerations—which, of course, should be read in a contemporary light—in the frame of great personal faith in music, which is attended by his confidence in the force of instrumental, absolute music of his day. A passage from his essay "Old and New Church Music" (1814) may serve to illustrate this:

No art arises so directly from man's spiritual nature, and no art calls for such primary, ethereal resources, as music. Sound audibly expresses an awareness [*Ahnung*] of the highest and holiest, of the spiritual power which enkindles the spark of life in the whole of nature, and so music and singing become an expression of the total plenitude of existence—a paean to the Creator! By virtue of its essential character, therefore, music is a form of religious worship . . . and its origin is to be sought and found only in religion, in the church.[94]

Hoffmann is referring to the Roman Catholic Church. Like most romantics, he is oriented to the Catholic tradition of Palestrina rather than Protestant church music. His adoration for music as *absolutum* then should be related to a certain concrete repertoire. And then it turns out, in proper ecclesiastic tradition, that quite a lot does not meet his standard. Thus Hoffmann rebukes, entirely in the spirit of Augustine, the "frivolity" of theater music, which is all about earthly gains and impressing the audience. Such music is the expression of "demonic forces," no less, holding man spellbound within his "miserable, blinkered world" that he mistakenly takes for the highest possible aim in his being. It keeps him from coming any closer to all that is "noble, true, and sacred," which is the source "from which in everlasting incandescence true works of art arise."[95]

For Hoffmann, the height of music resides foremost *not* in church music (the well from which it springs) but in Beethoven's instrumental works. They are the touchstone for absolute music. For Hoffmann, these works fulfill the function of a "monstrance" (in Wackenroder's words) of religious-metaphysical longing (infinite *Sehnsucht*) for Infinity. Just as with Jean Paul, Hoffmann's notion of Christianity is not related to confessional faith but rather to a kind of spirituality that evolves from a bursting tradition of Christianity but that is, ultimately, secular. Thus, he reasons that the superlatives of Beethoven's music not only transfer supreme music to the concert hall, but faith too. In the process, this faith is transformed into faith in art.[96]

The impression may have arisen that in its romantic shape, music as the highest art form has shaken off the supremacy of language. This is not the case, however. The theory of absolute music may free music from the subjection to word and program, but, as was briefly hinted at earlier, at a higher level it turns it into another verbal phenomenon: now as hyperlanguage or "language above language."[97] In *The Idea of Absolute Music*, Carl Dalhaus succinctly explains this move:

The change in the conception of instrumental music that took place in the 1790s, the interpretation of "indeterminacy" as "sublime" rather than "vacuous," may be called a fundamental one. Astonished wonderment has become wonderment filled with intimations; the "mechanics" of instrumental music become "magic." That the content of music can be determined not at all or only vaguely no longer demotes the allegro of a symphony (relative to the "moving" cantabile) but raises it to a sublime position. However, the pathos used to praise instrumental music was inspired by literature: were it not for the poetic conceit of unspeakability, there would have been no words available for reinterpreting the musically confusing or empty into the sublime or wonderful.[98]

The topos of music as "language above language," surprisingly, is derived from the art of poetry. The essence of music should be sought in its primal capacity to express (in indeterminate but elevated terms) what is beyond the reach of any language. In a paradoxical move, however, this reduces it to language again. It is either the language of essence, or the essence of language. In other words, music is either Hanslick's "mind (*Geist*) giving shape to itself from within," where, according to Dalhaus, mind is understood in practically unmetaphorical terms as language. Or the idea of music is, as later with Adorno, "the divine Name which has been given shape."[99] Despite its elevated indeterminacy, then, music is once again trapped by the primacy of rational and semantically defined language. The idea of absolute music does not free music from the shackles of the programmatic, but converts it in to the superlative of language: a hyperlanguage.[100]

### The Spirit of Augustine

In Balthasar, a similar motion can be discerned. The struggle for hierarchy in his case affects only the arts mutually. Collectively they are relative to a higher (but immanent) Sense. The struggle between word and music (the only art form able to vie with the word) appears to end in reconciliation, but Balthasar does not permit the idea of absolute music in uncontaminated form: "We see music as two-sided: Form of the higher and metaphysical, expression of the lower and representable. It oscillates between both sides without ever reaching one or the other."[101] Sense prevails in the end; it is located in the Form of the musical medium, which is like a "revelation from above" to Sense.[102] So far as music is directly in touch with the elevated, Balthasar explains this according to the model of absolute music. The degree of absoluteness is dependent on the intensity (that is, the success) of "information," which in turn, as the end product of the full evolution of world-immanent Sense, is ultimately identified with the Word. Thus, Balthasar rewrites a theory that was developed to grant music pure autonomy. In his version, that theory is cloaked with the material that had previously been cast off. Newly picked up, the robe does not fit, which is perhaps the most important lesson of his musical theology.

Yet the question remains whether this was really any different, ever, whether the verbal cloak of religion was at any moment capable of enveloping the body of music. The example of Augustine suggests that the problem was not so much historical as structural. The convergence of music and religion in the concept of *musica sacra* does not imply a simple junction of two powerful domains, but rather indicates a middle ground that is home to neither. Jean-Luc Nancy may be correct in his observation that "within religion itself, art is not religious," but then the phrase can perhaps also be reversed.[103] The value of Messiaen's music consists especially in highlighting this middle ground—or no-man's land. In this respect, it is easier to understand Messiaen with regard to his Franciscan predilection (and the preceding figure of Augustine) than in terms of Aquinas, whose musical theology is preeminently characterized by the subjection of music to the word or, if the word is unintelligible, to the intention with which it is sung.[104] It is fitting, therefore, to return briefly for the conclusion to this chapter to Augustine and review, for the twentieth century, the traces of his thoughts on music.

A remarkable voice in the musical theological debate belongs to Henri-Irénée Marrou, who used the pen name Henri Davenson in several books on music.[105] In *Traité de la musique selon l'esprit de Saint Augustin,* he argues for a renewed Augustinian view on music. The principle of his study is that musical theology should always respect the quality of sound, of musicality, in music.[106] He draws on Augustine's earlier work *De musica* (rather than on his *Confessions*), which introduces a numerically based hierarchy in music that connects the lowest, sounding levels in music with the highest, spiritual levels. Davenson is critical of the implicit reduction involved in the Augustinian hierarchy: the essence of music is reduced to something that is not music: to Pythagorean mathematics. Thus, in Leibniz's well-known phrase, music becomes the "concealed arithmetical exercise of a mind unconscious that it is calculating" (*exercitium arithmeticae occultum nescientis se numerare animi*). Davenson comments:

> Behold the fraud that is common to the philosopher, that is always implied by the dialectics of the aesthetic: the ineluctably vain attempt to explain art, emotion and the beauty of music by reducing it to some foreign principle (here number, there the Thing in itself, the primordial Will, no matter what), explaining in this way music by means of the nonmusical.[107]

He adds that the arithmetical description of sound structures does not even come close to explaining the musical function or significance of this material. The point that a fifth is based on the frequency ratio of 3:2 begs the question of the effect of this fifth in general or in the context of particular music. Davenson rejects, therefore, the Augustinian substitution of music by mathematics (or "acoustics") as "illusory and faulty," but wishes to retain his hierarchy of rhythms. His concern here is the idea of an inner ideal image (the *numeri judiciales* in Augustine) that would be reflected in the performance of music, and Davenson departs from the notion that "the musical does not derive from an unmusical [*amousia*] source but from music" (Plotinus).[108]

The practice of playing the piano serves to illustrate Davenson's point.[109] When learning to play a certain piece of music though repeated play of individual passages as well as the work as a whole, an ideal memory is formed that is like a pure and stilled image. The performance of the work is measured against this mental image, which in turn is honed in subsequent performances until "a musical image surfaces from the depths of the silent sanctuary of memory whose perfection, beauty, and purity is ideal." It is on a higher plane than the simple memory of this or that performance, and achieves its purest from in the music we inwardly hear after a performance, as music still reverberating in our ears. In this brief moment we can, according to Davenson, inwardly reproduce what we have heard as "silent music" that has a presence and motion that appears to be constantly renewed. It is this mysterious Presence that Davenson connects to the Augustinian *numeri judiciales*. It is, to Davenson, a music that is "perfectly actual and conscious, yet silent, purely spiritual, free from subservience to duration that shackles matter." This liberated music brings man to the state of beatitude resembling a religious epiphany: "It goes without saying that we can only taste the divine plenitude of this music in brief moments of our current life in the flesh." This music resides, according to Davenson, in the "pure Spirit" where, in the proximity of God, apophatic silence reigns.

For his interpretation of this void or silence as specifically Christian (rather than Schopenhauerian or Buddhist), Davenson, too, is dependent on the word.[110] The most decisive, "metaphysical" moment of music is plagued by indeterminacy; the best opportunity is always attended by the greatest danger. It thus appears that in the view of Davenson, music is always questionable in the theological perspective, necessitating continuous corrective checks. In practice, however, the affair is less complicated. Davenson knows exactly how to demarcate Christian from idolatrous music. The distinction is not determined by semantic considerations but simply by musical style. Strikingly, Messiaen is included in the specific examples Davenson refers to. His judgment on the composer is clear. To him, Messiaen's music certainly is subsumed in the category of musical idolatry, or "musicolatry," as Lacoue-Labarte coins it.[111] Discussing those composers who are inclined to "bulge" their music and "stuff it with indigestible elements," he mentions the name of Olivier Messiaen, "that dear boy . . . whose work in turn attracts and disturbs me because of its excess of willed spirituality."[112] It seems here that Davenson takes a course that he formerly rejected. Is not he in truth subjecting his theological judgment to an aesthetical judgment? Is not he really addressing the rhetorical force of music, its capacity to convince? It appears that Davenson exchanges the musical theological criteria for the aesthetic criteria of the faith in art. Why should he, from the perspective of musical theology, reject music for the musical-rhetorical reasons of padding and assumed insincerity? More generally, why should the lack of conviction in stylistic or rhetorical terms imply a lack of Christian truth? An uncomfortable suggestion arises from Davenson's thesis, which deserves to be more closely considered. Could it be the case—in a theological context, too—that it is more important that music is convincing than that it is true?

The conclusion to this chapter, then, must be that, apart from the position of certain Christian thinkers who take a stance against idolizing music, in most musical theologies the problem of the power of temptation in music is not fully addressed. There is room for maneuver in the musical theology of Balthasar. In the end, however, music is in various ways fashioned into the handmaid of extramusical, transcendent Sense. Speaking with Kierkegaard, it thus marginalizes the "demonic" potential of music by demanding the prior warrant that the experience of the music concerned be legitimate in Christian terms. Within the frames of such theology, one can listen to music without any qualms. The believing listener cannot be threatened by this music. There is, however, a prize to pay. Music is robbed of the far-reaching (and possibly too far-reaching) efficacy that makes it invaluable in the opinion of Messiaen and Augustine. Apparently presupposing that the value of music can be divorced from its dangers, Balthasar throws out the baby with the bathwater. Music represents neither opportunity nor danger in his musical theology. The beast is tamed, *musica sacra* as the middle ground, the no-man's-land, of music and religion is domesticated.

The next chapter will show, however, that this is sooner said than done. How can it be ascertained that music is or is not bona fide in Christian terms? The tried and trusted appeal to the notion of inspiration cannot serve to answer this question, because it raises more questions than it can possibly answer. "What is inspiration?" Messiaen wondered. "Is it different with a believer than with a nonbeliever? One can try to invoke the assistance of the Holy Spirit—perhaps then a work is crafted with a higher or deeper value. *How are we to know?*"[113]

# 4.    The Gift of Dazzlement

The notion of saturation surfaced more than once in the discussion of the dazzlement passages in Chapter 2. A saturated sound-image was created with Messiaen's so-called turning chords (*La Transfiguration*, Part VIII); along with that, different forms of chromatic saturation were mentioned, as with the sound field of the third movement (Part XII) or the fully chromatic chords in both chorales (Parts VII and XIV). Especially in these latter instances, saturation pertained to a parametric phenomenon: the notion referred to the fact that all twelve tones on the chromatic scale occurred in the sound field or the relevant chord form. This particular notion of saturation is based on the parametrical reduction of music.[1] In the former case, however, a different type of saturation is attained, a sonic excess that cannot be described as a summation of tones—even not of all twelve, and even not in terms of the whole that is larger than the sum of its constituent parts.[2] This particular notion of saturation, this sonic excess, will be the subject of this chapter.

As we have seen, the Christian element in Messiaen's music cannot satisfactorily be described in terms of representation (thematizing, symbolizing, sound imagery, and the like). Connecting the representation of faith to a music that is reduced, in the process, to sheer description in musical theoretical terms (see Pascal Ide's analysis of *Le corps glorieux*), leads to a construct that minimizes, trivializes, and eventually even erases both music and religion.[3] Any search for music and religion in such an analysis, any attempt to locate the musicosacral or the sacromusical, is doomed to remain sterile. But what if such a quest departs from the first form of saturation, that is, an excess that cannot be described as the effect of a parametric constellation? Could there be a relation between this excess, on one hand, and the phenomena of *éblouissement* (or dazzlement) and breakthrough on the other? Or, to reformulate this question, is Messiaen's experience of dazzlement perhaps concerned with an excess that is wholly different from the excess of chromatic saturation (experienced, for example, as relative to the surrounding modality)?

The latter suggestion is not merely possible but even probable, if Jean-Luc Marion's phenomenology of "a phenomenon saturated with intuition" (abbreviated as the saturated phenomenon or *phénomène saturé*) is considered, as shall be done presently. This is particularly so if Messiaen's music, or music as such, is considered in the light of Marion's phenomenology of the idol (Section 2) and the icon (Section 3). The opening offered by this approach to thinking Christianity in Messiaen's music introduces, however, a certain fissure between the aesthetic and theological possibilities of his music. This fault line between the aesthetic notion of the sublime and the theological notion of glory leads, at the end of this chapter in Section 4, to a renewed confrontation with the theories and concepts that were constitutive for the romantic religion of art or *Kunstreligion*.

## The Saturated Phenomenon

Marion objects to any kind of phenomenology that is based on the decision to privilege subjective constitution within the duality (intention/intuition, signification/fulfillment, noesis/noema, and so forth) of the phenomenon. As he argues, such privileging either leads to a reduction of the phenomenon, subsumed in the figure of the "poor phenomenon" (*phénomène pauvre d'intuition*, with the example of ideal and propositional objects in mathematics and logics), or to an objectification of the phenomenon (*phénomène de droit commun*, that is, the scientific object and technical-industrial product). These reductions then imply a representation of the phenomenon that excludes, in the philosophical sense (and in the theologically or musicologically inspired analyses of music too, as I have argued), anything that is historical, contingent, irrational, or overwhelming, thus impeding the phenomenological admittance to precisely those experiences and events that constitute our quotidian surroundings (Marion refers to "the beings of nature, the living in general, the historical event, the face of the Other in particular, etc.") and that would (and should) be the subject of thinking.[4] This analysis induces Marion to criticize metaphysics for its nihilism, as would become apparent in the fact of its orientation toward "the paradigm of phenomena that do *not* appear, or appear just a bit."[5] As was argued, this is a viable analysis that applies to similar tendencies in methods of musicography (and musicology in particular) as well, with frequent occurrences of idealizations or objectifications of the phenomenon under study. Such reductions hamper the analysis of the musical religious, above all when this concerns the singular character of Messiaen's testimony of breakthrough in (the experience of) his music, or the figure of a religious, miraculous breakthrough as such.

Marion does not advance his critique of phenomenology and metaphysics merely for the sake of it, but also with an eye on an alternative approach. His proposals to that effect will guide the discussion in this chapter. How to return to the things themselves? Marion formulates his response to this question as follows: by departing from the phenomenon's givenness (*donation, Gegebenheit*).[6] This turns out to be less Husserlian than it appears. The phenomenon manifests itself in its appearance, but according to Marion, it only does so to the extent that it gives itself. The inherent reflexivity in the expression of offering or giving itself (*se donner*) begs the question of thinking the self (*soi*) of the phenomenon that gives itself. This gift is thought as "the movement by which the phenomenon gives *itself*," but cannot be perceived directly, as it is shielded by the phenomenon's showing itself.[7] In addition, Marion states, it cannot be presumed that every instance of giving itself automatically leads to a showing itself.[8] The "self" in showing itself is not necessarily concomitant to the "self" in giving itself. Eventually, Marion argues, there is only one way for arriving at the latter, that is, to approach the phenomenon itself, and that is in trying

> to circle, in the space of manifestation, regions where phenomena show *themselves*, instead of letting them be shown simply as objects. Or again, to disengage the regions where the *self* of what shows *itself*, attests indisputably to the thrust—the pressure and, so to speak, the impact of what gives *itself*. The *self* of what shows *itself* would indirectly manifest that it gives *itself* more essentially. The same *self* that one would identify in the phenomenon showing *itself* would proceed from the original *self* of what gives itself. More clearly, the *self* of the phenomenalization would manifest indirectly the *self* of givenness, because the latter would operate it and, in the end, would become one with it.[9]

How does Marion envisage disengaging these regions?[10] First of all, by describing the phenomenon as an event (*événement*). This is a move that counters the delimitation, with Descartes and Kant, of the phenomenon as object. Kant, for example, specifies in the first of his "four rubrics that organize the category of the understanding and thus impose on phenomena the quadruple seal of object-ness,"[11] to wit the rubric of quantity, that each phenomenon must dispose of a quantity in order to become an object, that is, it should possess spatial extensiveness (the Cartesian *res extensa*).[12] This extensiveness involves that the whole of the phenomenon equals (and results from) the sum of its constituent parts. In addition, the phenomenon is inscribed beforehand, as object, in finite space. These two delimitations make it possible to know the phenomenon in advance: although we perceive at most only three sides of the cube at once, the other three can be inferred from its structure and the spatiality of its form.[13] "It is the same," Marion observes, "for all technical objects: we no longer see them, we no longer have even the need to see them, because we foresee them for a long time. . . . We reduce them to the rank of phenomena of the second order, of common [*de droit commun*] phenomena, without according them the full, autonomous, and disinterested appearance."[14] Thinking about the phenomenon in terms of objectivity mystifies the original phenomenality of the phenomenon.

The movement of thought suggested by Marion is precisely in the opposite direction: from the object toward the event. Its course is indicated by three characteristics of the event: irrepeatability, surplus, and possibility.[15] In the first place, the event is unrepeatable: "Each event, absolutely individualized, arrives only once (*hapax*) and once and for all (*ephapax*), without sufficient antecedents, without remainder, without return."[16] It escapes any attempt to determine its cause or to list criteria: it proceeds from itself alone. A second characteristic of the event is its surplus regarding any precedent. It is unlike any other, it has not been produced nor can it be reproduced; it "undefine[s] the world in the twofold sense of rendering it nonfinite and forbidding it any definition."[17] Finally, new horizons are breached by the possibility borne out by the event, and this is true for phenomena that are historically older as well. This is a possibility that is totally unrelated, according to Marion, to the possibility in metaphysics. That possibility is completely and beforehand subsumed in the economy of what can be realized, whereas in the case of the event this is a free, unshackled possibility that can be described in metaphysical terms as a leap of the impossible (that which is outside all causality, essence, or sufficient ground) toward facticity. Repeatedly, Marion emphasizes that the initiative to appear and become a fait accompli resides with the phenomenon itself, the phenomenon that offers, gives itself. Such giving itself inevitably happens in time, but not, as Kant wishes, before a transcendental ego that dwells outside time and produces it (just as space) in a majestic fashion. Marion argues his case by referring to an event that preeminently contains these three characteristics: my own birth. My birth is a phenomenon that presents itself to me in the manner of giving itself.[18] I have not witnessed my own birth, but I know about it from the testimony of others:

Since it is accomplished without me and even, strictly speaking, before me, it should not be able to show itself (if it were to show itself) to anyone at all, except to me. Nevertheless, I consider it rightfully as a phenomenon, since I do not stop aiming at it intentionally (wanting to know who and from where I am, undertaking research into my identity, and so on) and filling this aim with quasi-intuitions (secondary memories, direct and indirect witnessings, and so on). My birth is even offered as a privileged phenomenon, since my whole life is solely occupied, for an essential part, with reconstituting it, attributing to it a meaning and responding to its silent appeal.[19]

My origin presents itself to me in that it does not present itself to me. This aporia can be understood in two ways: first, I was not present at my own originating, and second, there is nothing original about my origin—in that it results from an indeterminate series of accidental events. According to Marion, then, my origin shows itself to me as the gift of what is to come: "My birth does phenomenalize itself, but as a pure event, unforeseeable, unrepeatable, exceeding all cause and rendering possible the impossible (that is to say, my life always new), surpassing all expectation, all promise, and all prediction."[20] And he concludes that "this phenomenon, which is accomplished in a perfect reduction of what shows *itself*, thus attests, in an exceptional and paradigmatic mode, that its phenomenality proceeds directly from the fact that it gives *itself*."[21] In other words, my birth is an example, a cardinal example perhaps, of a phenomenon that gives itself as an event and cannot be reduced to the coordinates of objectivity. It takes place prior to the transcendental ego, or, in giving me (*moi*) to myself it principally makes the ego (*Je*) possible. With this gift, the event opens an unprecedented range of temporal intuitions "for which I will seek without end, but always too late, meanings, concepts, and noeses inevitably missing."[22] The phenomenon, thought as event, is always a phenomenon that saturates the intention, or, in brief (but less precisely), a saturated phenomenon, a *phénomène saturé*.[23]

In describing the event, Marion takes issue with the limitations drawn by metaphysics and phenomenology regarding the phenomenon's (pure, absolute) givenness (*Gegebenheit*). Especially Leibniz's metaphysical law of sufficient ground is disputable because it attempts to determine every contingency (and possibility) by relating it to necessity. According to Marion, Kant subsequently endorsed this law, because Kant too subjected the possibility of the phenomenon to necessary preconditions, specifically that of the power of knowledge. Contrary to appearances, the phenomenon is no less restricted in phenomenology: Husserl may reject the law of sufficient ground, but spells out new conditions for the possibility of the phenomenon's occurrence. Marion analyzes these restrictions in relation to two denominators, the horizon and the ego.[24] The notion of the horizon is introduced to illustrate the idea that what is already known provides the background or context for what is as yet unknown: when I am perceiving three sides of a cube, and after rotation the other three, I will add up both perceptions in order to constitute a coherent object against a singular horizon (that presupposes the known). "It is therefore necessary that the irrepressible novelty of the flux of lived experiences, therefore of intuition, remain, de jure, always included within an already defined horizon where lived experiences not yet given could simply be united with the lived experiences already given (or already past and confided to memory) in one and the same objective intention. . . . Within the horizon, the unknown refers in advance to the known, because it welcomes and fixes it: 'Anything unknown is a horizon of something known.'"[25]

It is a phenomenological presupposition that such a landscape of phenomenality is presented to an observer who is situated outside time. Marion argues however that at closer inspection, Husserl's constant horizon of the phenomenon coincides with the observing subject, in other words, the horizon is the transcendental *ego*. There is moreover a case of "classical" revolution: the I, at first a witness of the phenomenon that gives itself, transforms into a transcendental ego that constitutes each phenomenon and demands of each givenness to justify itself as if "before a tribunal."[26] With Husserl, therefore, the phenomenon suffers from a strongly idealizing tendency. Marion advances a phenomenon that is "eventmental" (*événementiel*), that is, not based on the restrictions of a horizon or on (and this is the same with Husserl) the transcendental *ego*. Where these restrictions condemn the phenomenon beforehand to a poverty of intuition, Marion's phenomenology (if this still is the apt term) of the saturated phenomenon is an attempt to conceive precisely those appearances that "would receive a surplus of intuition, therefore of givenness, over and above intention, the concept, and the intended (*visée*)."[27] Marion uses (and subverts) thereto the four rubrics that, with Kant, organize the understanding. The first of these, quantity, has just been discussed under the denominator of the event (characterized by an excess of aspects and significations); the other three—quality, relation, and modality—are analyzed by Marion in a similar fashion, that is, indefining and deconstitutive, in terms of a more originary saturated gift (*donation*).[28] For each of these "regions" he gives a privileged example or type. After the historical event, these are in turn the idol (a saturated phenomenon in terms of the rubric of quality), the flesh (the rubric of relation), and the icon (modality). The types of the idol and the icon will be addressed in the next sections.

Before such a discussion of idol and icon, however, the theological (or theologizing) perspective on the saturated phenomenon needs to be considered.[29] To resume: within the area of the saturated phenomenon, Marion distinguishes four types, each responding respectively to one of the definitions of the phenomenon in the rubrics of the Kantian understanding. In principle, Marion presents these types as distinct but of equal value, "without intending any hierarchy," although he later wonders whether perhaps the case could be argued of a degree in saturation, or of gradual differences between the types, and whether apart from this, a maximum saturation are conceivable.[30] It comes as no surprise that the answer to the first question is in the positive, given his earlier plea for the icon (at the expense of the idol) in *God Without Being*.[31] The icon is the preferred type in *Being Given* and *In Excess*, if only because it unites the qualities of the other three and disposes of certain (religious) privileges that are related to the countenance of the other/Other. As for the second question, Marion's positive response is framed by two conditions: the maximum should not affect or cross the boundaries of the phenomenal; and the maximum should remain a sheer possibility, or as Marion puts it: "an ultimate possibility of the phenomenon—the last, but still under the heading of possibility."[32] He labels this last possibility as the phenomenon of *revelation* (subtly distinguished from theological Revelation) and describes it as the amalgam of all four types of the saturated phenomenon:

> It is a question of the last possible variation of the phenomenality of the phenomenon inasmuch as given. The phenomenon of revelation not only falls into the category of saturation (paradox in general), but it concentrates the four types of saturated phenomena and is given at once as historic event, idol, flesh, and icon (face). This concerns a fifth type of saturation, not that it adds a new one . . . to the first four . . . but because, by confounding them in it, it saturates phenomenality to the second degree, by saturation of saturation.[33]

The manifestation of Christ, as described in various locations in the New Testament, is paradigmatic for such a saturation to the second degree. Marion resorts again to Kantian rubrics (opposing them in the same movement) to depict the significance of this paradigm:[34] "According to quantity, the phenomenon of Christ gives itself intuitively as an event that is perfectly unforeseeable because it is radically heterogeneous to what it nevertheless completes (the prophecies). It arises 'as the lightning comes from the East and shows itself (*phainetai*) as far as the West' " (Mt 24:27). It makes an appeal to vigilance so far as this is connected to the notion of *kairos*, or decisive moment: "Take ye heed, watch and pray: for ye know not when the time (*kairos*) is" (Mk 13:33). Subsequently, with respect to quality, the Christ phenomenon is presented as unbearable (a qualification that, surprisingly perhaps, is related to the type of the idol, as will be argued extensively). Marion alludes to the description of the phenomenon of the Transfiguration of Christ, or rather of Christ in this moment of Transfiguration—an unbearable, indeed blinding light: "And his raiment became shining, exceeding white as snow; so as no fuller on earth can white them" (Mk 9:3). Not just the sense of sight is saturated by this phenomenon, but auditory perception is likewise overwhelmed, as Marion understands for example from this reference in Jn 18:6 (the capture): "As soon then as he had said unto them, I am he, they went backward, and fell to the ground."

As for the third rubric, relation, Marion argues, "Christ appears as an absolute phenomenon, one that annuls all relation because it saturates every possible horizon into which relation would introduce it. It saturates every possible horizon not only because its 'moment' escapes the time of the world (saturation in terms of the unforeseeable event) and its figure the space of the 'earth' (saturation in terms of the unbearable), but because 'My kingdom is not of this world' " (Jn 18:36).[35] In other words, the world does not know of anything that is comparable to Christ and that can serve as a horizon for framing the phenomenon. According to modality, finally, the phenomenon of Christ can be described as something that cannot be regarded (*irregardable*), "precisely because as icon he regards me in such a way that He constitutes me as his witness rather than some transcendental I constituting Him to his own liking." Marion illustrates this with reference to the parable of the rich young man (Mk 10:17–22), who is lovingly beheld by Christ, which transforms the young man into a witness and acts, moreover, as an invitation to surrender or abandon himself to this phenomenon of Christ.

The parable of the rich youth contains a double saturation, according to Marion. The first saturation is the given that the young man observes the biblical commandments that are concerned with respecting the other-as-other. He accepts that these commandments (and the other) are larger than himself. Saturation is doubled, then, in the constitutive gaze of Christ, which both prompts respect for the other (saturation) and, on top of that, urges self-abandonment to this other, a saturation of saturation. The phenomenon of revelation, which thus finds a paradigm in Christ, unites the four types in a quadrature that in the last instance is about pure givenness. It can even do without intuition; it is a phenomenon (and here Marion alludes to Anselm) "which is given in such a way that nothing more manifest can be given—*id quo nihil manifestius donari potest.*"[36]

## Saturation, Music, and the Idol

An outstanding example of the saturated phenomenon, given Marion's description of the event, seems to be music. Music is a temporal phenomenon that only exists in the singular, unrepeatable moment of its being brought to sound; it is a phenomenon that cannot be foreseen or recorded, no matter the frequency of repetitions or the technical accuracy of recordings; it escapes all definitive definition or interpretation. It is not often that Marion broaches the subject of music, but he awards it a special status in *Being Given*, be it in a brief passage, without much elucidation, on the saturated phenomenon as "counterexperience." The paradoxical formulation of "counterexperience" holds that it "offers the experience of what irreducibly contradicts the conditions for the experience of objects."[37] The phenomenon gives itself unmistakably in counterexperience, without however constituting itself as object: counterexperience "is not equivalent to a nonexperience, but to the experience of a phenomenon that is neither regardable, nor guarded according to objectness, one that therefore resists the conditions of objectification."[38] The abstruse elements in this phrasing are clarified by Marion's distinction, on the visual plane, between seeing (*voir*) and looking or regarding (*regarder*), which opens an interplay of the connotations and hidden meanings in regarding, or reguarding: grasping, relating, referring, maintaining, guarding. The saturated phenomenon cannot be disregarded, but at the same time it cannot be grasped or held, it cannot be constituted or repelled. Marion takes an example from photography: the excess of light that appears as the haze of overexposure, or the speed of a car that is captured as fuzzy motion. The eye "receives a pure givenness, precisely because it no longer discerns any objectifiable given therein."[39] And then he shifts his attention to music, Mozart's Symphony no. 41, the "Jupiter" (KV 551). The entire passage is worth quoting:

> It falls to music, or rather listening to music, to provide privileged occurrences of this sense of the phenomenon. The opening of a symphony—the

*Jupiter*, for example—reaches me in such a way that even before reconstituting the melodic line or assessing the orchestral fabric (therefore constituting
two objects from two givens), I first receive in my ear the movement (non-
objectifiable because giving) of the sonorous mass, which comes upon me
and submerges me, then my very belatedness to the deployment of this coming. A memory of previous performances no doubt allows me to identify the
melody more quickly and to assess the orchestral ensemble, but it does not
allow me to abolish the arising, therefore the event. The music offers the
very movement of its coming forward, its effect on me who receives it without producing it, in short, its arising without real content. Consequently, it
comes upon me in such a way that it affects me directly as pure givenness
mediated by almost no objectively given, and therefore imposes on me an
actuality immediately its own. The musical offering offers first the very
movement of its coming forward—it offers the effect of its very offering,
without or beyond the sounds that it produces. Let me name this phenomenological extremity where the coming forward exceeds what comes forward
a *paradox*.[40]

A number of things can be said about this passage. In the first place, there is
a striking parallel with Lyotard's notion of the "tone of the absolute" employed in his analysis of Augustine's *Confessions*. As we shall see in Chapter
5, this tone imposes on the mind without appearing as an object before this
mind. Secondly, the topos recurs of music's absolute (emotional and physical) proximity yet impalpability (conceptual and even cognitive)—this was
the double figure related to the phenomenon of melody by Schopenhauer,
Hegel, and Balthasar.[41] Marion writes that music moves him "directly," but
it remains "without real content" and is therefore conceptually impalpable.
It should be noted, incidentally, that Marion is concerned with the exterior
element of music, or the event as such of its becoming manifest. His phenomenology is less preoccupied with the proximity that is an expression of
the subjective, inner moment of listening.[42] Third, music here is represented
as an instance of the phenomenon's gift as such. It induces the experience
of its *quod* rather than its *quid*—the musical phenomenon's giving itself, as
departing from itself and preceding any constitution of the subject. The
music of the Jupiter, especially of the quasi-amorphous drone at the beginning (reportedly a prank to wake up the audience), is presented as (almost)
sheer matter (*hyle*).[43]

The "eventmental" character of music is supported by the trope of *anamorphosis*. Marion explains this trope as one of the general definitions of the

event, but employs it elsewhere too (as conversion of the gaze) in relation to the phenomenology of the icon (which is ranked higher). Anamorphosis is about crossing the "phenomenological distance" of the phenomenon's interiority: "the phenomenon crosses the distance that leads it (*ana-*) to assume form (*-morphosis*), according to an immanent axis."[44] The crossing constitutes the movement in which (and through which) the phenomenon gives itself and becomes visible, but it is not its first visibility: "Every visible (but likewise everything perceived, with whatever sense) by definition appears. It therefore has a form, as vague and unformed as it might be, but this appearing is not yet equal to a figure of apparition."[45] In this respect, Marion contrasts the fuzzy appearances of a phenomenon to the appearance of a phenomenon's individuation, disengaged from other phenomena that then become the background for the phenomenon in its *second* manifestation. "The *ana*-morphosis of the phenomenon insofar as it is given, thus designates its property of *rising* from the first to the second form—of passing from that which goes its own way (*va de soi*) (for a vague, unfocused gaze) to that which comes in its very own way (*vient de soi*) (of what shows *itself*). Or rather: from the depths of the phenomenon."[46] For an example of such a movement, Marion refers to the experiments of Iégor Reznikoff, musicologist, logician, and singer, in tracing the earliest sources of Gregorian chant:

> The scholarly works and virtuoso experimentation of I. Retznikoff [*sic*] have proven that the vaults of Romanesque churches (and even certain prehistoric caves) could resonate like stringed instruments, provided they were made to vibrate, by chanting, at a precise point. In each case, it was necessary, by a more and more precise approximation, to detect this point. The singer or the musician (and also the listener) had to move himself physically in such a way that the sound emitted would occur by itself in its fullness, would rise toward its total sonorous form. There is indeed sonorous anamorphosis.[47]

There is a parallel example in *The Two Ambassadors*, the famous painting by Holbein the Younger, where a smudge turns out to be skull when seen in the appropriate low-from-the bottom angle.[48] In both instances, the point is that such a phenomenon does *not* give itself unless the listener or viewer is situated in the right position, taking a stance right in line with the "immanent axis" of the phenomenon that enables the second form of the phenomenon to manifest itself. The listener or viewer does not constitute this phenomenon, as in cases of the subjective constitution of the object. On the contrary: projecting from its own inner axis the phenomenon gives itself from its own ground and on its own conditions. Once these conditions are met, the full, anamorphosized form of the phenomenon is revealed unto the spectator from the hyletic or proto-eidetic nature of the phenomenon as event.[49] What happens to the subject when no move is made, when anamorphosis is not admitted, can either be described, in Marion's words, as boredom (the purposeless gaze that wanders around in the world unseeingly, seeing through) or in terms of the idol: the gaze that is captured unexpectedly by the saturating spectacle that also bars the path toward the phenomenon.[50] The question of the significance of anamorphosis with respect to the ear is momentarily left aside; elements of this notion will be addressed in the final chapter. Because the spectacle of the idol is described, by Marion, as a dynamics of *éblouissement* and adoration, the question at hand is centered on what the phenomenology of the idol can teach us about the phenomena testified by Messiaen: dazzlement and "breakthrough toward the beyond."

The idol is a saturated phenomenon in the rubric of quality. Its essential characteristic is visibility and nothing but visibility. Marion illustrates this by contrasting the privileged example of the idol (painting, object) to the original it represents.[51] As was argued above with respect to the cube, the original does not present all its facets at once—these are, in Husserl's terminology, appresented.[52] Absent aspects belong to the object that is presented by force of the a priori conditions of experience. According to Marion, something close to the contrary occurs when the cube is depicted in a painting: "Here and here alone, the appresented tends to disappear and leave the way entirely free for the presented. . . . The painting no longer represents certain presentable aspects of an object (of the world) that would remain, for its other aspects, only appresentable; it reduces the object to the presentable in it, in excluding the appresentable."[53] Looking at a painting, then, brings fulfillment, according to Marion, and disillusion and absence are excluded from the gaze. The painting adds presence unto presence through the intensifying reinforcement of the frame, where nature preserves the spatial and hence appresentative absence. In Marion's words,

> Here is the painting: the non-physical space where the visible alone reigns, abolishes *l'invu* (the invisible by default) and reduces the phenomenon to pure visibility. The painting is the concern of the most classic and most strict phenomenology, because it reduces entirely the phenomenal to the visible . . . . The painting does not offer an example, interesting, but possibly optional, of phenomenological method of the reduction—it accomplishes it radically according to the quality (the intensity or the "intense grandeur") of the appearing. In reducing the visible to its atomic quintessence, in containing

in its frame the mad energy of the visible, the painting reduces what gives itself to what shows itself—under the regime of the idol. Phrased otherwise by Plato: ". . . in fact, only the beautiful has received, in terms of being [the phenomenon], the most apparent, the *ekhphanestaton*, and the most desirable."[54]

The idol captures my gaze that is wandering around in the world, bored and unseeing. Immediately visible in the splendor (excessive intuition) that saturates my gaze completely, the idol delimits the utmost of what I can bear in terms of visibility, it is dazzling me: "When the gaze cannot bear what it sees, it suffers bedazzlement (*éblouissement*). For not bearing is not simply equivalent to not seeing: one must first perceive, if not clearly see, in order to undergo what one cannot bear. It concerns a visible that our gaze cannot sustain."[55] Such dazzlement does not induce any suffering, lack, or discontent, but is concomitant to "success—glory, joy." It is related to the notion of being blinded by an excess of truth (as His Truth that we cannot perceive without dying; see Messiaen's "*excess de Vérité*" and communion of "la joie"), or to the Truth of Ideas, the Light projecting the shadows we commonly see—a Light and Truth that can only be witnessed by those whose eyes are already filled with glory.[56] The idol can also be experienced in less exceptional circumstances or by less fortuitous eyes, as is evidenced by the example of the painting and the work of art in general.[57]

The idol thus is the first object that the gaze can neither penetrate nor discard in boredom. Nor can it gather this supreme visible like a Kierkegaardian aesthete in an infinite range of fleeting, exchangeable impressions. The intense and exclusive visibility of the idol moves the gaze to adoration and fascination. Apart from the excess of intuition, two factors are connected to his dazzlement: in looking (*regarder*), the gaze tends to isolate the seen from the unlimited display of the visible, of what can be seen (*voir*) in the world; and in its focus on this isolated form, the gaze is fixed and allows itself to be fixed. Marion relates this to a certain weariness due to the enormous strain involved in seeing the divine: "The idol offers the gaze its earth—the first earth upon which to rest. In the idol, the gaze is buried."[58] In fact, therefore, the idol betrays a lack of intention in the gaze, which prefers (or is forced) to rest. Dwelling in the idol, the gaze thus demarcates the borderline between visibility (of the idol) and the opening toward the other dimension that remains, however, unattainable (*invisable*) for the gaze. The idol then acts like an invisible mirror in confronting the gaze with its own limitations or range (*portée*). This shows that the divine, so far as it is seen here, is experienced only within the span and the capacity of the *human* gaze. There is no case, in the idol, of the kind of anamorphosis or conversion that reverses perspective and that constitutes me through the gaze of the other. According to Marion, such a reversal still is the privilege of the gaze of the iconic face (for instance, the example of the rich young man). First and last, the idol is constituted by the gaze of the subject who is fascinated by his own reflection in the invisible mirror of the idol: "The decisive moment in the erection of an idol stems not from its fabrication, but from its investment as gazeable, as that which will fill a gaze. That which characterizes the idol stems from the gaze. It dazzles with visibility only inasmuch as the gaze looks on it with consideration (*Elle n'éblouit de visibilité qu'autant que le regard la regarde avec égards*). It draws the gaze only inasmuch as the gaze has drawn it whole into the gazeable and there exposes and exhausts it."[59]

Marion's examples are elucidating. The saturated (and saturating) color planes of Paul Klee and Mark Rothko provide an illustration of the idol. Marion mentions Rothko's painting *Number 7* (1951), which is at first sight strongly reminiscent of Messiaen's descriptions of synesthetic color experiences.[60] It is not only the colors of the painting that often recur in these descriptions—violet and its complementary, yellow; the blur of orange-red—the form and distribution of the color bands and the fuzzy edges of the color planes evoke the layered and fluid structure of Messiaen's sound colors as well.[61] Messiaen saw a relation between Monet and Debussy, "but not a [relationship] Cézanne-Debussy. In Cézanne there is a geometric aspect that doesn't exist in Debussy. Debussy is more fluid, more undulating, and less precise."[62] Marion, in turn, compares the colors in Rothko to Monet's water lilies—they appear to float on the canvas, rather than being sustained by it. They are self-borne, neither formed after any exterior definition not constituted as object, offering themselves in (and as) pure autonomous visibility, "silent, irresistible, adorable."[63] There are indeed more examples of the relation between the autonomy of color in the art of painting and certain aspects of music. It is interesting, for example, that Paul Klee gave musical titles to some of his art works—think for example of the intensely vibrating and saturating *Polyphonie* (1932). Likewise, as Simon Shaw-Miller has shown, there are many connections between other modernistic artists and music.[64] And the reverse is true too. From the start, musical impressionism distinguished itself with a characteristic use of timbral sound colors that did not depend on functional harmonics (as with Debussy); Schoenberg expressed his utopia of a *Klangfarbenmelodie*; Scriabin explored the possibilities of a synesthetic light organ for his *Prometheus*. The process of sound colors becoming more and more autonomous culminated in the

1970s in the so-called spectral music of Gérard Grisey and Tristan Murail. Composition of this kind of music is not based on tones and patterns, but on the spectral "interiority" of sound and its dynamic envelope that become the material of (and set the stage for) composition.[65]

## Spectrality, Spirituality, and the Icon

Jonathan Harvey, the British composer, called Messiaen a "protospectralist."[66] This is an apt description, in that Messiaen, early in his career, had already begun to experiment with manipulating the structure of overtones. The *Préludes* (1929) supposedly contain the first instance of such manipulations, as Harry Halbreich argues. In this largely still pre-electronic era, the nature of Messiaen's manipulations was indirect: so-called *grappes d'accords*, stacked chords in different modes, create the effect of fountains of colors in the *Préludes*. Yvonne Loriod-Messiaen, in describing the color effect of these chords as well as a sense of violence involved in the surplus of difference tones, speaks of an "avalanche of pebbles clinking together" (*pierreries entrochoquées*) reminiscent of Signac, Monet, or Robert Delaunay, "with circled patterns and color-chords" (*des dessins en cercles et les couleurs des accords*).[67] It should also be noted that the phenomenon of natural resonance is central to Messiaen's color-guided thinking about music, to the extent that it was fundamental to his theory of music:

> I believe that the majority of musicians and reference works on music have talked for centuries about so may things. They have discussed tonality, modality, the serial, aleatory music, repetitive music, electro-acoustic music, etcetera, etcetera, etcetera. And still, I am not quite sure if any of this is true. There is one thing that is true: natural resonance of sonorous bodies.[68]

Resonance alone does not suffice, however. The composer will have to (and want to) deploy this phenomenon. A popular version of the history of Western music holds that the application of resonance gradually evolved from the discovery, throughout the ages, of ever-higher overtones as a legitimate and supportive element in music.[69] Early polyphony was based on octaves and fifths, compounded by the gradual addition of fourths, thirds, and sixths in later centuries. Sevenths followed, and with the arrival of dodecaphony and serialism the smallest intervals were mixed in on the palette. In this version, Debussy provided the finishing touch with the addition of the most distanced interval, the former *diabolus in musica* or tritone.[70] Messiaen uses this particular interval so often and in such a structural manner that it determines the coloring of his music to an important extent. It takes up a key position both in his chords and in his melodies. Resonance of sonorous bodies (*corps sonores*) is respected, then, but only in the sense that the conventions of resonance are turned topsy-turvy with Messiaen. The most distanced interval, the tritone, becomes the touchstone of the ear.

Messiaen's manipulation of "natural" resonance was inspired, among others, by the possibilities of the organ. Entirely in the tradition and style of French music, he has a fondness for the *voix céleste* and the *gamba* and a predilection for mixtures and for thirds, sevenths, and other compound stops. These color stops appear to lead a life of their own with Messiaen, and surmount their function of adding sonority to the fundamental. Independently, they can furnish music with an unequalled clarity, transparency, and coloring; and then again with great obscurity, thickness, and complexity. In his later work for chamber music and orchestra, Messiaen deploys the possibility of supplementing strong bass tones to the higher chords, which then are modified into the partials of these bass tones.[71] Such *effets de resonance*, in Messiaen's words, are in their complex and inharmonic resonances much like church bells with their "false fundamentals" (*faux fundamentales*), their cacophony of combinatorial overtones and undertones. Messiaen uses these effects not only to regulate the arrangement of his harmonies, but also to simulate the timbre of bells. Hence, the presences of bells, xylophones, chimes, gongs, and last but not least, the pope of resonance instruments: the tam-tam.[72] These are the complex, sometimes saturated timbres that Messiaen ascribes "a certain mystery" to and which he uses for evoking the strange or the miraculous, as seen in Chapter 2.[73] With regard to the *éblouissement*-passages, especially Messiaen's "special chords" take up an important position, such as his "chord with contracted resonance" (*accord à résonance contractée*) and "resonance chord" (*accord de la résonance*). The majority of chords in these passages consist of such color chords and on the surface appear to account for the effectiveness of both chorales in Part VII and XIV.[74]

What then, and more precisely, is the relation between such spectral effects and the religious? Marion analyses the saturated phenomenon according to quality—the quality of dazzling intensity—as a phenomenon with religious overtones, in this case the idol. Jonathan Harvey might perhaps support Marion's religious analysis of the saturated phenomenon. He was among the first to work with the computers of Ircam and specialized in spectral music. Harvey relates the origins of spectral music not just to the rise of electronic music that enabled a direct manipulation of the frequencies of overtones, but also, and explicitly so, to spirituality.

Spectralism has effected a fundamental shift: music will never be quite the same again. Spectral music is symbiotically allied to electronic music; together they have achieved a rebirth of perception. Yet while electronic is a well-documented technological breakthrough, spectralism in its simplest form, as color-thinking, is a spiritual breakthrough.[75]

The spiritual is discussed in a mingled context of Anglican education, an interest in the thought of Rudolf Steiner, mysticism, and various forms of Vedic and Buddhist spirituality. As far as spectralism is concerned, Harvey is especially interested in the possibilities of this approach for elaborating on the relation between "the Many and the One," as well as between the spirit and the machine (mathematics, physics). According to Harvey, timbre is an *aesthetic* phenomenon, narrowly related to the construction of identity. Timbre explores the play of identity and difference: "The 'timbral experience' is fundamentally one of shifting identities. It occurs when we mistake, however momentarily, one thing for another."[76] The synthesis of the timbre of a flute serves to illustrate this idea. Easily identifiable, the aesthetic phenomenon of the flute timbre shields a mathematical universe that employs another language, the language of acoustics, mathematical principles and physics; of the spectrum and its constitutive formants, partials, harmonic and inharmonic series, and so on. The difference between these two universes is just as fascinating as the mutual transitions into one another and back again.

> To construct a flute timbre one must simulate all the clues the ear seeks to confirm the "fact" that someone is there blowing a flute: the breathiness, the jumpy micro-melody imposed one the player's vibrato by his or her nervous system, the sound of the lips starting up, and so one. When the "fact" is convincingly confirmed the mental picture of a flute is born which then unifies many sounds of very different timbre under the heading "flute."[77]

The fluctuating motion between the aesthetic and the physical opens the way for spiritual development: "This particular interchange between reason and soul is highly illuminating, and brings the 'indefinable' into ever-sharper definition. As Rudolf Steiner believed, man's endeavor should ever be to make things more conscious. That is spiritual development."[78] To that end, he arranges for *Inner Light*, a composition for seven instruments and tape (1973), a dialectics between harmony (structure) and timbre (spectrum) "to represent the expanded consciousness of mystical experience."[79] The indeterminacy of identity and difference, of unity and disarray, is linked to the notion of a mystic union: "The whole movement, whose idea is that of mystical union, constantly moves in and out of fusion and fission. Is an instrumental part only a part or a thing in itself? Such is the ambiguity, the teasing veil of identity."[80] There is always the one individual element (a formant, melody, harmony, and so forth) lifted from the oceanic whole of the spectrum.

> The aesthetic urge toward integration without losing individuality is my motive, a motive present from the integration of contrasting subjects in classical sonata form to Stockhausen's "ultimately I want to integrate everything." It is important because art is a means of expanding the tight ego to the larger, more compassionate one, or to the "egolessness" of Buddhism. Art's function is essentially ethical, ultimately spiritual. Any new consciousness born through experiencing, for instance, a timbral transition is a step in this direction, a life changed.[81]

With such a view on spectra, music and spirituality become a matter, again, of representation and cognition. Music then symbolizes a certain spiritual perspective (such as "the Many and the One") and ideally conduces to a change in consciousness or awareness. Marion, in contrast, opened the way for an analysis, in musical counterexperience, of the irreducible, for what cannot be paired down to such representative and cognitive functions. An important difference, for example, between Harvey's *Inner Light* and Kaija Saariaho's *Verblendungen* (Dazzlements) for orchestra and tape (1982–84) is brought about by the intensity of the spectrum, which possibly alludes to its givenness. Saariaho's composition is similarly inspired by the spectral and begins, in the words of Kimmo Korhonen, with "an enormous diminuendo beginning in an opening Big Bang and continuing throughout the work."[82] Gradually, a more contemplative, still music evolves from this big bang from which individual elements can be discerned: local harmonies, fragments of melody, an interchange between tape and musicians. From the center of the work a clear, metallic timbre emanates from the tape that forms the background to individual events. Such a spectrum can achieve great intensity, as in the final bars of *Verblendungen*, and can even become unbearable for the listener who is dazzled as if she looks directly at the sun. The spectralism of Saariaho reverts in this respect to Messiaen and his dazzling musical passages where (in contrast to Harvey) representations of faith are erased. The saturated phenomenon can especially be found, as far as the five *éblouissement* passages are concerned, in the closing chorale of *La Transfiguration de Notre-Seigneur Jésus-Christ* (Part XIV).

The last of the five passages, this is most like an exposition of sound-colors, which supplies the principal reason for speaking of saturation with respect to this work. It is less important here that the dramatic buildup of the chorale could be analyzed too—as in Part VII—because it is subsumed in the effect of saturation that unfolds in the course of the chorale, drenching, as it were, its form. To a lesser extent this is the case for the other passages as well. The theatrical focus that guided the analysis in Chapter 2 must be supplemented with an analysis of especially those effects that enfold or "envelop," in Harvey's words, the structure of music, and perhaps even precede those structures.[83] When Paul Griffiths remarks that "the objects and musical states that Messiaen offers to our inspection in *Les Corps glorieux* are so very singular that we may well be disinclined to accept them as invitations to meditate on something else, preferring to make of them the centre of our contemplation," he is right so far as the ear in Part XIV of *La Transfiguration* is captivated by an unequaled harmonic and spectral saturation.[84] It is a fascinating spectacle of the unique (the terrible too, as will be argued later on), one that does take part in the objectivity of the sound object as such, but pertains to the manner in which saturation is presented. At no point do these fascinating objects themselves (especially the color chords with their fully chromatic structures) materialize into stable and eventually repeatable structures that can be grasped by the ear. They are vibrant and moving. Spilling over continuously, their constitution as sound object does *not* come about. The saturation of sound image appears as the *ecstasy* of objectivity. This is exemplified in m. 10. Here, harmony surpasses its boundaries and is converted into a sound that can only be described as the ecstasy of harmony, a sound that is independent from the coordinates of the composed form (mastered by the intentions of composer or listener), that unfolds in musical time-space.[85] This is a sound sounding from and for itself, a fascinating and bewildering phenomenon that time and again fills the ear without ever being reduced to a musical object, no matter how unique this object might appear.

Another, slightly more durable occurrence of this effect is in the opening chord of the *Livre du Saint Sacrement*, Messiaen's organ cycle from 1984.[86] Here, too, a phenomenon sounds with no objectifying focus, harmonic directionality, or melodic propulsion, saturating the listener by its sheer being there. The thematics of the opening piece are related to the closing chorale in *La Transfiguration*: the adoration of God's glory, expressed here in the title of the piece, "Adoro te," and in the epigram, a fragment from Thomas Aquinas's similarly entitled hymn, "Devoutly I Adore Thee." In light of the idol, the divine is not unveiled: in both passages music does not signify, does not incorporate a *signum,* but is sheer fascinating saturation of the ear. The ear therefore is spellbound and amazed and it gazes, as it were, in adoration at this apparition, this breakthrough in objectifying, structural listening.[87] Is not this adoration a sign that the ear recognizes itself in the invisible reflection of the idol? And that, consequently, the passion of adoration and the intense joy in the glory of God are correlated to not seeing the divine in the idol? The ear, immersed in the apparition of this phenomenon, then would stumble upon the desired ultimate, the maximum of what can be heard, and would sense the boundary that acts both to block the passage to "face to face" experience as well as to bring the divine within reach of the ear.

This experience of joy and triumph is perhaps even stronger, with Messiaen, in a diatonic context than in a chromatic one. As can be discerned from the climax in the early work for organ *Apparition de l'Eglise éternelle* (mm. 33–37), the final triads in *La Transfiguration* and *Saint François d'Assise,* or the final chord of part ten of *Livre du Saint Sacrement* ("La Résurrection du Christ"), the auditive idol does not occur just in extreme chromatic contexts with Messiaen, but in extreme diatonic structures, too. The words that are sung at the gigantic, monumental (all too monumental, *ecstatic*) close of *Saint François* leave little to doubt about the composer's interpretation of the auditive idol: "*il* [Saint Francis] *ressuscite de la Force, de la Gloire, de la Joie!!!*" This latter word is exclaimed in an orgasmic, *tutti* C-major triad that admits no depth, distance, or ambiguity at all. A totalizing sound, in brief. Brigitte Massin designates the plenitude of Messiaen's music in the so-called Tristan period (1945–48); in *Saint François* this plenitude, this ecstatic enthusiasm, this will to express and to enumerate, is fulfilled and redoubled in the experience of the invisible mirror.[88] It is, however, a premature fulfillment, because the idol is constituted by the *lack* of intention. It is, in Marion's optics, the "burial" of the gaze (or, in this case, the ear), and the ear in the end celebrates—trembling—its own jubilation, rather than God's glory.

Nonetheless, Marion argues, the idol remains an option for the manifestation of the divine in phenomenality, because of the excess in intuition it is accompanied by. In the last instance, it is the unbearable blaze of the transfigured garment of Christ. In this sense indeed, the auditive idol induces, as Messiaen envisages, a moment of "breakthrough"—that is, a breakthrough marked by deficiency. But, as Balthasar wisely said, "even a dangerous road remains a road" (and may even turn out to be the preferred "narrow" road).[89] The musical idol dwells, in this context, in the (church) bell, which is, as we have seen, an important (if not *the* most important) reference point for Messiaen's thoughts about sound and music.[90] As if creating a kind of spectral music, Messiaen summons resonances and sound clusters in his works for organ, percussion, and even the piano that foreground the question whether his music is inscribed, through introducing the bell (or imaginary, otherworldly bells chiming with "artificial resonances"), in the most intimate relation Christianity can have with the (proto-)musical. In the allusion to these bell sounds, Messiaen's music then acquires a certain sacrality.[91] Marion, however, proposes a step beyond the blaze and daze involved in contemplating the idol for his definition of the saturated phenomenon. Despite the idol's honorable association with the adoration of Christ, he voices critique, for the idol would lack "depth," and hence the possibility to express the divine Name.[92] This would be the exclusive prerogative of the icon.

What are the implications for music? Is there perhaps another way to consider Messiaen's "breakthrough"? One that is, perhaps, less dangerous (Chadwick)? According to Marion, the idol reduces the given to what is shown, to mere audibility or visibility. The idol is a facade; it is mere flatness or platitude. There is no possibility for the appearance of another gaze, for the gaze or countenance of the other.[93] The countenance differs from the façade in that it does not become a phenomenon, that is although it is given, it remains invisible, nonmanifest. It procures me with counterintentionality.[94] Whereas the idol is being constituted by my gaze, and therefore is in fact a closed, potentially even demonic phenomenon, the countenance reveals to me the alterity of the other who constitutes me.[95] This involves a conversion of the gaze, or anamorphosis, described above as crossing the phenomenological distance in the phenomenon's interiority (see the example of Reznikoff). Anamorphosis then does not only designate the event, but the icon too, especially so.[96] The idol, however, may signal "a certain low-water mark of the divine," but blocks the passage to alterity, and will not lead to the Other.

This passage has both an ethical and an aesthetic nature. Only when my eyes are opened toward the perspective of the other and are receptive to the counterintentionality of the iconic countenance, can I truly perceive its beauty. Marion maintains that the mural canvasses in the Rothko Chapel in Houston are incapable of achieving this effect, because they are, in the end, mere facades (because of their banality, their platitude). The suggestion of an "intimidating secret" is not sustained, ultimately, by an ability to allow the appearance of the other. Although originally intended as a Roman

Catholic chapel, it was therefore understandably, according to Marion, converted into a nonconfessional, nonspecific sanctuary for meditation and prayer. The temple is, in other words, ultimately vacant.[97] The icon, however, makes an appeal to me and exhorts my capacity for respect, that is, it admonishes me to wield the perspective of the other in what I am seeing. It resists the reduction of countenance to sheer facade, to an idol with a flattened face, compressed into the visibility of surface. In line with the sixth commandment (thou shalt not kill), the icon is to be preferred over the idol, because it respects the other's alterity. It follows that it avoids the constitutive gaze of looking (*regarder*) that reduces the unattainable, the *invisable* to a definite, perceptible, and unequivocal object. The countenance of the other gives rise to an endless hermeneutics. Its final meaning is only revealed in the last judgment of the (wholly) other.

What can this criticism mean for music, more especially for Messiaen's auditive idol? On the face of it, this appears to be unclear. Marion's preferred model for the icon—countenance—seems to imply that the highest form of the saturated phenomenon (according to the fourth of Kant's rubrics, modality) accords with the predominantly visual metaphorics of the Greco-Christian tradition. This is not entirely the case, however. The icon may be described in terms of countenance, but Marion's turn of phrase in that description has the occasional musical overtone. One instance was the musical anamorphosis of the experimental compositions by Iegor Reznikoff. A second case concerned the description of the "eventmental" nature of the saturated phenomenon in relation to Mozart's Jupiter symphony. In fact, the discussion of this symphony in *Being Given* forms a part of his descriptive analysis of the icon. One may wonder, however, about the exact iconic nature of the blast that sounds at the opening of this symphony. It rather looks like a general aspect of the event that, as we have seen, is generally part of all types of the saturated phenomenon, including the idol that similarly appears suddenly and unannounced, saturating the gaze.[98] A third case that needs to be explored somewhat further is that of "endless hermeneutics" involved in understanding or reading expression. Seemingly echoing a formalist and romantic musical aesthetics, Marion argues,

> The impossibility in constituting it in an object and a univocal phenomenon must be taken seriously: the classic definition of truth (adequation, evidence), and even its phenomenal definition (to show oneself starting from oneself), become here inoperative. For the face only shows what it expresses, but it never expresses a meaning or a complex of defined

meanings. . . . This endless flux of significations . . . can never itself be reduced to the concept or said adequately.[99]

Expression, the indeterminacy of meaning, irreducibility: such terms punctuate any theory on musical significance and expression. Yet this alone does not suffice to justify the transposition of Marion's critique on the idol to the register of music. Better it is to focus on the essence of his critique, which appears to be centered on form, *figura*, or shape. The idol may reflect the blaze of the garment of Christ, but the icon confronts me with His countenance. In this, Marion sides with Balthasar, who had already voiced his preference for the Apollonian in his early *opusculum* on the theology of music. Schiller too, who, like Balthasar, was influenced by Goethe, speaks of music in terms of figure. He asserts, among other things, that music is the art that must "become sheer form (*Gestalt*) and affect us with the serene power of antiquity."[100]

In answering the question of what should be understood as *figura* in terms of music, Balthasar's thoughts are instructive again. He recognizes the form (*Gestalt*) of Christ not only in the image (*eikon*) but also in rhythm, as it develops in the course of time: "the form can also be a temporally flowing rhythm or a theatrically developing plot."[101] Elsewhere, he describes the melodic contour as a shape whose "sum is greater than its constitutive parts," whose meaning is "immediately evident" and in a logical sense "impalpable."[102] As we have seen, this antinomic structure is interpreted by Balthasar as the manifestation of the divine—in the form of melody—in music. This form then might be taken to represent, apart from the curves of rhythm, the iconic in music. Such a shift toward the formal in music comprehends, in the last instance, a philosophical-theological decision. The idol resides primarily in the domain of the senses; it is an atomistic phenomenon. The icon, rather, is connected to philosophical hylomorphism and to the theological primacy of the image (*eikon*). It seems that both Balthasar and Marion take up this tradition, where form is the source and carrier of any and all splendor, blazing, blinding, dazzling, idolic luster.[103] As form in music is melody (according to Balthasar), this would imply that the dazzling *sons-couleurs* in both chorales are to be interpreted as a means of inking in melody. The luster of sound then is subservient to the formal and religiously privileged principle of form. In short, the iconic moment of the chorales consists precisely in this: the glorious appearance of melody as constitutive of the witnessing ear according to the process of anamorphosis.

To what extent is it plausible, this primacy of melody? In a contemporary perspective, it can reasonably be argued that melody represents the personal or the "countenance" in music. Melody is often used and understood as the lyrical, subjective element in music, addressing the listener in a meaningful way, from or by itself. This is especially true for music from the sixteenth century onward, when the subject made an entrance in music and the dominant paradigm of polyphony made way for homophony. Listening to an accompanied melody requires a certain "conversion" of the ear, in that the melody is no longer perceived as a phenomenon but is appreciated from the perspective or counterintentionality of the melodic line. In such cases, melody is expressive of something; it is, as Edward T. Cone famously argued, the voice of an indeterminate but unmistakably present "persona."[104] Accordingly, if Messiaen's music is to escape the entrapment of an all too hazy phenomenality of the idol, it will have to subordinate the idol to melody which then makes appear, as it were, the countenance of the other. It could be argued that this is indeed Messiaen's intention. The tenets from his melodist creed (cited in Chapter 3) are abundantly applied, and in other respects, too, his music is characterized by the use of forms such as his *neumes* and *personnages rythmiques*. Melody is assigned a prominent role in *La Transfiguration* (in the chorales and copious bird songs), which supports the impression that Messiaen adheres to the principle that Balthasar held too, in referring to Mozart. In this line of reasoning, the unmistakable Christian moment in Messiaen's music can therefore be grasped when listening is guided by the perspective of melody (music's iconic "countenance").

On the other hand, the fact of the religious ambivalence in musical form cannot be denied.[105] With Balthasar, the idea of form is derived from Greek antiquity, not from Christianity. The indissolubleness of form and content, which constitutes the spine of revelation as form for Balthasar, is for Hanslinck the designated hallmark of autonomous, purely *musical* (and so not at all theological) beauty.[106] Furthermore, if melody is privileged at all, it is so in two different directions. Melody is not just the most memorable of musical elements, or in speaking to us after a fashion, the most personal; it is the most demonic, too. Do not we all recognize the temporary experience of melody as the uninvited guest that cannot be shaken off, because it simply sneaked in and now insidiously inhabits our mind?[107] Finally, in a more general sense, the question might be raised as to why precisely *musical* form should be entitled to a privileged position. The analogy to mystery that sustains such privileging (that is, the simultaneous manifestation of irreducible proximity and distance) is also to be found elsewhere. Think, for example, of the rhetorics of Gorgias, where the deployment of figures cannot be wholly understood although they do have an intrusive effect on the listener.

It was Kierkegaard who pointed out that language can be just as disconcerting as music.

The position of melody is just as ambiguous with Messiaen. The paradigm of Mozart that frames the discussion of all these philosophers and theologians little resembles the patterns of *La Transfiguration*. There is no Mozartian melodic line, clear and of distinct form, and no melody that is homophonously accompanied. On the contrary, the melody of the closing chorale (Part XIV) and the words sung to it, appear to dissolve at crucial moments in the spectral surface of the idol, even though they occasionally seem to arise from this surface. In Chapter 2 this crisis of melody was analyzed in terms of the difficulties it encountered as it was swamping through the mire of chromatism. Melody is a great touchstone for the dissolution of musical time and space, because it has, in terms of Marion's poor or common phenomenon, both temporal linearity and two-dimensional spatiality. The saturation of music dissolves, at certain moments, its own coordinates, as for example when the tone of melody is disseminated (the effect is ecstasy of melody, as in mm. 10, 15, 37–38) or when the tone of melody disappears into the spectral universe it is surrounded by (the effect of eclipse, cf. mm. 17–18). Neither effect is related to any special occurrence in the melody, but is connected to the acute saturation of the actual musical phenomenon concerned. On the basis of this chorale, then, there is no reason to follow Balthasar in his interpretation of melody. Although in this chorale, too, melody can be viewed as the formal principle providing the scaffolding of colors, it is, as form, only of distinct significance when in crisis, in ecstasy, or even indeed when disappearing (into the spectral saturation of the idol).

Balthasar's formal turn (the *figura*, Gestalt, and so forth) is significant for other reasons, however. As was remarked earlier, Messiaen has, where his own music is concerned, little sense of the fluid indefiniteness he so admires in Debussy. Seldom does his music acquire that floating quality that is the hallmark of Debussy's music (and relates it to certain color-field paintings). Messiaen's colors are also, in general, different from those of Debussy. They are bathed in the harsh tones (and forms) of Gothic church windows, in contrast to the soft pastel shades of Debussy's idiom.[108] Colors with Messiaen are nearly always framed, in a local context or in the conceptual form of the composition, which is reflected in the presentation of color chords in the five *éblouissement* passages. The chorales form the exception to the rule, as we have seen: here no blocks of color music bordered by sharp (vertical) transitions toward contrasting music or (horizontal) framing drones and chords. In the conclusion to Chapter 2 it was therefore maintained that "breakthrough" is mostly about the transitions through these frames, in and out of the passage. The content of these passages are as such less important. This links up to the notion of the difficulty to imagine the saturated phenomenon. The transitions cause what otherwise remains imperceptible to appear, just as with the sudden opening chords of the Jupiter symphony. The listener, bearing witness, is always late (*sero te audivi*). The musical event has already occurred before it can be registered by the mind (*animus*). It is because of this structure that the illusion is created that a window is opened on something that normally is indiscernible because it overreaches or "underreaches" perception.[109] This "counterexperience" might be designated, with some reservations, as the iconicity of the passages. The term in that case does not strictly refer to Marion's icon, and should certainly not be confused with its conventional musicological meaning of tone painting or madrigalism.[110]

John Tavener (b. 1944), the British composer with the explicit objective of composing the musical equivalent of the icon, would probably contest this interpretation. In his view, Messiaen's formalism, due to his close-knit ties with modernism, has a devaluating effect on his music (especially with respect to religion). Distinguishing the "esoteric" from the "exoteric" approach, Tavener holds that the latter is doomed to remain superficial. This, then, is Messiaen's fate too: "Messiaen, I think, is a supreme example of a modern composer who really never goes beyond the exoteric. Yet I have to concede that that is the Western way of doing things. It is incomprehensible to me that any composer who is concerned with the sacred should proceed in such a way."[111] He appears to be saying that the exoteric approach cannot but lead to idols.[112] Instead, Tavener—who is of Presbyterian background but was received in the Russian Orthodox Church in 1977—envisages, in musical practice, the ideal of the icon in music as the culmination of the esoteric. This is in stark contrast to the alleged idolatry of modernism:

> To me [the icon] is the most transcendent form of art that exists in the West—that is, if you can call it art in the conventional sense. Whether you can write music that is truly like an ikon, whether you can prostrate in front of a piece of music, I simply do not know. I suppose the closest you get to it is in the chant that goes with the ikonography of the Church. I might also say that an ikon dissects us, and I think truly sacred music should do the same.[113]

His own music is a kind of "liquid metaphysics" and intends to make heard the "divine prototype."[114] Such esoteric music "speaks of an everlasting and unchanging reality and it exists on a higher plane. It is not subject to human manipulation. Different, higher, elusive by nature, it comes in a different way. The reality of the other dimensions tears through the screen of our earthly body, penetrating our feeble nature."[115] In this line of thought, music, that is *true* music, is not created but revealed. The composer merely mediates in this process of revelation and should efface his own self. He truly must obliterate the self in an attempt "to gradually annihilate the personal emotions and conscious deliberation in my music."[116] Nothing can be predicted beforehand about the resulting music, but it is the only way: "If it's just one or two banal notes, okay, then it's just one or two banal notes. But I guarantee that if one continues with this, gradually a music starts to form inside one, and who knows, we might start to realize that another kind of reality does after all exist."[117] His belief in the gradual inward process that is confluent with the move away from exterior and formal principles does not seem to warrant, as he also realizes, musical iconicity any better than the formalist and perhaps all too modernistic shock effects of Messiaen. In both cases music, as the result, will have to achieve this impression about its origin, that it is indeed "revealed." Intentions, no matter their sincerity, are no criterion for evaluating the degree or sense of revelation in music. The musical idol can be described in phenomenological terms, but in the end the musical icon remains hard to conceive.

The discussion of the possibility of such an icon and of its quadrature (the saturation of saturation) in the phenomenon of musical revelation appears to principally come down to the question of what can be described in positive terms as a specific Christian phenomenon in music. The idol falls short because, in the analysis of Marion, it cannot speak the Name, it cannot do justice to the countenance of the other/Other. The structures brought in by Balthasar (melody, rhythm) are indeed positive terms, but are on the other hand too general and too open to interpretation—and, as for the *éblouisse-ment* passages, too much beside the question. Greater accuracy is needed, in other words, in describing what is specifically Christian in (and through) Messiaen's music.[118]

## Glory and the Sublime

The music of the closing chorale in *La Transfiguration* is, as we have seen, at times saturated "according to quality." Hence it is characterized as an auditive idol. The mixture of admiration and amazement that this music evokes further testifies to its idolic nature. The way the ear is saturated and completely enthralled by the auditive idol has no precedence, but such fascination for the sound phenomenon is not unaccompanied. It is paired to its opposite, terror. This sensation is caused by the surplus of intuition in the idol. The ear is overwhelmed by the idol and is brought to the brink of its own limitations. The ear is deafened without becoming deaf; it is, in fact, dazzled.

By means of Marion's phenomenology of the saturated phenomenon, this experience-without-experience or counterexperience was described as a *religious* experience. It testified to a more or less diluted sense of revelation. The pure gift is manifested in the idol, even though it is veiled by the excessive visibility (audibility) of depthless surface. This leads to a further question. As Marion's phenomenology pretends to the sheer philosophical and is only developed to open a space within phenomenology for thinking the phenomenon of revelation (and, although this strictly remains the domain of positive theology, of Revelation), the phenomenon of the idol should perhaps be understood as a mere aesthetic phenomenon. Is not the idol, in combining the effects of fascination and terror, the theological substitution or alternative for that other effect of overwhelming transport—the sublime? What is the quintessential distinction that notches the theologizing explanation of this phenomenon (in terms of idol and dazzlement) by Marion, on the expense of the aesthetic notion of the sublime?

The aesthetics of Messiaen's music very often seem to invoke the sublime. Not only do Messiaen's titles, motto's and commentaries refer to classical examples of the sublime, such as starry heavens, the abyss, or alpine mountains; also the very style and design of much of his music is prone to typical gestures toward the sublime, such as the sensation of overpowering, the majestic, and the unimaginable. Messiaen's music is not only music of beautiful proportion, elegant design, and good taste; it very often seeks to transcend human measure. It aspires to the divine, or at least to the worldly traces thereof, through an arsenal of grand musical gestures, some of which may be quite violent and repellent to the ear. This music brings forth *negative* forms of representation: it presents that which cannot be presented in positive form (in an analogy from the domain of language: the name of God) through shattered or shattering forms (for example, faltering speech, a fractured language of the ineffable) or by falling silent altogether. Traditionally, the sublime has been thought as that which overpowers the human mind and may be thought to testify to (and perhaps, as Messiaen suggest, lead the mind toward) the ineffable domains of divine mystery.

In Kant's *Critique of Judgment*—the *locus classicus* of modern aesthetics—the sublime is analyzed according to Enlightenment aesthetics by setting a limit to the domain of sense perception with regard to religion.[119] The sublime is construed as a feeling, which indicates that the object of perception is unrepresentable to the subject's imagination. The sublime shatters the mind's power to synthesize the intuitions it receives into a unified representation of the object, in other words, to give it a unified form. According to Kant, the first moment of the sublime is characterized by the experience of displeasure (*Unlust*), which accompanies the overpowering of the imagination. After this initial moment, reason responds to this negative moment by making available to the subject its supernatural destiny, which is expressed by reason's three transcendental ideas: God, Infinity, and Immortality. In this second moment, the subject elevates itself above its finitude and subordination to the forces of nature, and thus pleasurably (*Lust*) overcomes its initial painful break with the world by realizing the superiority of its own destiny (that is freedom). The idea or feeling of the sublime has been a major source of inspiration for artists, in particular with respect to the romantic movement of the nineteenth century.[120]

In his classic book on the relation between religion and art, the phenomenologist theologian Gerardus van der Leeuw describes a variety of ways in which the sublime may be present in music:

> Music attains sublimity by slowness of tempo. But this is not the only means, nor does it offer a guarantee for true sublimity, as many "religious" composers seem to think. To slow tempo belongs majestic reserve, chaste restraint. And even this remains nothing unless everything points to an emotion which admits no more violent expression. . . . If we ask whence it comes that the massive, the sublime, often moves us religiously, indeed seems to be an expression of the Holy, we find that this lies in its overpowering character. We cannot escape it; we find ourselves in the presence of the wholly other.[121]

For listeners to Messiaen's music, this might not sound unfamiliar. Two short examples could be given, both from his early organ repertoire. The first is the extremely slow piece *Le banquet céleste*, notated in quaver 52 mpm, with its endless final chord, especially as in Messiaen's own recording. The second example is *Apparition de l'Eglise éternelle*, a piece that is characterized by the gestures of laborious swelling and expansion from its first seconds onward, and that reaches its tremendous, triumphant climax on a giant C-major triad midway through.[122] Van der Leeuw insists that if art is to express the Holy by means of the sublime, both of its constitutive moments, the *fascinans* and the *tremendum*, should be present. It is not enough for art either to "enchant, captivate, illuminate, remove a burden from the heart" or to "oppress, bring fear, cause horror and terror." As he puts it, "it may be that terror dominates, but fascination must not be absent. It may also be that we are so enchanted that we revel in bliss; but if every tremor is lacking, it is a false bliss, even if we may be confronted with real beauty."[123]

It is not difficult to locate passages where either the one or the other is predominant in Messiaen's work. Many forms of the sublime can be appreciated in his work—as far as form is an adequate term when speaking of sublime. The element of the monumental, for example, pervades *Et exspecto*: its five parts are highly segregated and it contains allusions to pyramids. Then, there is also the sublime of order: sections or 'verticality' as in *Couleurs* and *Et exspecto*; the sublime of temporal homogeneity (*Catalogue d'oiseaux*); the sublime of harmonic excess (*Transfiguration*, Part XIV); and the sublime of loudness (the tam-tam in *Et exspecto*). The joint occurrence of the *fascinans* and the *tremendum* are predominant the *éblouissement* passages. The brusque transitions to brief, blissful passages in Part IX and XII can be called to mind. Or both chorales, where it occurs in the combination of the continuous alteration between terribly dissonant chromatics and enlightening, graceful diatonics as well as in the melody, which is always on the verge of being drowned in saturation but persists nevertheless. The triumphant close on the major triad is entirely in accord with the elevating and ultimately affirming conclusion of the Kantian sublime.[124] The sublime evidently expresses the Holy, with van der Leeuw, but his terminology seems to be drawn from quite a different source, one that precisely distinguishes the sublime from the Holy or, as it is called in that context, the numinous. Thus, one may wonder whether the sublime in music really relates to the presence of the Holy or the numinous at all.

A study on the Holy that precedes van der Leeuw's *Sacred and Profane Beauty* and can be taken to be one its background sources is Rudolf Otto's *The Idea of the Holy*. Otto analyzes several "moments" of the numinous, departing from the central notions of the *tremendum* and the *fascinans*.[125] He traces these two aspects in the numinous. The numinous as awe-inspiring mystery or *mysterium tremendum* is the mystery that cannot be expressed in words but is felt nonetheless. Its elements can be recognized in Messiaen's oeuvre. Mystery as such is tremendous or awe-inspiring; but there is further the majestic that impresses man with a sense of his own diminutiveness and dependency; the dynamic that relates to God's active numinous presence, his wrath, love, and deeds; and finally the famous "wholly other," mystery ineffable and beyond human comprehension.[126] The aspect of fascination in the numinous urges, in contrast to the sense of humbleness spurred by the *mysterium tremendum*, a sensation of actively participating in this mystery. It is a figure not of absence, of the void, but of presence and fullness. With Messiaen, this is often articulated in the modality of amazement about the sheer miraculousness of it all and is characterized by his somewhat naive enthusiasm and fervor, which appears to find its way in the abundance and excess of his music: yet even more birds, colors, yet even longer works, and so forth.[127]

Otto's bipartite analysis of the moments of the numinous may look adequate, but these different aspects, just as the manifold *determinations* of the numinous, should a priori be suspected because of the reductive nature of such an analysis. The wholly other is condensed to what can be conceptualized or experienced, in other words to the qualities of sameness; an appeal on feeling or mood (*Stimmung*) is to no avail because they in turn are also aspects of experience. It could be argued, therefore, that so far as the numinous is presented or expressed in words or, as with Messiaen, in music, it is being corrupted. It follows that whatever his music expresses, it is *not* the numinous. This is a problem that returns in Otto's discussion of the sublime. The sublime and the numinous are similar in many respects, but not wholly identical, given Otto's insistence on the radical alterity and absolute originality of the numinous. What then is the relation between these two phenomena that, perhaps not in experiencing them but certainly in Kant's description, are so alike? Otto sustains the distinction between "the feeling of the sublime" and "the numinous feeling," even though recognizing the "external analogy" between the two that would testify to the fact that "there is more . . . in the combination of 'the holy' with 'the sublime' than a mere association of feelings."[128] Taken with the stability of this relatedness, the analogy would signify the "schematization" of the sublime with respect to the numinous. The former then is the aesthetical elevation, but nonetheless a pale reflection of the original, an irreducible and unforgettable *ur*-feeling (*Urgefühl*) of the numinous that stems from "the rational spirit of man and its *a priori* capacity."[129] It follows, according to Otto, that the appeal on the sublime, such as with van der Leeuw, can at most be an appeal on the indirect, secondary and weakened manifestation of the numinous. They are more dissimilar than alike (*maior dissimilitudo in tanta similitudine*). The question returns again: Could we conceive of a more originary trace of the numinous in music? And could such a trace in fact be heard? The answer to

the question starts from the theological aesthetics of Balthasar, more specifically his central and eponymous concept of glory (*Herrlichkeit*).

At first glance, the biblical concept of glory (*kabod, doxa, gloria*) appears
to be articulated in contrast to, amongst others, the aesthetic sublime. Despite his qualified appreciation of Kant (which "halts at the threshold of
German idealism and its aesthetics of identity and bears traces of a sense of
the Cross"), Balthasar is unequivocal in his judgment of the self-glorification
of the enlightened mind. In exalting the enlightened mind, the glory of God
is effaced from thought. Thus, Balthasar maintains that "'critical idealism'
leaves . . . no room for experiencing Worldbeing as the manifestation of
God's glory" and that "'glory,' as a consequence, is superseded by ethical
*sublimity.*" Such sublimity is blind to the glory of God and can only, when
experiencing the cosmos, appreciate the sublimity of the mind and its laws.
With Kant, glory is superseded by the *ethical* sublime, of which the aesthetic
sublime is merely an "expression," according to Balthasar. This line of
thought then "catastrophically" culminates in the works of Fichte, where
the absolute subject gradually replaces God, with the dire result that "'glory'
is not only reduced to worldly beauty but to the prayerless self-glorification
of the Mind."[130]

A comparative study of glory and the sublime yields, according to Reinhard Hoeps, three types of justification for such an opposition. First, glory
is a term derived from the theology of manifestation in the Bible, whereas
the sublime (*das Erhabene*) has its source in rhetorics and derives its contemporary meaning from the Enlightenment. Glory refers to the divine initiative that cannot be made comprehensible; the sublime demarcates the limits
of the powers of knowledge.[131] Second, glory is about the movement
toward the image, whereas the sublime moves in a contrary direction, away
from the world of representation (*bildlichkeit*).

> Glory is the answer to the question how the highest Being or the highest
> truth can be present in the world of appearances. The sublime moves in the
> opposite direction. It searches in the world of appearances for the possibility
> of representing the highest Being. Although the sublime remains entrenched
> in intuited Nature, it does strife to overcome it. In contrast, glory descends
> into Nature and breaks it apart. The problem of intuition is here a problem
> of becoming image (*Bildwerdung*), whereas the problem of the sublime is one
> of exiting the realm of representations. Hence, their orientations and move-
> ments are contrary, even though they can appear to the beholder as one and
> the same phenomenon, and are related to one another in their common
> seriousness.[132]

Third and finally, the sublime is distant from glory because it rejects the idea of ordered nature or cosmos and is prone to endorse the contrary, chaos, in welcoming the "possibility of experiencing the manifestation of the divine."[133] For Hoeps, the first of these distinctions is, quite rightly, the most important: "There is a fundamental distinction between the concepts of glory and the sublime, marked by the enlightened consciousness of critical reflection."[134] Still, the two figures are narrowly related to one another and at times barely distinguishable. Frederick Bauerschmidt, for example, shows that it is not only the sublime (in the sense of Lyotard's postmodern sublime) that is characterized by a moment of negativity, but glory too, in that it creates absence in concealing or withdrawing the Holy. The Holy is not manifested *as* form, but *in* form. Revelation takes shape not as an independent image of God, but as a unique, hypostatic union of archetype and image.[135] Thus, Bauerschmidt argues that "the sublime archetype is in the form; one might say that the form is the 'real presence' of the archetype."[136] This is, however, a broken presence. The ultimate, most important form, with Balthasar, is the form of Christ (*Christusgestalt*), which has the tripartite shape of a fractured *corpus triforme*.[137] Bauerschmidt maintains that this form consists of the natural body, the body of the Church and the Eucharistic body. A fractured form, it is nonetheless one and whole in the (exegetic) tradition.[138] This sheds some light on what was advanced by Hoeps: glory descending into nature and breaking it apart (without canceling the unity of body, Church, and Eucharist).

The double motion of glory can be taken to confirm visible form as such, as well as the alterity of the invisible (presented nevertheless) and, concomitantly, the unrepresentableness of visible form.[139] The fact of the unrepresentable constitutes a moment that is very similar to the negative moment of the sublime. In other respects, too, the two figures are remarkably alike. In glory, according to Hoeps, there is a distinct oscillation between the tropes of concealment (distance) and revelation (presence), both at the level of conception as in actual perception. A similar dynamics would also occur in the (Kantian) description of the sublime.[140] Apart from that, it is interesting to note that Balthasar retains the distinction between the notions of glory and the Holy in describing these dynamics, identifying the Holy as the element in withdrawal, present in its absence. Glory, then, is secondary to the Holy, which creates a situation that is not dissimilar from the position of the sublime in relation to glory in the writings of Otto. If both the sublime and glory are connected to a certain concealing revelation of something that, in theological and philosophical terms, surpasses all pure determination in positive terms (the wholly other)—what then is the meaning of a discussion on how the two are related?

The most pertinent distinction between the two, brought to the fore by the interposition of philosophical Enlightenment, may provide the answer to this question. However, this distinction is not finite. Thus, Hoeps believes that Balthasar's description of glory falls short and should be *complemented* by the idea of the sublime:

> Against the backdrop of critical philosophy [the sublime] highlights the relation between appearing and seeing which is expressed by this biblical notion. It is precisely by marking a coming-into-presence that glory presents its very difference from the notion of the Holy (*Heiligkeit*)—a distinction that Balthasar seems not to have pursued rigorously enough when he plays out the human conditions of perception against the unconditionality of appearance. The insistence on unconditionally appearing objectivity and unity of revelation is only one aspect of what the notion of glory seeks to describe. The strength of this notion is in the way this aspect is enmeshed with its opposite, constitutive signification through human perception. It is in this sense that the topos of glory bears within itself the seed of that of the sublime.[141]

For Marion, too, the philosophical notion of the sublime is not extraneous to theology. He does not hesitate to denote the Kantian sublime as a saturated phenomenon *avant la lettre*. The sublime carries all four characteristics of this phenomenon and "permits us to broaden the field of application for the concept of the saturated phenomenon."[142] As for the *anamorphosis* of the icon (that is, the saturated phenomenon in terms of modality), Marion states that also in Kant's description of the sublime the gaze is converted. In a move that disrupts the conventional interpretation that the Kantian sublime is an internal affair of the subject, Marion advances that the ego's capacity for evaluation is countered in the sublime to such an extent that eventually the phenomenon is regarding the ego rather than being constituted by the ego (just as in the case of the icon), and with respect (*Achtung*) to boot.[143]

In the conventional reading of the Kantian sublime, however, the privileging of the subject appears to rule out religion in any significant sense. This has led theologians to distrust the Kantian sublime, because in such self-affirming, self-constituting subjectivity, the other, the wholly other and especially the wholly Other are excluded. The two extremes of the subject, namely its demonic enclosure in self-constitution on one hand and its opening unto witnessing or being gifted (*adonné*) to the phenomenon-giving-itself on the other hand, do not affect the sublime and glory alone. They are also essential in interpreting dazzlement and breakthrough in Messiaen. Either the ear is demonically enclosed within the economic circulation of the auditive idol, or the ear opens unto ("breaks through *toward* the beyond") a phenomenon—icon or revelation—that in overpowering the ear simultaneously constitutes it.[144]

How can such a distinction be conceived? In the event of a musical experience, how is the decision made that the phenomenon gives *itself* in showing itself, that this is a case of counterintentionality, and not, as with the idol, a mere illusion of giving itself, that is, a mirror effect that is not recognized as such by the subject? This dilemma is reminiscent of Descartes's hypothesis of the evil genius: how are we to know that in the anamorphosis of the icon we are not being misled, in the Cartesian sense, by a demonic genius into believing that here we are facing the phenomenon of revelation? The musical counterpart to this dilemma is in the enforced distinction between the romantic theories of *Kunstreligion* or religion of art, discussed earlier, and the aforementioned alternative suggested by the approach of Marion. The cult of music in the religion of art is to an important extent enabled by the concept of absolute music, a music absolved from all nonmusical content, and so from all ties with the extramusical (such as its functional subjection to the word or the Church), thus, according to this religion, rising above the phenomenal world. This music, realized as instrumental music, is one of pure form, pure signifier, devoid (*kenosis*) of all extramusical meaning. It is an empty shape, perfectly suited to the association with the sublime because it is adaptable to the projections of a desire for Infinity, for what lies beyond the veil of Isis. As Daniel Chua beautifully shows, it is no great step from this absolute, sublime music to the idol and its reflections. Writing about self-deification, he notices,

> The empty sign is . . . the precondition for the subject's plenitude. The ego surreptitiously enthrones itself in the space made vacant by the draining out of meaning and reorganises the empty signs as a trace of its own divinity. "Music names the subjective inner self as its content," says Hegel. Indeed, it was only by committing the acts of aesthetic violence against music that the Romantics could demolish a space for the ego to inhabit; the obliteration of content by form and then the shattering of form by the sublime is the continual manipulation of the subject to know itself as infinite. "*Form*," says Schumann, "is the vessel for spirit"; it is an inner teleological structure for the subject to know itself as autonomous and surpass as infinite. Musical *kenosis* becomes the real presence of the subject.[145]

In the romantic period, this implied for music that it could be absolved from any programmatic determination; it was absolute. The ensuing emptiness (which could also be perceived, in the Kantian sense, as empty play, hollow virtuosity, or sensuousness) could then count as the materialization of metaphysical form (Idea, Spirit), taking on in its indeterminacy all worldly content (concrete meaning). The emptiness in music was not therefore understood to be regressive or presignificant, but rather transsignificant or hypersignificant; the emptiness in form is fullness in the highest, transcendental sense. In this, the analogy of music with the sublime is suggested: formal and senseless overpowering, shifting to metaphysical plenitude and insight.

In light of this, Balthasar's appeal on the notion of absolute music and his idea that form is "revelation from above" is an understandable but suspect move. Is not this really about creating maximal space for the subject, or from a different angle, about minimizing the phenomenon and its intuitive givenness? Are not the concept of religion of art and the notion of absolute music it is founded on extreme examples of reducing music to intention, given the manifold significances, theories, concepts, noeses? Is the religion of art, all things considered, about music at all? And if the answer is positive, then what insight may this theory engender in what is specifically Christian in (or through) music?

The humanist bearings of the sublime complicate the answer to this question. Adorno argued that in modernity, the sublime is connected with "the bourgeois spirit" that sticks to the "illusion" of "the unhistorical immortality of art . . . the belief in genius, that metaphysical transfiguration of bourgeois individualism," and the idea that "great men can achieve great things at any time and that the greatest achievements are always available to them."[146] This bourgeoisie, which includes thinkers such as Kant, Hegel, and (despite himself) Adorno, clutches to the idea of a humanist dream of human grandeur to which the holy is, in the last instance, subservient.[147] It is an ideological preference that creates the possibility for a dialectics of sublime self-elevation and melancholic self-pity that is abundantly celebrated in early romantic music.[148] The subject and its vicissitudes form the center. Breaking through toward the beyond can then only be conceived of as an intrasubjective event and is conditionally predetermined by subjectivity. This leaves no room for the notion of the saturated phenomenon, which is principally not conditioned by any determinants. However, it is the question whether the saturated phenomenon can be distinguished clearly and convincingly from these notions of sublimity and from human subjectivity, as the empty form of absolute music, an outstanding object for all kinds of pantheistic worship of the Infinite, suits the description of the saturated phenomenon remarkably well. There is no end to its meanings, and just like the icon or the event it invites an infinite hermeneutics. Empty form, the object of the religion of art (aesthetic theory in the extreme), appears to double, then, as the kenotic-Christian *Gestalt* that is pivotal to the alternative theological aesthetics of Balthasar.

This resemblance is more significant than may appear at first sight. Because it can indeed be argued, with reference to the notion of repetition (see the next chapter), that the icon (countenance, form) too must observe the logics of iterability that prescribe that it should be possible, for the icon to be meaningful at all, that it be repeated in different contexts. A precondition for the possibility of meaning, however, such repetition runs the danger of becoming mechanical, hence vacant, hollow, an empty husk, a vessel for just any meaning: or, in other words, "absolute" music, *Kunstreligion*. The diaphanous icon then degenerates into an aesthetic-theological idol, which, according to this logic, would belong to the very structure of its constitution.[149] Thus, an impasse is reached in the analysis of Messiaen's music by means of the phenomenological approach of Marion. How to decide that the phenomenon presents *it*self in the manner of giving it*self* if this self is subject to repetition?[150] In the final two chapters, I will look into the possibilities of emerging from this impasse.

# 5. The Technics of Breakthrough

## The Artifactuality of the Beyond

The varied and conflicting vocabularies Messiaen uses when speaking of his own work are a reflection of the complex cultural-historical background that informs it: secularization, individualization, modernism, postmodernism, and technology, to name a few. In the opening paragraph of his *Conférence de Kyoto*, Messiaen blames the lack of understanding that often informs the reception of his work on the decline of faith. He laments the fact that as a "Christian and a Roman Catholic," he speaks of "God, Divine Mysteries, and the Mystery of Christ to unbelievers or people who have little knowledge of religion and theology."[1] This sounds like a tragic fate for a composer who states, as we have seen in Chapter 1, that the illumination of "theological truths" is the most vital characteristic of his work. The question arises, however, why it is that Messiaen chose to express such illumination in art at all, and especially why, once this road was taken, he sought to establish a context beyond and outside the church, where, in all probability, at least a greater understanding of his thematics would have been warranted. For a believer, Messiaen has done the improbable and the unexpected: his religious intentions are conveyed into a domain of art with a noticeable history, dating back at least to the early nineteenth century, of divergence from the church. But he also joined, and by no means reluctantly, the most progressive representatives of his art form and shared their focus on the compositional-technical aporias of their era. Paul Griffiths contends that "at this stage of Western culture religious art is impossible except as a spiritual exercise for the creating individual."[2] If this is correct, this would lead, in the case of Messiaen, to the question of the relation between the technical nature of the exercises that he would have created for himself, and their religious, more specifically Christian, meaning.

Paradoxically, Messiaen is one of those whose musical views are not primarily guided by religion. His views on composition are steeped in the twentieth century tradition of musical-analytical formalism. An important guiding principle in this formalism is making a clear distinction between, on one hand, the autonomous domain of music itself, and on the other, everything that is associated with it. Relying on this principle, Messiaen often differentiates the musical artifact, which is characterized by its technical dimension, from preferences, feelings, and needs that are not completely dissociated from the artifact but should nevertheless be considered as "extramusical." In the preface to *The Technique of My Musical Language*, he writes, "Though I have written a good number of works—religious in a mystical, Christian, Catholic sense—I shall further leave aside this preference; we treat technique and not sentiment."[3] A similar distinction is made in conversation with Almut Rössler, when he remarks that "music is to a certain extent a specialty, a technique, whereas faith, piety, is a need."[4] When probed, he adds, in the spirit of Eduard Hanslick, that form and content are inseparable in music, but in general his sayings are clearly pervaded with a brand of one-sided analytical formalism that rests on the distinction between technique and intention.[5] It is as if music is divided against itself with Messiaen, as his words both produce and reproduce the very dissociation of form and content he deplores, in a sense, in his *Conférence*.

The separation of music and religion this formalist approach amounts to, is reflected in the literature on Messiaen, and is extended, occasionally, toward the domain of the creative spirit. Again, an example of this line of thought can be drawn from Griffiths, who frames the music of the composer in an aesthetic and psychological matrix, as distinct from a religious one. He clearly maintains that music "is a contribution to art before it is a contribution to theology," and can therefore best be considered as a "mental" art, that is, an art that produces "experiences."[6]

> We may do better to consider his as a mental art rather than a spiritual art, one providing experiences for the imagination that go beyond the natural in ways suggested by his religion and his ornithology: experiences of weightlessness, great clarity and timelessness, of flight and joy (hence the great number of works dealing with resurrected existence). Moreover, to understand Messiaen in terms of his religious intentions would seem to be going at things the wrong way round. If Messiaen's is a religious art, then its subject is vastly more important than its substance, and it would seem an exercise of doubtful value to bring the whole theology of sin and redemption to bear on the analysis of *Les offrandes oubliées*, for example.[7]

Griffiths does not take up the implication in his latter remark where he appears to suggest that the underlying concept of religious art is in fact senseless. The contribution of Messiaen to the tradition of religious music—a term Griffiths does not hesitate to use, by the way—would especially consist in his deployment of sacred texts "that may hugely challenge the imagination to the extent that they are appalling or awe-inspiring."[8] The work for organ *Livre d'orgue*, with its appeal to the extraordinary visions of Ezekiel, is a point in case. Nevertheless, Griffiths argues, Messiaen was always oriented to the *cultural* norm of diatonic tonality. The contrast between religious text and (cultural) diatonics, then, would serve to understand Messiaen's notions of dazzlement and breakthrough as sheer musical-mental occurrences within the realm of humanism.

> The diatonic system is by long convention, if not by inherent nature, a humanist language. Music that would speak of the divine has to wield its triads in other ways or else avoid them altogether, which is perhaps because we accept the major-minor system as some sort of musical reality and associate excursions from it with experiences beyond the normal. Messiaen himself may be thinking in these terms when he says that music can encompass "an opening towards the beyond, towards the invisible and unsayable, which can be made with the help of *sound-color* and amounts to a sensation of *dazzlement*."[9]

In other words, Griffiths gives a certain slant to Messiaen's testimony. The musical reality of Messiaen's work, such as Griffiths analyzes it, runs parallel to the religious imagery conveyed by Messiaen. Thus, the music of Messiaen can be interpreted as an allegory of the "beyond," but it can just as well be understood in terms of an immanent play with musical conventions, in dissociation from the realm of religion. In effect, with such a move the position of the religious in the art of Messiaen is marginalized and reduced to an accidental and optional program, an elective frame for interpreting musical structure. Prime attention should be focused, according to Griffiths, on what happens in sound and time; when discussing Messiaen's music, the religious can—and should—be barred.

Actually, there are two remarkable elements in Messiaen's discourse on breakthrough that support Griffiths's stance. Breakthrough would occur "with the help of" (*à l'aide de*) sound-color, which implies a shift of attention: music as the *cause* of a religious *effect*. This strange logic qualifies religion as one of the effects of music. Second, Messiaen's appeal on the religious is a little suspect when considering the fact that two of the five assigned passages of breakthrough are repeated in a kind of "musicalizing" variation. God's ways may be mysterious, but it is rather unlikely that

He—or one of his representatives—will be bothered by musical circumstances, let alone raise twice to the composer's bait.[10] It is advisable, then, to follow Griffiths, who proposes to concentrate matter-of-factly on "what [music] parades in sound and time," and to treat the religious testimony of Messiaen with some caution.[11] If necessary, this testimony can always be implicated in a parallel (symbolical or allegorical) reading of the musical-technical and the aesthetical-psychological dimensions of this art.

There is, however, a drawback to Griffiths's approach (which he shares, incidentally, with others): it makes Messiaen's claim that music can be about the extraordinary, and to some extent *privileged* alliance with the religious, incomprehensible. In other instances it would perhaps not matter if the composer's statements were judged obscure and ignored, but here the consequences are rather immense. It is not the representation of the religious that is addressed by Messiaen, but its *presence* as an event (and even its "liveness" in the sense of the French *actualité*). With Griffiths, the religious is at best conceivable, in terms of its public aspect, as an historical phenomenon (a *representation*), but in the worst case it is merely, from the viewpoint of presence, an empty figure. In seeking to solve the conflict between the miracle of breakthrough and the objectivity of the musical artifact Griffiths reverts to reducing, if not eliminating, the marvelous. Music is art, a construction made human hands; experiencing Messiaen's music is a "mental," not a religious affair. Presence, essential for the existence and sense of music as a phenomenon that sounds and is listened to, is only of secondary importance. Likewise, Griffiths's favoring representation of breakthrough—verbal-musical—is on the expense of actually experiencing the breakthrough Messiaen speaks of. Thus, the question is whether there is an alternative to Griffiths's brand of hermeneutic musicology. Is it possible to conceive of a theoretical medium that allows for the conjunction of different dimensions, for the musical touching on the religious, the technical on the theological?

The identification of such a medium is complicated primarily because of the different temporalities that are involved. When referring to the music of dazzlement in a formal sense, both Messiaen and Griffiths make use of the medium of writing. The place in music pinpointed by Messiaen as the alleged location for religious breakthrough does not refer to a particular moment in experience, but to a point in the score. In other words, the moment of breakthrough is a coordinate in the spatiality of notation, and as such it is alienated from the experience of time. As a matter of fact, the dimension of time is converted into a spatial dimension, a dot on an imaginary line with-out spectator, subject to the regime of temporal unity and homogeneity.[12] Bernard Stiegler argues that such a conversion, the hallmark of the way we have known "objective" time since Aristotle, is also characteristic for what he dubs "technological time."[13] In the technological time of the score, music appears as a calculable and architectonically transparent phenomenon that has the score as its blueprint. However much we acknowledge that the score is not the music itself, the technicality that is evoked in the notation of music is not just the representational externalization of a musical duration that is internally experienced. Musical writing constitutes an essential mo-ment in the music, because it exists in its textual form. This is a general characteristic in a certain tradition of the musical West, whose significance comes fully to the fore when music asserts a claim on presence. With Messi-aen, this is the case in a special way. His discourse on breakthrough traverses the distance between the extremely formal-technical determination of the musical object on one hand and the most singular experience of music as religious immediacy on the other. *Eblouissement* is conceived as being at once a dot on a line and a withdrawal from all spatio-temporality, at once affirming and negating music as a technical phenomenon.

Messiaen's presence is not unadulterated but in the order of *artifactuality*. This portmanteau term was introduced by Jacques Derrida to highlight the idea that our sense of ("live") presence is informed by, among others, politi-cal debate and current affairs programs on television, and is therefore in fact a constructed "liveness." Actuality, he posits, is "not given, but actively pro-duced, sifted, invested, performatively interpreted by numerous devices which are *factitious* or *artificial*, hierarchizing and selective."[14] Such an invisi-ble and filtered construction of presence is a feature of Messiaen's discourse on breakthrough, too. The immediate experience of the beyond is part of a technical amalgam of musical construction, rhetorical evocation, artistic presentation and performance, dispersion in different media through digital technology, and so on; processes that involve a similar filtering as in the construction of public liveness. In a sense, the experience of dazzlement is also a form of public liveness, although Messiaen points out that as such it is dysfunctional in that it is not an experience shared by the composer and the audience. It is more interesting, however, to dwell on Derrida's insight in the alliance between technology (notably in the visual media) and the topi-cal present. This alliance is mutually reciprocal. Presence is not only a tech-nical effect, always already produced, anticipated, and stored elsewhere, but technics in turn are also induced by presence, especially where access unto itself is involved. When Messiaen speaks of *éblouissement*, it is not the experience as such that is at stake (in so far as this "as such" is conceivable at all), but an indissoluble circuit that comes about in the instrumental-musical domain of sound-color and the (synesthetically) listening ear-eye. The ecstasy of dazzlement is a transport that is not restricted to the condition of the soul (as certain Bergsonian interpretations of time and duration with Messiaen appear to suggest), but extends into the circuit between the ear-eye and sound-color. As a consequence, the actual experience of breakthrough is always and inevitably inscribed in the temporality of technology, and evokes it.

This chapter is centered on the question of what insisting on presence, as Messiaen does, means for theorizing his music *as a phenomenon*. The next chapter will then address the issues of what is involved in *listening* to such a phenomenon. Here, the endeavor to understand the intervention of presence in the domain of musical technics will be prepared first by determining the nature of this presence. The next section therefore proceeds with a discussion on the phenomenology of musico-religious touch, guided by the later writings of Jean-François Lyotard. Temporal displacements such as syncopations and the play of memory are shown to be important elements. The different forms music can take under pressure of liveness will be addressed at the end of this section. Next, the thematics of the technological mediation of Messiaen's music will be addressed. Here, the religious will be related to economical and psychoanalytical motives with the objective to track the modulations of breakthrough, all through the very context Messiaen brings into opposition to his intention of illuminating simply religious themes alone. The final section is concerned with the philosophical implications of Messiaen's repeating and "musicalizing" the unique moments of breakthrough in his music; a repetitiveness whose effect is multiplied at another level, through the sheer fact that music is absorbed in a repetitive movement through scores, rehearsals, performances, recordings, memories, and so on. Here, the argument centers on the question whether the religiosity—more precisely, the Christianity—of Messiaen's music of breakthrough really is at odds with this technically mediated possibility of repetition. To what extent can we say that a serial breakthrough still is Christian? What criteria can be developed to ascertain this at all?

## The Tone of the Absolute

The touch of the absolute is one of the recurrent concerns in Jean-François Lyotard's book *The Confession of Augustine*. In positioning this theme, he makes use of the dualities of Kantian representational thought. Touch is a figure of (and for) the mind, or *animus*, a portmanteau term for everything that enables the subject to form representations. This power presupposes, however, another dimension that escapes such representing, namely the soul or *anima*. With Augustine, the subject of Lyotard's writing, both terms refer to the soul, but in general anima is taken to connote the soul's vegetative and appetitive functions, while animus refers to the thinking soul or the mind. Chris Doude van Troostwijk explains the difference between the two terms in Kantianizing fashion:

> Prior to the entry of impressions into the representative registers of the *animus*, there is *anima*, the sensitivity to naked existence. The *animus* takes care of the objective constitution of reality: sense impressions acquire form and meaning and are localised in a recognisable world. But not only is ability required for *what* the things are, the openness for the fact *that* things are is also necessary. Impressions presuppose impressionability. The "being"—the *that* of things—is not derived from or stored in frameworks of imagination. It only makes itself felt, here and now, like an actual occurrence. This primary presence is noted by an ability which can be distinguished from the representative *animus*, yet is not an entirely separate entity. The *anima* is nothing more than the feeling (*affectus*) which exists only in the actuality of the impression (*affectio*).[15]

Augustine addresses God's presence not only in his ear but in the other senses too. It is as if there is a "fivefold assault," in Lyotard's words, on the subject who suffers it like a penetration or a ravishment. Why such words of violence? Because Lyotard reads in Augustine how the divine penetrates man by force: "Placing your outside within, you converted the most intimate part of him into his outside. And with this exteriority to himself, your, an incision henceforth from within, you make your saint of saints, *penetrale meum*, he confesses, thy shrine in me."[16] The absolute forcefully breaks through the aesthetic frames that constitute the animus; it is a "something" outside space, time, and synthesis that nestles in an inner space that is more interior than man is unto himself (*interior intimo meo*). Here the anima resides, the soul that is partnered by the elevated divine: "The absolute, absolutely irrelative, outside space and time, so absolutely far—there he is for one moment lodged in the most intimate part of this man. Limits are reversed, the inside and the outside, the before and the after, these miseries of the mind."[17] Divine touch, insofar as Lyotard conceives it, occurs at the level of anima.

There is only actuality and singularity at this level. The "inner human" or anima "who is neither man nor inner, woman and man, an outside inside," is grazed by this meeting with the Other (the *affectio*). The anima does not witness the experience of touch because it does not possess the objectifying conditions for testimony (temporality, spatiality, memory, synthesis, and so forth). "The inner human does not bear witness to a fact, to a violent event that it would have seen, that it would have heard, tasted or touched. It does not give testimony, it is the testimony. It is the vision, the scent, the listening, the taste, the contact, each violated and metamorphosed. A wound, an ecchymosis, a scar attests to the fact that a blow has been received, they are its mechanical effect."[18] Thus, sensation only exists in the actuality of the impression as such, not in its repeatable retention or in its recording. Still, Lyotard maintains, this singular *affectio* is not detached from the animus. Although unmediated repetition or remembrance of the singular is not possible, the mind bears traces of being touched by the Other. The notion of fissure is among the tropes used by Lyotard to refer to such traces. The fissure continuously disrupts the neat oppositions the mind needs to maintain order and structure.

> A fissure zigzags across all that lends itself to writing, to the great vexation of animus, whose binary clarity is humiliated. The caesura does not take place, has not the time. The here and now, the stretches of time, the places, the lives, and the I present themselves as fissured, or rather, fissure continually. The field of reality, discourse included, fissures in its entirety, like a struck glass.[19]

The absolute is neither present nor absent, but "cuts its presence into the shallow furrow of its absence."[20] What is the form this fissure may take? Lyotard tracks the fissure in several distinct locations in the discourse of the *Confessions*: unfathomable memory, the topology of interiority, the expanse of time (*distentio*), the habits of the body. It is always about an irreducible differend, what is askew (*dissidio*), dissipated (*dissipatio*), or the highly inflammable sequence of "conversion, reversion, inversion, perversion."[21] Doude van Troostwijk subsumes the indirect connections between the actuality of the anima and the syntheses of the animus under two different perspectives. The first is of a *libidinal* nature: "The *anima* is grieving the loss of the actual 'thing' it was touched by in a syncopic moment. This encounter leaves no memory, strictly speaking, but a 'deception' . . . The *anima* bears this sense of deception, grief and loss for the animus as well. A desire (*libido*) for the 'thing' is settled in the subject."[22]

The second is *ontological*. In Lyotard's words: "The object is only there to the extent that it is not there, it passes in transit, its present nickname does nothing but streak with the tiniest of flashes the interface between two clouds of nonexistence, the not yet and no longer."[23]

References to music are early and frequent in Lyotard's book. The soul, touched, will not cry out when violated, but breaks out in psalmodies: the flesh "chants, brings to each assault [by the absolute] rhythm and rhyme, in a recitative, a *Sprechgesang*."[24] The animus does not break out, in other words, in the melisma of madness, but embodies the testimony of the anima in the minimal inflection of psalmody. In the text of the *Confessions* a similar intervention takes place, according to Lyotard, of the anima's actuality and singularity in the form of the musical. In a passage cited earlier, he describes the *Confessions* as follows: "The work, before being narration and meditation, is *mélos*, a poem in which the chord of disquiet and that of rest, the chord of death and the of true life, of question and response send out their assonant and dissonant vibrations to the address of the Absolute."[25] The fissures in the logical-discursive text of the autobiography transform it, momentarily, into a score. They constitute a moment in the text where the account of his life is interrupted by the performative evocation (in the anagogical or mystagogical sense) of the absolute. As Lyotard puts it: "The argumentative 'disorder,' the sequential dissonance of the questions, to which other questions 'respond' are to be understood foremost as music that the soul strives to *tune* to the harmony of the involuntary will, and with which the soul strives to pay it homage."[26] By means of this "cryptography," Augustine would attempt to recreate for the reader, in a momentary syncope, the order of "primality," that is, "the rare experience of naked existence" (*sentiment d'exister*).[27]

The musical thematics alluded to by Lyotard in discussing Augustine recurs elsewhere in his writings. The connective link is, in this case, in his use of the notion of tone. He states, for example, that the "tone" of the *Confessions* is invocative (*invocatio*), and this turns out to be a node in an elaborate network of musical imagery. Listen to the following crescendo:

> The tone of *invocation* is that of *laudatio*, of praise that the work addresses to its authentic author. The tone is given by a rhythm, which is that of the *Psalms*, the book being quoted profusely in the recurring stream of invocations. The psalm constitutes a song of praise, sung with the harp. The harp is the instrument of the guiding chord, and Augustine is something like the psalmist working the strings, the vibration of which calls forth the voice of

the Lord. The psalm rises up, it takes the work out of its immanence, it gathers up its interior transcendence, concealed more deeply than the work can show. The invocation is an act of praise, and this praise is a melody.[28]

The complex musical metaphorics in this quotation, and indeed in the entire section it was lifted from, needs some clarification. What does Lyotard mean exactly? Augustine is the psalmist; the psalm he chants is, according to Lyotard, both a laud and a melody. Augustine is playing the chords, that is, he is singing (*chordes vocales*). He is praising the Lord and invokes Him, hoping that His voice will reverberate in his own. But this song ("my tone") is directed by another ("the tone"), the tone that is set by the introit, a "leitmotif, a guiding thread," and sounded by the harp.[29] This instrument is also being played by Augustine, who is "working the strings" so that the tone of the harp incessantly "rivets my tone to the order of your omniscience."[30] What kind of miraculous tone can this be? In any case, it is a tone that directs for Augustine the way to God, a *sacred* tone. Within Lyotard's frame of thought, this then can only be the tone of *timbre* or *stridence*: the tone of the absolute. A nuance, rather than the phenomenological or aesthetic tone of the harp. As Doude van Troostwijk explains, "The *Confessions* are an account of the quest for the singular moment that escapes any form of repetition. Music and confession are shaped by the 'tone of the absolute.' This is not the *aisthetic-phenomenological* tone that can be trapped in an empirical framework, nor the *aesthetic* tone tracing the forms of feeling. The tone Lyotard speaks of is 'timbre,' the singular colouring of sound-material, or 'stridence,' a barely perceptible shrill tonality."[31]

According to Lyotard, the "timbres of piety (*timbres de la piété*)" reverberate in psalmody.[32] Nuance and timbre have been addressed elsewhere in Lyotard, for instance in "God and the Puppet."[33] In this essay, Lyotard juxtaposes the three tropes of the divine Other, death, and the tone of the absolute (or absolute tone). The well-known epicurean formula that if I am not here, $x$ is not either, and if $x$ is not here, neither am I, is true for each of these figures.[34] Lyotard does not answer the question of whether this means that it is possible to identify the absolute alterities of tone, death, and God. Principally, he is concerned with the resemblance of the divine (or more precisely "infinite divine grace") to a specific instance of the mechanical, which would preeminently come to the fore in his notion of musical nuance.[35]

Again, Lyotard takes the course of delocalization in order to localize this nuance, withdrawing the aesthetic from the forms of space (and time).[36] He constructs, thereto, an opposition between, on one hand, the logics of identical repetition that condition the comprehension of music in terms of synthesis, form, and identity, and, on the other hand, the logics of analogy that precisely preclude any form of conceptuality. The difference between the two types of logics is analogous to the traditional distinction of form and matter, or, in Kantian terms, the cognitive finality of the understanding (knowledge) and the finality without a concept of the imagination (beauty). However, this distinction is subverted by "timbre," as he calls it, "or rather . . . the nuance of a sound or a set of sounds."[37] Singular in the most radical sense, this nuance is neither located in form, in the sense of parametric synthesis, nor in matter as preconditioned by the *aisthetic* (space and time). This nuance escapes all repetition. It is the uniqueness of what sounds in absolute (because completely detached) presence, what cannot be anticipated, remembered, registered or noted down, and what is incomparable. No matter the number of rehearsals spent on a musical work, it is impossible to prepare for the singularity of a performance in an actual concert. This, then, is the analogy between musical nuance and death: both exclude the subject endowed with synthetic powers. When there is nuance, there is no me, and vice versa: "For if the pure matter of sound, its nuance, can reach the subject, this is at the cost of surpassing, or 'sub-passing,' its capacity for synthetic activity. This would be a definition (a negative one indeed) of matter: what breaks the mind."[38]

Lyotard's thoughts on this matter are less radical than they appear here. In "Anima Minima" he argues, for example, that there are ways, neither straightforward nor unequivocal, in which matter may pierce through the "resistance" of the mind and its forms.[39] Are these the fissures he signaled in the discourse of Augustine? So it appears. A further consideration of "God and the Puppet" may clarify the issue some more. The writing of Ernst Bloch draws his attention; in it, he argues, the nature of breakthrough is not aesthetic but ethical or "spiritual."[40] The structure is, however, identical: the pen searches for what is "not inscribed." This, Lyotard argues, is true for all writing, including writing (composing) music. In what manner, then, can the radical alterity of matter break through the screen of the mind? In an earlier quote two different models were mentioned: nuance can either overreach or underreach the synthetic powers of the subject. In the first case, this is the idea that the ear (music remains the main subject) is struck by a sound that is the result of excessive synthesis. This would be like the sound heard by Leibniz's God: all the possible sounds of this world and all other worlds reverberating as a condensed, single, and timeless chord. The idea bears some resemblance to the classic concept of the harmony of the spheres, but a more contemporary analogy would be the idea of primal sound (a "white noise," "terrible for our human ears") that becomes scattered after an imaginary Big Bang and is dispersed into a time-space where musical objects such as pitch, melody, and harmony come about.[41] Composers are not mentioned here, but Lyotard links this idea with a kind of music that offers the possibility of the "magnificent deployment" of the power of synthesis, enabled by the ineluctable "resonance and consonance" of matter.[42]

The second case is concerned with hypo- rather than hypersynthetical sound. Now, the ear is not struck by what is overly complex but what is overly simple. Lyotard explains the idea of underreaching the subject's synthetic powers with reference to Kant. There is a significant correspondence to the idea of the *anima* being touched by the absolute Other (or, who could tell, the Thing?) in Augustine's *Confessions*. Just imagine, Lyotard's reasoning goes, that the subject receives every time only a single oscillation. "It hears only one wave, and it does not know that *it is only* one wave."[43] It is touched in a mechanical fashion, as one billiard ball hits another. There is no recollection of being struck, as the synthetic instrument of retention that would be required for memory is, precisely, precluded from this event. Even a consecutive touch does not lead to the intuition (*Anschauung*) of synthesis, however primary. Hence, there is no music, because this would require the association of several elements. What is heard, then, in the flash of being struck? "Timbre" is heard, or "nuance," which is to be imagined as "an absolute sound-cloud, with no relation to any other."[44] It is the tone of the absolute or absolute tone, which comes before all memory, anticipation, appropriation, or the attribution of sense. If the first case still could be associated with a kind of music that reflects the magnificent deployment of synthetic faculties, the music that fits the second case will expose the shortcomings of these faculties, or their "impotence of holding to a material instant, the pain of an impossible sainthood."[45] The common denominator of these two models is the notion of trace, a trace felt like a sublime *je ne sais quoi* that brings the listener in touch with radical (overreaching or underreaching) alterity.[46]

Nuance in the strictest sense is in withdrawal from the activities of the animus, which implies that the trace of its breakthrough into consciousness cannot be entirely retrieved. It is not surprising, therefore, that Lyotard discusses the music where such a breakthrough occurs only in negative terms, by referring to the *impression* of the synthetic faculties in (or mirrored) music. In the first case, this impression is affirmative, "magnificent," as in the Kantian sublime. In the second case, it is negative and painful. Whether this is caused by the material nuance of music (and which nuance?) will always remain an unanswered question. In fact, because the singular according to Lyotard cannot be perceived directly, and is only indirectly inferred, the problem of reduction is insurmountable. The listener is struck, no doubt about it, but by what? Lyotard's privileging certain music is therefore, notwithstanding the felicity of such a courageous attempt, rather precariously suspended. It hangs on a thin thread—and these are always difficult to tune. Taking up Derrida's concept of *tonos*, one might say that the pitch of the string between music and its referent (the singular nuance that according to Lyotard is sought by all writing) is rather unstable: now too high (does not Lyotard say way too much about a nuance that of necessity escapes the mind?), then too low (the all too hazy reference, via feeling or mood, of a discursive disarray to something that cannot be pinpointed). In *The Confession of Augustine*, Lyotard speaks of the reverberation of "strident tones [that] resonate within him without a source" that eventually "makes everything ring false, the illusory and the true."[47] Just as in Derrida, for instance, there is no case of the mind preliminarily projecting a stabilizing *Stimmung*.[48] There is only overstrained jubilation, as with Augustine, that joyous exclamation because of the certainty of faith, which is invaded by the "sluggishness" of the sexual that will come to inhabit it without ever overtly contesting it.[49]

When so much is out of tune, then, the question whether being touched actually involves being in touch with God is difficult to settle. It leads to a series of other questions. Because, will not the animus forever arrive either too soon (*avant-coup*) or too late (*après-coup*, syncopation) on the scene to properly witness the event? Are the signs (*signa*), as far as they can be made out, readable at all?[50] And what about the libido, this *other* longing for the actual, which forcefully but insidiously resists the desire for submission to the absolute Other? "Two attractions, two twin appetites, almost equal in force, what does it take for one to prevail upon the other? A nuance, and accent, a child humming an old tune? Who speaks here of transcendence when divine grace is placed at the same level as charm?"[51] What is the use of psalmody when the choir is *divided*, the voice *broken*, and the pitch *imperfect*?

> Antiphons, confessions, responsorials as much as psalms: the fissure runs
> between waiting and anxiety, a most shallow furrow that is irreparable for
> ages, before the soul's reunion with itself in death before God. Until then,

the uncertainty that is faith must be woven, one must knot together the two strands that God's incision in the tessitura of the soul had undone: the soul still belongs to the self, it already belongs to god. Pain and Joy. And therefore threatened by two sins: either the I reveling in its own distress, or assuming to fawn upon the good lord to prize salvation out of him. The show of suffering, the bragging of praise. How can this creature find the right tone unless God helps him? But how shall it know that he is helping unless his signs are decipherable? If, indeed, it is still right to attribute the trances to his love, and not perhaps, to a cunning error, thereby putting them out of account.[52]

Augustine's reply might have been that he does not invoke his God because he knows Him, but because he desires to know Him: "The invocation is a quest and search for you, you who have already found me."[53] The question of nuance, however, remains unsettled. Or, returning now to the context of Messiaen, how can the ecstasy of dazzlement as the flesh's *auto-affection* (the delight of the *sucré*, the icing on the cake) be distinguished from dazzlement as the effect of being touched by the absolute (the delight of the *sacré*, the sacred)? What nuance in music would be decisive in toppling the balance either way? And what might be the significance of the fact that dazzlement does not effectuate the complete blotting of the senses but terminates, as in Messiaen's *Lecture at Notre-Dame* stained-glass example, in the *aisthetic* sediment of a haze "all blue, all green, all violet"?[54] Here, perhaps, there is a trace of the force introduced by the *anima minima* into the cognitive spectacle (the animus) of breakthrough. How could this trace be read?

## The Technics and Commerce of Musical Christianity

The possibility for music to decide in any way on that question is mediated by its technicality. Musical nuance, even when it results to be a *signum* of the divine, remains a work of art and is forever already intertwined with its (possible) musicalization. A certain form of violence is part of the fray; the violence against the singular that is brought up against the structural possibility of its perversion (musicalization, technologization, commercialization, and so forth).[55] Such originary violence affects both music and religion and concerns inscribing the singular in the animus, (enlightened) reason, science, and technology. Derrida traces these serial movements in one of the most important interventions in the debate on religion in the 1990s, "Faith and Knowledge: The Two Sources of 'Religion' at the Limits of Reason

Alone."[56] This essay suggests, in the manner of thinking through the relation between religion, technics, and technology or techno-science, new perspectives on the appearance of religion in the domain of music (considered here in its technical guise). Derrida especially points out the recent changes in the way life, death, and technology are related to each other, which in turn affects the manner of constructing the credibility of Messiaen's music as religious music.

Traditionally, the relation between religion and technology is rather strained, as is shown by Jay Newman and Emmanuel Mesthene.[57] The religiously inspired resistance against technology, most vociferously represented by Jacques Ellul, indicts it for its detrimental instrumentalizing effects, which cause humanity to constantly readjust to ever-changing technics it is increasingly dependent on; for its general role in the process of disenchantment; and for encouraging idolatry: "Technology tempts us like the snake of old, promising that if we partake sufficiently in its fruits we shall attain equality with God."[58] Fabricating the golden calf and building the Tower of Babel (and Messiaen's project is to some extent not dissimilar to such undertakings) are among the archetypes of technological idolatry. Technology, the argument goes, is to be feared because it threatens to become a rival to religion, or even its substitute: "Technology's very success in contributing to the realization of ideals such as freedom, knowledge, happiness, and peace—ideals that most defenders of religion see as historically associated with the traditional ethicosocial program of religion—may lead the practical observer to believe that technology is a proper successor to religion."[59]

Derrida also acknowledges the danger of substitution (appearing as repetition, translation, computability), but with him it is a danger that is *always already* a component of religion. Not only as in the doubling of the root of religion (the "two sources" of religion in Henri Bergson), but also in the inevitable implication of (and prerequisite for) the singular, "untranslatable" religious as well.[60] Or, in the words of Hent de Vries, "The fear of ritualization, automatization, the artificial, empty husks, or just words—and hence of idolatry, blasphemy and indeed the lie—is . . . not entirely unfounded but cannot be evaded."[61]

Thus, the positive relation between religion (that is, the three Abrahamic religions, and mainly Judaism and Christianity) and technology, the description of technology as a form of religion, and even the description of religion as a technological enterprise, are all rooted in the Bible, and most conspicuously in the technology of writing or *scripture*. In fact, the recently established links of official Christianity with new technologies of communication, such as the Internet, the creation of "dedicated software," CDs and DVDs, television and radio, or the frequent use of modern modes of transport introduced by Pope John Paul II, perpetuate the biblical technological tradition of God's creative work.[62] Incipient in His instructions for building Noah's Ark, the script of clay tablets, or building the arc and the tabernacle, this technological tradition ranges to the carpenter's Son and Worker of Miracles who was *created* in God's likeness and in whose name medical technologies gave shape to the notion of *caritas*. It flourished in the technologies of transport that built and improved the Mission's hull, wheel or wings; in the art of printing that aided in disseminating the Scripture; in communicative technologies uniting the community of the Church; and finally in the Catholic tradition of the *works* of charity (feeding the hungry, burying the dead, and so on).[63] According to Newman, God's blessing of mankind, in "let us make man in our image, after our likeness: and let them have dominion over the fish of the sea, and over the fowl of the air, and over the cattle, and over all the earth, and over every creeping thing that creepeth upon the earth" (Gn 1:26), was taken as an assignment, in Christianity, to finish Creation, to the extent that mankind has made the world a lot more "Christian" by means of technology. Thus, not only has technology enabled the manifestation of Christianity, but as such, Christianity is also the epitome of successfully realizing the mediating nature of technology, especially tele-technology. One should think here of its appeal on the hyperbolic idea of telecommunication with the beyond (in prayer, with angels, and so on), and more specifically of the figure of the Incarnation, that preeminently exemplifies the mediation between immanence and transcendence, the here and the beyond.[64]

Along these lines, it is conceivable that religion should be sought precisely in the calculative domain of technology, or more generally in the domain of repetition in various guises (animus, the concept of the artwork, notational techniques, and the like). Religion may be found in a machine or appear to be the product of a machine (a deus ex machina) as though it were a golden calf of sorts.[65] This includes the "common phenomenon" discussed in Chapter 4, which according to Marion is best exemplified by the technical-industrial product.[66] According to Derrida, the machinic (the mechanical, the automatic) resides within and in between the two roots, or sources, of religion: on one hand, the appeal on, or the experience of, faith and confidence, and "the experience of the unscathed, of *sacredness* or of *holiness*, on the other."[67] Each is characterized by the possibility of its repetition (like life itself, sacred only "in the name of what is worth more than it," that is, sur-vival (*sur-vie*) after death; or the act of testifying in the absence of what was originally witnessed), and each experience automatically evokes the other.[68] The tropes of religion and technology converge, then, but at the same time they forcefully repel one another. The most significant form of their meeting is the *miracle*, where their filiation (both interdependence and competitiveness, hostility even) is manifested. It is no coincidence that this is the term reserved for the promises implicit in technics, and to connote both its credibility and its unassailability, but at the same time the notion of the miracle concerns the divine manifested or self-(re)produced as the very event of religion (as the double respect for the two pure sources of fiduciarity and sacrality). The multiple significance of the figure of repetition sketched here will recur in the last paragraphs of this section, when the unique "miracle" of breakthrough toward the beyond in Messiaen will be addressed with reference to traces of the logics of iteration in his music: commerciality, the mechanical, resurrection, and so forth.

The double figure of the miracle—religious and technological—is problematically constellated in relation to a third area: the world of commerce. The musicologist Richard Taruskin criticizes the emergence, at the brink of the new millennium, of a "new spiritualism."[69] Taruskin locates this phenomenon, among others, in recent theatrical music such as by Philip Glass or John Adams, and contrasts this new spiritualism with the religiosity in Messiaen's opera *Saint François d'Assise*. Taruskin believes that the movement of the new spiritualism is supported by an emerging cultural elite consisting of well-to-do baby boomers (so-called bobos, for "bourgeois bohemians") finding satisfaction for their craving for social and cultural "content" by picking and choosing from the manger of religion. The new spiritualism, then, does not represent a form of ethical–religious reorientation, but should be interpreted as the assertion of a new social order, a powerful economic elite, to flaunt moral commitment, en passant giving new impetus to the ailing but coveted world of classical music. Taruskin's criticism is mainly directed at the "topically slanted nativity oratorio" *El Niño*, a collaborative product of Adams and the director Peter Sellars that premiered in Paris in 2000. He objects to Sellars's statement that in order to survive, classical music should offer "something that is not otherwise available," which would be "spiritual content, which is what's missing from the commercial culture that surrounds us." Apparently, Taruskin concludes, "spiritual or sacred entertainments have become the most marketable and profitable genre the literate (or "art") tradition of music can boast at a time when its end . . . has become foreseeable."[70]

Although Taruskin acknowledges that religion and commerce have of long been intertwined—he cites Handel's oratorios, on which *El Niño* was modeled—he apparently envisages the possibility of a credibly noncommercial religious music. For the century that was closed by Adam's oratorio, Taruskin most strongly recommends the example of Messiaen's work: "Messiaen, supremely sophisticated in technique yet naively direct in expression as only a believer could be, works throughout the opera [*Saint François d'Assise*]—indeed worked throughout his career—at the ticklish borderline of cliché" (118).[71] Instead of exploiting the cliché, as Adam allegedly does, Messiaen allows his audience to experience the risk of platitudes and kitsch in order to bring them on the verge of religious ecstasy: "The fact that, despite its many near approaches to it, Messiaen's opera manages after all to avoid kitsch while retaining its naiveté is perhaps its most impressive feat—and at the present cultural moment, dominated by a profusion of extremely artful spiritual kitsch, an enormously provocative one."[72]

The context of commercial and aesthetic exploitation can indeed pervert religion, but Taruskin is convinced that the instance of such perversion can be pinpointed exactly, with the notions of risk and naivety acting as signposts. Taruskin is convinced of the veracity of Messiaen's music when it is risk taking (bordering on kitsch, bathos, or insignificance) or when the sacred is evoked by means of "uncanny otherness." Messiaen's naïveté then supplies the seal of credibility, in any case in those instances in which his music, either or not calculatingly (this is a possibility Taruskin will not discard and that shall be addressed below) distinguishes himself from the "shabby topical hypocrisy" of the younger generation of "spiritual" composers. At least Messiaen stacks sufficient credit, in Taruskin's eyes, for going over the top in other instances. Fiercely critical of the *Turangalîla Symphonie*, Taruskin describes it as "one of the great monuments of sacroporn in its attempt to marry Christian mysticism to the Kama Sutra with side-by-side titles like 'Joie du sang des étoiles' and 'Jardin du sommeil d'amour.'"[73]

The appeal on the authority of religious persuasiveness and the composer's intention is, in fact, a late echo of the conflict between theatrical and sacred music that played such an important part in Augustine. Throughout the ages, this conflict has colored the Christian, and especially ecclesiastic, view on music. Augustine was critical of theater musicians (*theatricos operarios*) who performed solely for gain and applause, which they thought could be acquired through mere feats of virtuosity and memory.[74] Music is priceless, according to Augustine, inestimable and of great value, but theater musicians do not shrink from base negotiations.[75] Music, in other words, is external to the order of economic circulation, and is in this respect related to life itself, which Kant situated, using similar terms such as *Würdigkeit* (value, dignity) and *Marktpreis* (market price), above the economic order.[76] Theater musicians, however, are not attuned to music's spiritual value; material gain is their sole interest.

As Taruskin mentions in a significant aside, Messiaen's ignorance, or naïveté perhaps, may to a certain extent be calculated.[77] Insofar as the sacred is merchandised, by his music, as a product of musical (and theatrical) technics, a scandal materializes: when reduced to a mere effect of musical rhetorics, the sacred is made profane. By foregrounding the rhetorics of music and hence the alliance with technology that constitutes the machinery of techniques of persuasion, the essentially *commercial* nature of rhetorics is revealed. Over and over again, Messiaen's music is demonstrably highly effective in putting a spell on the audience, as Paul Griffiths acutely observes in the remark that has been mentioned before: "The objects and musical states that Messiaen offers to our inspection in *Les Corps glorieux* are so very singular that we may well be disinclined to accept them as invitations to meditate on something else, preferring to make of them the centre of our contemplation."[78] To the extent that the sacred is reduced to a force in the market of economical (commercial and technological) exchange, it is a commodity (a techno-commercial *effect*) that is produced and reproduced with advanced means and traded with similarly sophisticated musical strategies. This is scandalous not only because of the profanation of the sacred that is involved, but also because of the *skandalon* (that is, temptation) this economic circulation implies. Manufacturing the divine then is in the hands of man. A shift of balance occurs in the *admirabile commercium* between man and God to the benefit of man, whose power to impose with profitable artifacts and *art effects* is almost boundless.

With Messiaen, the scandalous is not limited to the tropes of dazzlement and breakthrough. In his later work again, religious transcendence is proximate to technological repetition and the economy of commerce (rather than of religion). Messiaen had thought that he had reached the end of his career as a composer with his opera on Saint Francis. Thoroughly spent by his immense labor on this musical spectacle of more than four hours' length, he became, according to his wife, Yvonne Loriod, "very depressed—he was unable to eat or walk or indeed do anything. And he told everyone that he'd finished with composing."[79] Resurrection from creative death followed only a year later, with his most extensive composition for organ (*Livre du Saint Sacrement*, 1984), which was succeeded by a series of shorter pieces and his last great work, *Éclairs sur l'Au-delà* . . . (1988–92). An aspect of Messiaen's music that had been present all along becomes more manifest now: it is as if his music is assembled from a limited set of tried and tested parts, both musical (chords, melodic styles, structures, and so forth) and biographical-referential (the Celestial City, landscapes, stained glass, birds, and the like). Composition then becomes, as Boulez once remarked about his former teacher, juxtaposition, and the recombination of these recursive elements (see, for example, the piece for piano, percussion and wind orchestra *Un vitrail et des oiseaux*, 1986).[80] Messiaen's mechanical modus operandi in this period is not unlike the form of a scholastic tract, where a single method is applied to suit each and every problem.[81] As he remarked himself, this approach serves to assimilate all sorts of diverse experiences. "In each of my works, there's a moment which I've experienced, landscapes I've loved, things, souls, people, birds, trees, which or whom I've encountered, and every time I hear or read through these works again, I find these moments, these people, birds and trees again—that gives me a great satisfaction; it's as if I were shown a film or photographs of earlier times."[82] It is as if, in the final years of his career as a composer, music disappears behind the program, and the program behind the picturesque. It becomes semi-automatous, wrapped in the *couleur locale* of the programmatic. Hence the question whether Messiaen's objective of representing a certain *content*, let alone making a *musical* sound, is fulfilled at all. Are not both subjected to the mechanical logic of his own procedures, so that the *repetition* of formulae (spawned by his own tradition, his own canon of materials, techniques, thematic topoi) leads to an emptying, if not erasure, of both music and program?

Such machinery spills over in the textual accoutrements to Messiaen's music, as Paul Griffiths's liner notes to the recording of *Éclairs* testify. Reading these notes is an increasingly unbearable experience. Yet again the commonplaces about Messiaen's music in general are paraded, in order to zoom in on the structure and biographic program of *Éclairs* (Australia, the lyrebird, the Celestial City) in particular.[83] The story of this music is just too good to be true, or rather, it really tells us little or nothing, it is the vain spin of eternally recurring topoi. Reiterative, repeatable, and mechanical, the music, in the words of Griffiths and Loriod (not to mention Messiaen, the instigator of a rehearsed standard version of his own life story and invariable explanatory notes), becomes a specter that haunts the audience like the restless ghost of the deceased. This nervous narrative, this ineffective machine, challenges its own credibility; it is unreal and helpless, condemned to infinite regress, unintentionally infinite. Thus, Messiaen's music, which is, as we have seen, focused on illuminating the truths of faith, of Life or what is most Alive, duplicating this Life in effect because this is the priceless, unmarketable music of the spirit—this music now is inscribed in the logics of Return or Resurrection. The analogy between the noneconomical position of Life and that of spiritual music perhaps allows then for the thought that similarly Messiaen's "messiaenic" music is always attuned to the apocalypse, to Resurrection and the beyond. It could only retain the "possibility of religion" or the possibility of a religious, deferential stance toward the beyond through the possibility of its repetition, mechanization, automation, and the like.[84]

The alliance of Messiaen's music with precisely those technologies that might be thought to involve tarnishing religion is no reason to contend the religious claims of the composer. On the contrary. For instance, Paul Griffiths's remark that Messiaen has achieved "a special radiance" in his last apocalyptic work stands uneasily, but inescapably, to the message on the cover of the CD on the technology of recording *Éclairs*: "4D Audio Recording—A new dimension in clarity and realism."[85] Another example is derived from the notion of the "phallic" that Derrida associates with "the automaton (exemplarily 'phallic'), to technics, the machine, the prosthesis."[86] The array of connotations the phallic can be associated with includes the sense of triumph and potency, the idea of a final struggle, and in the last instance the entire gamut of the Apocalypse as it is read by Messiaen. An analysis of one of his earliest compositions, *Apparition de l'église éternelle* from 1932, can reveal the phallic affirmation that is enclosed in the vocabulary and climax of this piece. It is a gesture that will recur in a variety of sites in his later work, as for instance in part VI of the *Méditations*. Derrida relates, in this respect, the phallic (and the erection) to the sphere of tele-technoscience, in that these tropes of life are disengaged both in the *phantasma* of the phallus, which tends toward (and climaxes in) the *virtual*, and in the erection as "colossal" automacity, reflex, and mechanism. Both tropes are intimately connected to religion in the sense of "faith in the most living as dead and automatically *sur-viving*, resuscitated in its spectral *phantasma*."[87] Resurrection is, in other words, associated with the figures of the specter and (technical) virtuality and automacity. What is dead and mechanical, he posits, in fact appears as the most living. The trope of swelling, both in erection and in pregnancy, at once expresses life and lifeless mechanicity; in short, the phallus is exposed to circumcision. Messiaen's attempts to mold the phallic in his music certainly reflect this oxymoron, and explain the different possible reactions of those who are listening (or exposed, in turn) to his music, which range from awe and wonder to disillusion when this music is understood to evoke the sacrosanct in a mechanical fashion. Consequently, in Messiaen the sacred always is a function of what is impaired, the *circumcised* phallus. Nonetheless, this is how the sacred fully partakes of the discourse and logics of the sacro-phallic "automaton."

Derrida's unfolding logic implies, in a sense, that the divine will (or may) necessarily appear in the form of untruth or illusion, because each apparition involves an alienation from the divine. With respect to music, if music and the effects of dazzlement and breakthrough were not to appear, possibly, as constructed and effectuated, they should be doubted anyway. This reverse logic turns the relation between religion and construction upside down, in the sense that illusion becomes the hallmark of truth. The importance of this hypothesis when thinking about the music of Messiaen, may again be illustrated by taking recourse to the "last things" in his life as a composer, in particular *Éclairs*. Like *La Transfiguration*, this work sounds in many instances like the music that accompanies cartoons, as if it were part of Disney's world of imagination. Indeed, this brings to mind Messiaen's love for the fairytale, the "Naïvité du Seigneur," that he never wholly relinquished. The serious attempts of Messiaen to express certain truths in his music cannot be dissociated from the imaginary, in the shape of the idyllic (*Turangalîla*; *Éclairs*, parts V and XI; *Des canyons aux étoiles . . .* part VIII), the phallic (*Apparition* or *Éclairs*, part I), or the cartoon (fairytale, adventures; see *Éclairs*, part III and X; *Des canyons*, part VII; *La Transfiguration*, part XIII). In this last instance, only the reality (or the reality *effect*) of human singing seems to shield the music from the sheer fictitious.

If *jouissance* is the domain of both the cartoon and of *ekstasis* (the radiance of stars joyfully celebrating their Creator), can the line between amusement and religious adoration be drawn at all? There is devotion in Messiaen's music, but visual fantasy (posing as visionary) as well, and a penchant—at least in way his music sometimes sounds—for the salon music of the 1920s (as with the strings in *Éclairs* V and XI). Does this mean that the vanity of amusement is concomitant to our ultimate raison d'être (see the last things in the book of Revelation)? Again, the cover of the CD's booklet is again suggestive of an answer: the idea of an *au-delà* is evoked, in an illustration reminiscent of the work of the German romantic painter Caspar David Friedrich, by an imaginary theater. Opened curtains appear to indicate a remote stage, as if a breakthrough to the other side of the footlights has just occurred. There is a strong suggestion of veils (to be pierced, as with Isis) and a double horizon that throws the viewer of his feet, as he contemplates this tunnel-like vision that acquires an erotic-religious depth because of the hymenlike structures that surround the distant sun. The scenery is set alight in illustration of the way the promise of reality and its profound truths is staged. It is an apt illustration, all in all, for Messiaen's music, with its strong element of the theatrical and the related idea of performing and arguing musically the essences of faith. It is suggested that the sacred is unimpaired, by means of transporting the listener to a domain where evil (and all other flip sides) can be lost in oblivion. Here are amusement, phantasm, occasionally even sentiment—no truth, but naïveté and sweet enchantment.

Who would suggest, incidentally, that the occurrence of truth—say, epiphany—is barred or even distanced by such modes? The exposure to temptation is fundamental to the structure of Christianity, according to Emmanuel Levinas. In one of his Talmudic readings, "the temptation of temptation" is described as the promise that everything, including evil, can be experienced without the threat that there is no way back: "[the tempted ego] can listen to the song of the sirens without compromising the return to its island."[88] This adds another dimension to the Augustinian conflict between temptation of pure vocal beauty and the moral appeal of the words that are sung. For Levinas, the problem is different altogether and located in the structure of temptation as such:

> The temptation of temptation is not the attractive pull exerted by this or that pleasure, to which the tempted one risks giving himself over body and soul. What tempts the one tempted by temptation is not pleasure but the ambiguity of a situation in which pleasure is still possible but in respect to which the Ego keeps its liberty, has not yet given up its security, has kept its distance. What is tempting here is the situation in which the ego remains independent but where this independence does not exclude it from what must consume it, either to exalt it or to destroy it. What is tempting is to be simultaneously outside everything and participating in everything.[89]

If it is indeed temptation that conducts us to the Christian moment in Messiaen's music, or perhaps we should rather speak of Messiaen's music putting us in such a situation, then there is nothing accidental in the "sacroporn" Taruskin signaled in Messiaen's oeuvre. In that case, there is nothing accidental in the deplorable slips Taruskin construes as minor details that are easily forgotten once the provocative-naïve religiosity of *Saint François d'Assise* becomes apparent. Rather, these "slips" are a structural asset. Messiaen's music exposes rather than shuns the structures of temptation; it reveals that Christian music is not confined to only the most dependable sonic signs of faith. In this respect, his music bears a relation to the notion of sacred prostitution (*prostitution sacrée*) in Baudelaire, the idea of seeing eye to eye with the danger of substitution and acknowledging that the same is part and parcel of the structure of Christian religion.[90]

Such a reading of the relationship between music and religion in Messiaen suggests a radical revision of my earlier analyses that concern the relationship between the singular, on one hand (thought as cipher for what is the bare essence of both music and religion) and the domain of repetition and iterability (with the entire range of technological, vitalizing and commercializing effects), on the other. In the following, I will attempt to sketch the lines of thought that construct (in the sense of *Zusammendenken*), rather than contrast, the many guises of repetition in (and of) his miraculous and singular "breakthrough" music. As I will argue, these repetitions are to be regarded as effects that originate in the same powerful momentum (movement, version, conversion) as the effects of singularity, of miracle and breakthrough.

### Repetitive Breakthroughs

When considering the techno-commercial context of what appear to be nonreligious phenomena, the music of *La Transfiguration* and the concomitant testimony of breakthrough toward the beyond come into view. As we have seen, the fact that in two out of five of such passages the music of dazzlement is repeated (part IX and XII), strongly challenges the suggestion of religious breakthrough. It was argued that if breakthrough is a repeatable (and hence all too falsifiable) effect of music, the supposition that something truly special or miraculous had happened should be rejected. The miracle of breakthrough is associated with the singular and depends theologically on the unique initiative of the transcendent Absolute breaking through into the dimension of time and history (as in the "historical" event of Incarnation). Aptly named breakthrough, it subverts, breaks through, the laws of nature.[91] A "true" breakthrough, one could argue, ought to belong to the order of the miraculous and is, therefore, preeminently singular.

As we have seen, however, in and surrounding these two passages there are many instances of repetition, techniques, reproductions, machines, and imitations. There is not just repetition of the passages themselves, but also in their internal configuration. In part IX, this emerges right with the introduction to the passage, which consists largely of a repeated pattern of chords and accompanying figures. This is subsequently followed by the overwhelming complexity of mechanically revolving three-layered patterns, each layer consisting of an ostinato of, among others, "turning chords" and a repetitively (that is, nonretrogradable) structured sequence of deçî-tâlas.[92] The principle of ostinato is less central in part XII (even though, in the absence of repetitions in the strict sense, mechanical movements can be discerned) and the sonic totality is determined especially by repetitively structured color modes and the insistent present of the unison. Apart from their proper configuration, the context of these passages is repetitive as well. The strongly marked transitions toward these moments, mirroring each other, form a schema of their own; the content of the passages pivots on the principle of duplication at work in mimesis or representation; the work as a whole is a diptych and the *éblouissement* passages formally reflect each other; the notation of music is meant to represent the work as a selfsame entity, and is reproduced in print; performance again is another multiplication of particular concretizations, stored in endlessly repeatable digital recordings, and so on. All things considered, who would dare to speak of such a singular event, in this music, of a breakthrough toward the beyond? Is not this rather a case of a musico-technological *special effect*, such as, for instance, the old and well-tested surprise effect?[93]

This casts perhaps for a more nominalistic light on Messiaen's music, justified in a sense by Messiaen's own postulation that a musician worthy of the name is foremost a "rhythmician": "*Un musicien est forcément rythmicien, sinon il ne mérite pas d'être appelé musicien.*"[94] A broad circuit of terms and notions is involved, for Messiaen, in the concept of rhythm, but in *Traité de rythme* three are finally distilled because they would "recur constantly in the mouths of rhythmologues": periodicity, irreversibility, and symmetry.[95] The first of these terms is the most important, according to Messiaen, in the sense that it best indicates what rhythm is, and what it is not. As he put it elsewhere: "schematically, rhythmic music is music that scorns repetition, squareness, and equal divisions, and that is inspired by the movements of nature, movements of free and unequal durations."[96] Repetitiveness then should be avoided not just for programmatic reasons but also for reasons of musicality. Indeed, unadulterated repetition is usually avoided in Messiaen, except perhaps in the iteration of schematic forms he frequently takes recourse to (as in *Méditations*, for example). Rather, the intention is to achieve continuous variation in the mode of Debussy, a "*variation perpétuelle,*" that is not characterized by the mechanical return of the same (*le même*) but by the voluntary return of semblance (*le semblable*).[97] Rhythm then is conceived of in terms of difference. Implicitly, Messiaen decides which of the other two rhythmological terms he prefers—whereas symmetry demands sameness, difference entails irreversibility (that is, dissymmetry, to be distinguished from the nonretrogradable). The objective temporality of notation dissolves into the "perpetual becoming" of resounding temporality.[98]

> The true periodicity of sea waves is . . . the reverse of pure and simple repetition. Each wave is different from the preceding one and from the following, with regard to its volume, its height, its duration, the lengthiness or brevity of its formation, the power of its climax, the prolongation of its fall, of its flow, of its dissipation. . . . This is varied periodicity. Regarding absolute periodicity, which adds the same to the same and more of the same, as it is currently practiced in music by means of rhythmic pedals and ostinatos, it should be remarked that there is a difference between each textual repetition: no term is in the same place in the sonorous unfolding. . . . Although they resemble each other, they take place in a perpetual becoming.[99]

What Messiaen has to say about the repetition of elements from an ostinato can a fortiori be applied to the work as whole. Here, a notion completely different from the unified work-concept of formalism can be introduced, based on Messiaen's notion of varied periodicity. In essence, music is not about extracting, isolating, or distilling a transcendental "work-identity" (a platonizing self-identity), but about the repetition of performances that are *semblable* (alike); they are metonymically or allegorically differentiated and do not constitute, nor can be reduced to, an autonomous self-identical form. Here Adorno would speak of musical nominalism, although he reserved the term for transhistorical musical forms (such as the sonata) rather than works.[100] The recurrence of Messiaen's *éblouissement* passages should be understood as the presentation of repetition, never in identical terms (neither in the score of *La Transfiguration*, as each repetition contains a slight variation, nor in performances, each having their own unique nuance and context) but as the return of the *semblable*. This logic does not just affect the difference between the passages in part IX and XII and their respective slightly altered repetitions, but also the unity of the *hic et nunc* of breakthrough itself, including the idea of epiphany as a moment in time.

A reference to Augustine's classic analysis of time would suffice to deconstruct the notion of a perceptual now-moment.[101] With Saint Paul, too, the moment, preeminently conceived as the critical, eschatologically filled time of *kairos*, is not a singular, palpable "now" but a plurality of times. As Hent de Vries observes, "in the New Testament . . . the *kairos* is mentioned not in the singular but in the plural; its privileged moment or rather momentum is 'one of a kind,' to be sure, but this singularity is not or no longer characterized by its being *one* or indivisible."[102] The (Christian) significance of Messiaen's breakthrough toward the beyond does not reside, then, in the moments assigned by Messiaen (their *hic et nunc*) but in the multiplicity, the differential, and the temporal modality of their appearances. An important shift of perspective on Messiaen's suggestions and indications ensues. The significance is not so much in parametrically establishing breakthrough as such, or in the relationships that can be extrapolated from such coordinates.[103] The crux is in the way that breakthrough, and the manner of its constitution, is either inscribed or not in a specifically Christian temporal modality such as the New Testament notions of *kairos* and *parousia*. It is my intention to show that this modality can be discerned in music too, especially, of course, with reference to Messiaen.

An instructive example to begin an exposition on this topic is supplied by a work of another composer. *Archipelago II, for viola, cello, and double bass* (1985) by the Dutch composer Daan Manneke, manifests, according to Rokus de Groot, certain musical "moments of grace" that can be experienced as "numinous," and bears some striking correspondences to Messiaen.[104] Manneke studied with Ton de Leeuw (1926–1996), who, in the late 1940s, had studied with Messiaen in Paris. *Archipelago II* centers on a chord of mostly superimposed fifths, flanked by an introductory ascending line where fifths again play a conclusive part, and a descending motion that ends it. Such a technical description of this brief passage neglects one aspect that according to Manneke is inexpressible. He illustrates his point by referring to the Transfiguration of Christ on Mount Tabor. As de Groot argues, Manneke's way of paying tribute to the wonder of this sacred moment is in restraint: "In the words of the composer, 'one has to let go of this moment, one cannot abide there, no return to it is possible.' As soon as the moment arrives in the music, it is left."[105] After the moment, then, an elongated heterophonic melody sets in to announce "a return to daily life." In referring to this passage, Manneke speaks of a unique moment of grace, but de Groot shows that, just as in Messiaen, this moment is repeated and elaborated later in the piece. He compares it to the response of the apostle Peter, who, when witnessing the Transfiguration of Christ, cries out for a monument to retain this unique event: "if thou wilt, let us make here three tabernacles; one for thee, and one for Moses, and one for Elias" (Mt 17:4). Such commemoration or retention betrays, according to de Groot, the sacrality of this moment, as the repeat dislodges the music from what was (perhaps) attained in a moment of grace. Along similar lines, such a disqualification would affect Messiaen's reiterative passages as well: in repetition the sacred is betrayed. However, this begs the question whether repetition can in fact be evaded at all. Can there ever be a pure testimony of unadulterated presence, which then, only in second moment (in repetition) is corrupted? Another point is that the Christian moment appears to be preeminently constituted by repeated declarations in the New Testament (Matthew, then Mark, then Luke, and so on), in other words, precisely by the reiterative dissemination of testifying to the Transfiguration. This is acknowledged, in a way, by de Groot when he notes that the "return to daily life" involves, in the life of the composer in any case, a return "now with the consciousness that it is a sacred daily life, permeated by the numinous."[106]

Thus, the technological forms of repetitiveness have a unique bearing on Christianity. In the concluding pages to this chapter, I will argue that something similar is the case in temporal terms: a special alliance (though not unequivocally stable or stabilizing) between the trope of repetitiveness and Christianity.

Jean-Luc Nancy postulates that the "original structure" of Christianity is the proclamation of the end, or "more precisely, it is the end as proclamation, as something proclaimed, as Gospel, as *evangelion*, 'the good news.'"[107] The end in Christianity, however, is not predestined. Rather, Nancy reaffirms—in line with, among others, Nietzsche's conclusions—that the gospel, quite literally paper-thin, borders on nothingness, on *presque rien*, containing little more than the gesture itself of proclamation.

> What is Christianity? It is the Gospel. What is the Gospel? Not the texts that go under this name, but what is proclaimed. What is proclaimed? Nothing. Marcel Gauchet has drawn attention, as did Nietzsche before him, to the slenderness of the four Gospels: almost nothing. And the fact that these few pages sublate all the earlier *biblia*, the fact that one can call hardly anything at all (*trois fois rien*) properly Christian writing, consists in tracing extremely quickly the contours of the proclamation, in saying that "it is proclaimed" and that someone has lived in such a way that he has proclaimed, cannot be considered closely enough.[108]

Nancy describes the end that is announced in Christianity—and which is its quintessence—as open-ended, or the Open: "It is the Open as such, the

Open of the proclamation, of history and faith that, through the living God, is disclosed at the heart of Christianity."[109] The Open is also (here Nancy follows Hölderlin) "the free," a notion that leads to a series of questions. How to think the free? Is it what is detached from any determinant, external to any economy, trapped neither in inscription nor incarnation, appearing *ex abrupto* as a miracle, out of the blue? Is the free, in other words, something that signals the sudden transition to which a number of Messiaen's passages appeared to be reducible to?[110] When considering the New Testament, the reply is negative. Because the One who, as Nancy puts it, "has lived in such a way that he has proclaimed" was proclaimed, or announced, Himself (by John the Baptist, the archangel Gabriel, and so forth). Is not the New Testament precisely a reading of the Old Testament in view of the proclamation, and the prophecy of proclamation, that is, of an infinite regress of proclamations constituting the proclamation proper? Is not *parousia* itself introduced by the arrival of an imposter, the Antichrist posing as a miracle worker, who is only discerned and distinguished from the true Second Coming of Christ by the righteous?[111] The in-between time of Christianity itself appears to be suffused with the trope of return, the second coming, which despite its unique, "historical," and no doubt miraculous nature is inscribed already in the Incarnation that proclaims it, and thus, as Nancy adds, in the dialectic or integrating momentum of the history of salvation.[112]

The repetitiveness of Messiaen's trope of breakthrough and its elements is not incompatible with a Christian notion of temporality. On the contrary, in enacting a reiterative dynamics, repetitiveness partakes of a motion that is one of the founding constituents of Christianity. This is not restricted to the different notions of return, rebirth, second coming, reiterated proclamations and insistent message in the Gospel, or to the Pauline theme of the demonic double, but involves a more philosophical, Kierkegaardian thematics of repetition as well. Nancy's idea of "the Open" or "the free" can to a certain extent be interpreted in light of Kierkegaard's reflections on repetition as, on one hand, synonymous to faith and, on the other, as a feature of the demonic. Nancy relies on Kierkegaard, for instance, when he relates the sacred to "openness to proclamation," contrasting it to the "sinful condition" of a self "as related to the self and not as distended and open to the other."[113] Kierkegaard elsewhere censures such self-preoccupied closure for its demonic exclusion, in rigid uncertainty, of all externality.[114] With reference to music (the act of listening will be the subject of the next chapter), this would be similar to the closure of music brought about by pure self-repeating, curving it backward in a "demonic" imprisonment. In Messiaen, an example of such closure can be found in the seventh tableau of *Saint François d'Assise*, the expression of the sacred violence of stigmatization.[115] The music here tends toward a purely mechanical repetition that drives away all difference, all suggestion of openness or indeterminacy. In fact, Messiaen intends to evoke in this passage the idea of sacred, rather than satanic, violence, but that difference is dramatically imperceptible.

Another form of demonic repetition is, according to Kierkegaard, in the less conspicuous but no less dangerous category of "the aesthetic." Boredom sets in easily here because the dull repetition of the ephemeral—including friendship, marriage, profession, and so on—draws the sap out of all life. As the youth in *Either/Or* exclaims, "Boredom is demonic pantheism. If we remain in it as such it becomes evil; on the other hand, as soon as it is annulled it is true. But one annuls it only by amusing oneself—ergo one ought to amuse oneself."[116] As was discussed, the fraught notion of amusement takes on various forms in Messiaen's work. For instance, he expressed the imperative that rhythm, foremost in the mind of the musician, never implies pure repetition but entails a slight variation, which seems to propagate the idea of distraction, charm, and amusement.[117] In the repetitions of breakthrough passages, moreover, the specter of "aesthetic" self-irony haunts the music and signals the experience of distance, deflation, boredom, and melancholy. The narrow ties between amusement and a certain logics of religion that was pointed out before now lead to another dimension of this association. The will to avoid pure and simple repetition, and the emphasis on entertainment, conceal a more profound doubt about music, an attitude of *contemptus mundi* and the experience of accidie (sloth, inertia, indifference). This leads to the verso of breakthrough repetitions, and makes room for arguments against Messiaen's idea of dazzlement. But it sheds only some light on a single aspect of the perpetual motion of return that envelops music in general, and this music of the miraculous and singularity most specifically. Taking one further step, Kierkegaard even posits that music is quintessentially demonic because "the erotic sensual genius" is its true object.[118]

The notion of repetition that Kierkegaard advances against forms of repetition that involve the aesthetic, amusement, the demonic, or boredom, is "a religious movement by virtue of the absurd, which commences when a person has come to the border of the wondrous."[119] Repetition here is modeled on the narratives of Abraham and Job, Abraham recovering his (to be) sacrificed son and Job recovering the double value of all that he had lost in adversity. Whatever their value as psychological studies of religious life, these stories also illustrate the potential for renewal of the world and of life, as in the words of Christ, "Behold, I make all things new" (Rev 21:5). Abraham and Job do not simply return to an earlier condition but are made new. This is not a case of rehearsing or repeating an event or experience, and cannot be compared, according to Kierkegaard, to for example rereading a book or otherwise repeating an experience (in this context: the repetition of breakthrough through rehearsal and repeated experience of music). Still, both biblical stories center on the return, in its full singularity, of what was uniquely lost. There is nothing abstract or metaphysical about Abraham recovering his one and only son, *this* son, Isaac.[120] Repetition then is, according to Kierkegaard, the paradoxical return of the actual-with-a-difference, and it is the absolute prerequisite for any ethics, metaphysics, or dogmatics.[121] The significance for music of such an aporetic notion of repetition was discussed before, but now a new and unique dimension is added on. Repetition in the sense of Kierkegaard cannot be construed, according to Edward Mooney, but is a gift received in grace.[122] It is the preeminent figure of openness or receptivity for the miraculous, the absurd, or the paradoxical (as emblematically in the trope of Incarnation).[123] It involves a readiness to accept the fact that anything is possible with God, even the impossible repetition of the singular.[124]

Messiaen's gesture of repeating the unique event of "breakthrough toward the beyond" entails the plural inscription of this singularity into the domain of repetition and partakes of the logics of this impossible possibility. The breakthrough breaks through in (and as) repetition, although the locus in time and place of being touched or struck cannot immediately or with any certainty be indicated. To twist one of Messiaen's similes: listening to this kind of music is like gazing, at the lakeside, at ripples whose cause (a pebble) was unseen.[125] There is no originary moment to what is reiterated, just the undulation of (its) varied repetitions. This is not about reiterating the same, repeating the original, but about possibly preparing for the Open (*trois fois rien*), for repetition in Kierkegaard's transfigurative sense, for Messiaen's breakthrough. Thinking such iteration shall always, however, entail the possibility of an antichristian idolizing of music, as Hent de Vries has argued. Repetition, thought in this way, paves the way for the religious possibility of Messiaen's music but in the same movement creates its parody as well, making it devoid of the sense (*Sinn*) Balthasar insists on. Referring to Kierkegaard's love of the farce, Samuel Weber puts it as follows:

Repetition is a condition of meaning. There can be no meaning if it is not repeatable in some sense. But this condition itself doesn't just produce meaning, it produces the double of meaning, the shadow of meaning, the theatrical farce, the unserious series. Farce is not just something you can take or leave. If you want meaning you will, in one way or the other, also have farce, something you may not want to admit.[126]

In the theological reception and interpretation of Messiaen's work, this comedy of repetition—this farce of duplication and duplicity, this doubling the point that inevitably entails alteration—is neglected, to the effect that the religious (and, as we have seen, musical) space his work opens onto is barred. When duplication is allowed, however, the Augustinian aporia of experiencing music returns with full force: it is *dangerous*, but, conversely (that is, returning at the same time, in the same movement, in repetition), also *indispensable*.

# 6.  The Circumcision of the Ear

## Testimonial Mode

Messiaen's discourse on *éblouissement* and the possibility of a breakthrough toward the beyond is surprisingly radical. This is not only because the composer calls attention to the actual possibility of religious music—and in a certain sense hyperreligious music, for Messiaen places it above religious music—in an age when, to all appearances, this possibility had definitively turned into its opposite, but also because of his surprising move of connecting the domain of religious experience directly to the coordinates of the musical artifact. In this way, he suggests that a religious experience can be evoked by musical-technical means, countering the theological presupposition that grace will be bestowed only at the initiative of the Invisible. In his definition of musical religious experience, Messiaen is more radical than any other composer before him; not only that, but by employing certain concepts that overcome the strict division between art and religion, he also explodes what had become an accepted notion since the nineteenth century, namely that these constitute two separate domains.

In his *Lecture at Notre-Dame* and elsewhere, Messiaen opted for a testimonial (or confessional, as some would prefer) mode in order to speak of colors seen by no one else and a musical religious spectacle that is one of a kind.[1] As a testimony, it makes an appeal to the belief of the reader or listener, who will just have to trust that what is being said is true (or correct). There is no point in verifying Messiaen's testimony beyond the mere consistency of his statements. This final chapter will focus on the philosophical underpinning of the possibility testified by Messiaen, that is, the transition from a musical to a religious experience. In contrast to Chapter 4, the issue here shall not be what Hans Urs von Balthasar designated as the "objective evidence" of religious faith. Rather than focus on those manifestations that would ground faith in the object of perception (*Wahr-nehmung*) it is the "subjective" movement of faith itself that is at issue. That is, insofar as these dualistic terms, subjective and objective, still fit the discussion of the phenomena under consideration.[2]

Departing from the words of Messiaen, I will focus on the subjective movements of musical-religious belief proper.[3] Messiaen notably does not merely refer to *son-couleur* or breakthrough, but he also indicates the direction of breakthrough, which is "*toward* the beyond," in other words, a movement from here to there. His words indicate that such a breakthrough is related to an external phenomenon (sound-color), but that the dazzlement that occurs because of this phenomenon should be distinguished from the proper experience of breaking through. Messiaen therefore describes the latter in subjective terms. It does not lead to confronting an unsuspected religious *object*, but it prepares for faith, and it is precisely this transition or passage that constitutes the real breakthrough: "Touching at once our noblest senses: hearing and vision, it shakes our sensibilities into motion, pushes us to go beyond concepts, to approach that which is higher than reason and intuition, that is, FAITH."[4]

How should this strange passage from musical experience to religious belief be interpreted? The role played by phenomenality in this passage is rather ambiguous. As a composer, Messiaen would be the last to minimize the importance of what is composed, but in his description of this ultimate, hyperreligious music, it is as if music is turned into a disposable utility for reaching another domain. The sound-colors and other means Messiaen uses in the relevant works are employed to create a modulation of musical experience and ultimately to surpass the domain of musical immanence. After all, even the experience of synesthetic dazzlement (*éblouissement*) only provides the stepping-stone to what lies beyond it, that is, according to Messiaen, "faith." The divine, dazzling light may proceed from the musical phenomenon as such, but the question remains—in Messiaen's words— whether the listener is able to perform the movement to breakthrough toward the "beyond." The musical phenomenon on offer is then, relatively speaking, of minor importance. Paul Griffiths therefore maintains in his book on Messiaen that the distinction between sacred and profane music is decided, in the last instance, by *how* one listens to music. The decisive moment (or *momentum*, turn or conversion) is arguably located in the ear.[5]

Thus, Griffiths acknowledges the possibility of a religious musical experience, but he implies that the listener may refuse, misjudge, or negate the sacred or may just be indifferent to it. In his view, the phenomenon of religious music involves a certain liberty in choosing to perceive a given piece of music in a religious sense. But as it might be objected, the term *religious* appears to be rather deflated, in that case. What is left of religion when the sacred or religious experience is made to be dependent on the finite and deliberately chosen *perspective* of the listener? Griffiths seems to testify to the contemporary banishment of the religious to the private sphere, where it is a matter of personal choice to decide what is, and what is not, religious. On the positive side, however, his position begs the question of understanding how, in the process of listening, the enigmatic passage from musical to religious experience in the music of *éblouissement* actually takes place. What kind of passage is this exactly? What is it, in listening, that testifies in the sensation of *éblouissement* to breaking through, to the transition of a common way of listening to another, exceptional way? And in what sense is this indeed a religious experience, rather than the experience of aesthetic transgression, that commonplace of modernist art?

In answering these questions, I shall confront Messiaen's provocative assertions with two theological *topoi*, namely the reference in Jeremiah to a circumcision of the ear and the theological notion of the spiritual senses. In order to construct a theory of listening capable of rendering a contemporary answer to these questions, the two topoi will also be related to the recent debate on the concept of structural listening.[6] Only the mere contours of a possible "conversion" of the ear will be sketched here. In conclusion, we shall turn to the question of what could constitute, on the basis of Messiaen, faith—in music.

## The Circumcision of the Ear

In Jeremiah 6:10, the prophet asks the Lord of hosts: "To whom shall I speak, and give warning, that they may hear? Behold, *their ear is uncircumcised*, and they cannot hearken: behold, the word of the Lord is unto them a reproach; they have no delight in it." This verse alludes to the precondition the ear must meet in order to hear the word of the Lord: it should be circumcised. The uncircumcised ear is only bothered by the word of the Lord; the circumcised ear is delighted. Such delight, the verse suggests, is related to a certain fidelity or obedience to the word. Listening does not refer only to the capacity to hear (as the uncircumcised can hear perfectly, or they would not be bothered by the word), but also to the capacity for understanding and obedience.[7] As Mathew Henry explicates,

> I cannot speak *that they may hear,* cannot speak to any purpose, or with any
> hope of success; for *their ear is uncircumcised,* it is carnal and fleshly, indisposed

to receive the voice of God, so that *they cannot hearken*. They have, as it were, a thick skin grown over the organs of hearing, so that divine things might to as much purpose be spoken to a stone as to them.[8]

The image of the thick-skinned ear is an interpretation of the Hebrew text, which only mentions circumcision (*hinee arelah aznaim*). Commentators have agreed unanimously on its meaning. In the words of William McKane, for example, "the image of uncircumcised ears does not indicate total deafness but selective deafness—receptivity to illusions and incapacity to hear the truth."[9] And William Holladay points out that the circumcision of the ear corresponds, in Christian terms, to the baptism of the ear. The latter term, however, is nowhere used in the New Testament, in contrast to the circumcision of the ear (cf. Acts 7:51).

What, then, is the structure of this circumcision, which prepares the ear for the delightful obedience to the Word of the Lord? And what are its implications for listening to music? Jacques Derrida, preeminently the thinker of circumcision as a philosopheme, thematizes this figure in many places. In his text on Paul Celan, "Shibboleth," the figure of circumcision refers to the transition from a *Diesseits*, a "this-side-of-the-beyond" to (compare Messiaen's breakthrough *toward*) the beyond.[10] It is the mark of belonging to the (Jewish) community, and it therefore serves to mark difference or exteriority to other possible communities as well. Circumcision is also an event, however, a unique and decisive moment in life that signifies that a community is joined, that one enters in the law. It is a rite of *passage*, a movement from outside to inside (and vice versa) that lifts existence from its particularity and inscribes it in the community. Hence, when the ear is circumcised, this should indicate a passage, a transition, an initiation—just as Messiaen's breakthrough is an initiation.

Still, the question remains of where this passage made, that is, to what exteriority or interiority a transition is being made. A first interpretation of the "circumcision of the ear" in contemporary terms is the passage of the ear into the *inner room* of the sensorium, a possibility that will be considered in this section. The second interpretation that concerns passage to the sensible *outside* will be considered next, followed by a third section where the formula of "faith in music" will serve to analyze the circular movement implied in spiritual listening.

Following Derrida, Byung-Chul Han argues that the ear is the location for auto-affection, which he relates to the anatomical closure of the ear (the tympanum) and its position in between the inner world and the exterior.

This complacent middle position is symbolized, in Han's view, by the notion of the middle ear.[11] Although the anatomical being-near-and-with-itself of the ear is an image for its self-reflexivity, the ear's auto-affectivity remains indissolubly connected to a certain orientation on sound. That is to say, not on exterior sound, but on an *inner* sound or the announcement of such, as in the "brazen voice" of Kant's moral law, or the "voice of reason." Han refers to a privilege that is often attributed to inwardness in philosophy (and elsewhere). Just as Eryximachus proposes, at the beginning of Plato's symposium, to dismiss the girl musician with the *aulos* (a kind of double oboe) from the banquet to make room (that is silence) for the *logos*, so will thought prefer to shut its ears for the sounds of the world. Nietzsche acknowledged the application of wax in the ears as a—suspect—precondition for philosophy.[12] The voice of reason always is a voice without apparent sound, as Derrida shows with reference to Husserl, a voice that cannot be perverted by the alienating reverberations of the exterior physical voice.[13] In the intimacy of thought or in the silence of pure inwardness philosophy hopes to hear *more*, what is more authentic or more original. In the words of Han, "one longs to be deaf or desires it for others, so that our hearing is improved and we hear better, more, and more originally, as if deafness is undone by 'more-hearing' in an economy of compensation."[14] The passage then does not lead through an opening toward exteriority, toward what is listened to in community, but consists of a withdrawal toward interiority. Thus, the ear sacrifices itself in an attempt to be inscribed in the universality of what cannot be publicly heard: the voices of reason and moral law.

## Structural Listening

These tropes are merged in the interpretations of Beethoven's exemplary deafness by Heidegger, Adorno, and Wagner, among others. Heidegger remarks that Beethoven, in his deafness, "may hear more and grander things than before."[15] The demise of the auditory organ forms the doorway to a completely different dimension, formed by a constellation of elevated inspiration, truth, and pseudotheological notions such as revelation or calling. The circumcision of the ear, then, is not a circumcision of some thick skin covering the ear but a circumcision of the tympanum itself, which will bring liberation from any outer temptation (distraction, misdirection, and the like) in the silence of actual deafness. Such a circumcision is the ultimate consequence of the Kantian resentment for—as he saw it—the obtrusive and noncultural nature of nearly all kinds of exterior-sounding music. The circumcision of the tympanum brings a much-desired silence to the crypt of reason, where the word (*logos*) desires to be heard. And it creates silence for the Muse, the inexhaustible and unique inner source of the Beethovenian, clairaudient prophet-musician.

In his historical analysis of listening, Peter Szendy describes how the cult of interpreting Beethoven's deafness had originated in the 1830s and culminated with Wagner.[16] "The deafness of the genius," Szendy writes, "is inseparable from his originality. It is even the *condition* for it: it is this deafness that founds the genius in its inner clairvoyance, in its *clairaudience*. Deaf, the genius is all the more *transparent to himself* when he closes himself off from the noise of the world."[17] In his tribute *Beethoven*, Wagner had compared the deaf musician to the blind seer and had attributed to his music the qualities of a divine revelation. Beethoven's music, in particular "these Symphonies in A major and F major" and more generally "all tone-works from this godlike period of the master's total deafness," aroused repentance and atonement in the listener.[18] Szendy refers to Edward Dannreuther's study on Beethoven in order to show how this clairaudience is accompanied by a desire to transfer the heard to the listener. The idea is that in listening to the work, the listener is taken step by step through the development of the compositional idea and is thus taught how this piece of music should be heard. While she is listening, the simple listener is transfigured into a clairaudient as well.[19] The circumcision of the ear is carried out by the initiated on the one who hears, the listener, as a passage leading into a transcendent order.

It appears that Adorno, too, is concerned, in a rather paradoxical way, with this subtle communication of inner worlds via a musical structure. In his typology of listeners and modes of listening, the aural perception of musical structure figures as the *via regia* toward music. In Adorno's case, the rite of passage does not consist of the ear's closing the shutters to the sounds in the exterior world, but precisely in opening the ear to the structure of the sounds of music. Adorno refers to "the concrete musical logic" that he situates in music's technical dimension. "The location of this logic is technique; to one whose ear thinks along with what he hears, its several elements are promptly present as technical, and it is in technical categories that the nexus of sense (*Sinnzusammenhang*) is essentially revealed."[20] The capacity for "structural listening," Adorno stipulates, appears to be developed only with professional musicians, and even among them with only a few.[21] The initiation into this higher art of listening consists of a musical-technical training.

Structural listening is, in Adorno's words, a listening that is "completely adequate." He refers to the "fully conscious listener, who tends to miss nothing and at the same time, at each moment, accounts to himself for what he has heard. . . . Spontaneously following the course of music, even complicated music, he hears the sequence, hears the past, present, and future together so that they crystallize into a nexus of sense."[22]

This description of structural listening only seems to suggest an opening of the ear to the estimable reality of music. At closer inspection, it appears that the reality of this ideal listening is more complex. The standard for different types of listening is not set by the inner experience of sound, according to Adorno, but by the objective artifact of the musical *work*, which serves as a correlative for determining the adequacy of different listening attitudes. His typology then ranges from "fully adequate listening" to "a total lack of understanding and complete indifference to the material."[23] However, the standard offered by the concept of work stumbles on an internal problem, largely neglected by Adorno: the objective work *as such* already presupposes a particular type of listening on which it is based.

Adorno maintains explicitly that works are "objectively structured things and meaningful in themselves, things that invite analysis and can be perceived and experienced with different degrees of adequacy."[24] However, one might argue that the concept of structural listening is the *condition* for the historical origin and development of the notion of work. The genesis and cultivation of auditory attention (*Andacht*) for music *as such* have formed the condition for the blossoming and growth of those instrumental genres that would later constitute the standard, the masterpieces, for listening.[25] How then can it be determined—in this circular logic—what it is to be open to music, what listening is authentic and what inadequate? In addition, Adorno's typology betrays the predilection for a type of listening that is based on warding off anything outside the functional closure of the work. Just as the work is characterized by the fullness of its synthesis, so Adorno demands of his listener that she disposes of a strong ego to reflect this synthetic fullness. The "entertainment-listener" is reproached for "a weak ego" (*Ich-Schwäche*); and the ability to give full attention to music (its structure, the work), is accompanied by a strengthening—through training—of the subject's synthetic capacities.[26]

Structural listening as an initiation—a circumcision—into the elite of "experts" involves imprisoning listening in the ironical position of the autonomous subject, without which the musical work cannot exist as the abstract object it essentially is. Adorno seems to have no conception of the possible *transfiguration* of listening, fixed as he is on reaching a *Gestalt* (a form, structure) in listening. Interestingly in this regard, the composer and director Pierre Boulez distinguishes three different stages in the encounter with a piece of music:

> The first encounter with a work you are puzzled because you don't know it. You have to learn to know it. In this first phase you are in darkness, you are in the dark. Then, in the second phase, you analyze the work, you know it. You know the construction, you know how it is made. You have made something of it. Then you think you know it because you have perceived everything. But when you go further and you want to know how and why—beyond the how, *why* it was done—then you are in the dark again, because you will never know why a thing is really better than another thing.[27]

It seems that Adorno is focused too much on the second stage. He offers an insight into *aesthetic* listening (in the Kierkegaardian sense), which precedes analysis, and in the logical-technological nature of this analysis, but not in the just as mysterious experience that occurs after, or through this analysis—in philosophical terms, after or through the constitutive syntheses of the subject. Adorno wishes to constitute the ideal listener, wishes this ideal listener to be constituted. To take distance from structure can only be, in his view, a form of regression.[28]

The constitutive listener observes music with ironical distance; she surveys the world of the musical work from a stance that masks the emptiness of the work. Only in the synthesis of the subject can music acquire its nexus of sense and become whole, and as a whole then be transparent to understanding. In contrast to what transpires from Adorno, this synthetic completeness is *projected onto* music; it is the fruit of the labor of structural listening. Taking up the role of signifier, the listener is free—"negatively free," as Kierkegaard would say—because the emptiness of the sound can at will be transformed into the fullness of a nexus of sense.[29] By maintaining a distance to music, the listener retains the freedom to construct sense, but ultimately the *lack* of sense that is overcome in structural listening can barely be concealed.[30]

It is not surprising that the structural listener therefore is sensitive to nihilism, melancholy, and boredom—more so even than the average listener.[31] She is not just aware of the lack of sense in the music she is listening to; she is also conscious of the contingence of her analyses, which are shattered in and through a series of ironizations. The fate of the structural listener is the fate of Kierkegaard's ironic subject. She realizes that the reality of music consists in a lack of sense, and acquires with this perception the freedom to construct sense. On one hand, this involves a break with reality, whereas on the other hand not a single analysis achieves fullness, so that in turn sense itself is emptied out. Step by step, the structural listener ascends to the position where she can listen with an ear *as if* it were the ear of God.[32] Imprisoned in the serial expropriations of irony, all grip on the music, on the possibility to experience sense, is eventually lost. The experience of the fullness of a nexus of sense changes into the boredom and melancholy of nothingness, and loss respectively.[33]

Structural listening appears to coincide with the ideal of the entirely open ear, an ear that hears, in Schoenberg's words, *everything*. This fiction of a (potentially religious) totality turns out to contain, when the conditions are more closely inspected, the movements of withdrawal, in the last instance even an imprisonment of the ear in the irony of the autonomous (or "strong," as Adorno would probably say) *ego*.[34] In this respect, structural listening touches upon the clairaudience of the deaf genius: both forms of listening presuppose the autonomous subject of the Enlightenment, and both return to this subject that is endemically totalizing, or potentially demonic.[35] Is this the movement Jeremiah refers to with his notion of a circumcision of the ear? The contrary is perhaps more probable. Not the subject's turning in upon herself leads the way to the word of God, but being open unto the appeal of this word that, in accordance with the Christian logic of the Incarnation, approaches the subject from *outside*. The circumcision of the ear involves an unmistakable orientation on the exterior, that is to say, on what is offered beyond the subject dwelling with and by itself.

## BODY, AFFECT, AND FLESH

How can this exterior be envisaged? The circumcision of the ear points in the direction of exteriority, but one that is different from the musical object. Where could it be located? Jean-Luc Marion suggests a possibility for envisaging such exteriority by departing from the concept of the individual and the notion of flesh.[36] According to Marion, the flesh is a gift, in which the ego is bestowed. This implies, according to Marion, that the ego is not autonomous, on the contrary, it comes along as the *adonné* (the gifted) in a more originary experience. "Flesh gives," Marion writes, "nothing other than the *ego* itself, at the same time that every given gives itself to it. It fixes it in it as an *adonné*—that which receives itself from this very thing that it receives."[37] An example of the movement in which the *ego* is bestowed by the flesh is the moment of birth, where the self is given (to itself) even before we can speak of autonomous self-constitution. "My flesh is distinguished from every object of the world, therefore from every body, in such a way that *before even being able to perceive itself as a possible external object in the world*, it perceives; before even making itself be felt, it allows one to feel; in short, before making itself be seen and appearing, it makes me feel (myself) and appear."[38] The Cartesian mind-body split fails to acknowledge the originarity of the flesh. In Marion's view, the body is not an attribute to the ego, as is suggested in phrases such as the "proper body," that is, the body that I have appropriated. Rather, it is in and through the unity of feeling and the felt (seeing and the seen, hearing and the heard) that the *ego*, as *adonné*, is bestowed unto itself.[39]

The *ego*, then, is not an autonomous principle that takes on a body, according to Marion, but a heteronymous and ecstatic movement of giving oneself, always already inscribed in the bestowing flesh, which by (and through) its gift bestows the *ego* unto itself. The flesh is distinguished by its possibility to be touched, "to receive impressions, original or derived, whatever they might be—intuitive impressions, but impressions that are significant as well," a possibility it has on its own.[40] The principal presupposition of the flesh is that it feels itself, that it is auto-affective: "The affection refers to no object, according to no ecstasy, but only to itself; for it itself is sufficient to accomplish itself as affected."[41] The auto-affection of the flesh is not only immediate (preceding each act of synthesis), but singular as well (there is no one who can feel my flesh in my place). Most decisive is that the flesh is *absolute*: it avoids any relating horizon that constitutes the object. In contrast to the body, it gives without becoming manifest: "The body appears, but flesh remains invisible, precisely because it makes appear."[42]

If, as Marion suggests, one should reckon with such a prereflective unity in hetero- and auto-affection in listening, too, a new possibility for interpreting the circumcision of the ear arises. In line with his thought, hearing (since it is oriented toward a sonic phenomenon) is then an intentionality that is always already inscribed in auto-affection, an aural being-given, that precedes it. At this level of auto-affection there is no orientation on a sonic object presenting itself either inwardly or in the exterior. There is, first of all and in the originary sense, an absolute affection, a touching of the ear that precedes its relation to listening understood in terms of reducing, intending, or signifying. Obviously, this notion of affection has much in common with the idea of the touching of the soul—the *affectio* of the *anima*—that Lyotard traces in Augustine, even though Marion does not refer to this source. "The absolute, absolutely irrelative, outside space and time," Lyotard writes, "so absolutely far—there he is for one moment lodged in the most intimate part of this man. Limits are reversed, the inside and the outside, the before and the after, these miseries of the mind."[43] Both Marion and Lyotard refer to an immediacy that circumvents synthesis, for which the spirit (*animus*) always arrives too late for registering, signifying, or organizing it.[44]

In the light of Marion and Lyotard, the passage figured by the circumcision of the ear is relocated. It is no longer a passage toward music as object, or toward the resonant crypt of the autonomous subject. It involves a step beyond the syntheses of the ego and its objects, that is to say, beyond (structural, intentional) listening and beyond the objectivated musical work of art—a passage that follows, fittingly for a circumcision, the birth of the *ego* as an *adonné* from the saturated phenomenon of the flesh.[45] The ear is touched, in this transition, at a place that logically precedes the subject and eludes the topology (inside, outside) of experience. On one hand, then, *affectio* and flesh alert to the possibility of a hetero-affective encounter with the musical exterior; on the other hand they allude to the possibility of the self meeting itself, a kind of auto-affection ranging with Lacan's *jouissance*. The circumcision of the ear oscillates between these two passages, because the subject and object of touch cannot yet be decided at the level of affection and the flesh. The exteriority of these passages does not warrant presence or sense. The listener is not so much devoted (as, for instance, Aquinas's theology of music would like to see her) as *expelled*: the circumcision of the ear as part of the body leads toward listening as an undecidable *affectio* of the flesh.

## The Transfiguration of the Ear

The images employed by Messiaen for sketching the breakthrough toward the beyond show, rather remarkably, a certain circulation of the sensory. As we have seen, this breakthrough departs from the vicinity of the sensory sound, passes through a bedazzlement and arrives at faith (written in upper case), to end up with opening a new and distinct perspective of the senses. In a passage that follows the one on breakthrough and faith cited at the beginning of this chapter, Messiaen writes,

> Now FAITH and its logical continuation, true Contemplation, the beatific Vision after death. Our resurrected body, notwithstanding its glory, its spirituality, will conserve this same flesh that has clothed us and accompanied us,

with the same faculties of seeing and hearing: and we must be able to see and to hear well to appreciate all the music and all the colors which are spoken of in the Apocalypse![46]

The resurrection of the body as a *corpus gloriosum* involves a transfiguration of the senses, as for instance the transfiguration of ear and eye mentioned by Messiaen.[47] These transfigured senses are the same as those belonging to our body in our current existence, now glorified and made new. With these senses, we will experience the beatific reality of the beyond which we were unable to notice before. The breakthrough toward the beyond can apparently be described as a change—a transfiguration—in our sensory perception of reality, all through the passage of death. At the same time, however, Messiaen postulates the extraordinary experience of the *corpora gloriosa* on this side of death, in the synesthetic experience of music. Such listening resembles the synaesthetic experience after death, which, in Messiaen's view, is the hallmark of knowing the truth. He writes, " 'Eternal life,' we read in Saint John (Jn 17:3), 'is to know Thee, Thou, the only true God and Him whom Thou hast sent, Jesus Christ.' This knowledge will be a perpetual bedazzlement, an eternal music of colors, and eternal color of musics."[48] Messiaen's breakthrough, therefore, is not simply a matter of passing to the other side but involves the experience of a transfiguration that in a certain sense has *already* taken place. Nevertheless, we learn from Messiaen that this breakthrough is about a passage. The question, then, is what the relation is, in listening, between breakthrough, with its attributes of interruption and singularity, and repetition.

## The Aporia of the Spiritual Senses

The problematics of this relation leads, first of all, to the tradition of the church fathers. The being-there-already is—as I will argue—the *precondition* for the possibility of transcendence and follows as such from the theological tradition that Messiaen implicitly refers to. The transfiguration of the ear is a notion from the theology of spiritual senses (*sensus spiritualis*), originating in the thought of Origen, the third-century church father.[49] The notion of spiritual senses bridges the gap between, on one hand, John's word that no one has ever seen God (Jn 1:18), and on the other hand the idea—supported by the Incarnation—that God is not completely divided from humanity, and accessible in one way or another.[50] Origen does not reject the latter, but he opposes the idea—put forward by the anti-Christian thinker Celsus at the end of the second century in a document that was lost—that Christians would believe that God can be known in a physical, sensory way. He speaks indeed of five senses for perceiving the divine, but these are qualitatively distinct from the senses of the body.[51] His spiritual senses are no particular transformations of the senses of the body, but are pure "senses of the spirit." They even exclude the body, as the story of Adam and Eve exemplifies. According to Origen, Adam and Eve would have delighted in the pleasures of Paradise "with the eyes of the soul," until Sin opened the eyes of the flesh and they were left with the crumbs of experiencing the world only in the physical sense.[52] This effect of sin also explains why so few possess all five senses. Most can dispose of only one or two, and some may lack them altogether (as with unbelievers). Although they are purely immaterial, Origen stresses the fact that these spiritual senses must be trained regularly— prayer would be a good opportunity—just like the physical senses. Their receptivity for things spiritual is a fruit not only of grace, but also of their application.[53]

Purely spiritual perception is concomitant with a closing (that is the *death*) of the physical senses, with Origen, to whom the senses are always of two different kinds.[54] With later Christian thinkers—as with Messiaen—we find attempts to envisage the physical and spiritual senses as a continuum. Such attempts are motivated by "the aporetics of spiritual senses," according to Hans Urs von Balthasar, who believes that Christianity is concerned with the "human-spiritual manifestation of God in Christ." The Christian, then, is dependent on the physical senses to perceive God amid the worldly reality. Such an orientation on the world, however, not only threatens to degrade Christianity to a religion that is too concrete and merely mythical, but it also forces the believer into a stalemate position: it seems impossible to reconcile the appeal on the physical sensory—as in relation to the dogma of Incarnation—with the appeal to the spiritual. It is not for nothing that Paul admonishes the Christian to "walk not after the flesh, but after the Spirit" (Rom 8:4).[55]

The aporetics of the Christian sensory are addressed by pseudo-Macarius and Bonaventure with the postulate of a transfiguration of the natural senses. Such a transfiguration would occur through the intervention of the Holy Ghost or through Christ. Pseudo-Macarius calls these Christian, physical senses "spiritual," but he envisages them as based on the natural senses.[56] Bonaventure also refers to the Holy Ghost, who is "poured in" the natural senses. His thought is more closely related to Messiaen than that of the other sources discussed here. The senses would reconstitute their original fullness because of this spiritual pouring in, and in the obscurity of what is beyond the rational or the comprehensible (compare Messiaen's description of *éblouissement*), God is met and experienced. Bonaventure distinguishes in this the ecstasy of love, where such meeting is always a possibility, and the so-called *raptus*, which is an exceptional and passing event (as is *éblouissement*), as with Saulus on his way to Damascus. In the ecstasy of love (the *apex affectus*), the soul is touched by God, but the intellect is not involved. It is about meeting or touching in darkness, in more than one way comparable to the topos of the dark night in Saint John of the Cross.[57]

Such meeting in darkness implies a certain inward turn (*conversio*). With Bonaventure the awakening of the senses involves a process of inwardness that is strongly reminiscent of Augustine: "For in this stage, when the inner senses are restored to see the highest beauty, to hear the highest harmony, to smell the highest fragrance, to taste the highest sweetness, to apprehend the highest delight, the soul is prepared for spiritual ecstasy."[58] Augustine was caught in a double bind when listening to religious chants: under the spell of the beauty of the hymns, he was also snatched away by a conscience that was admonished by the words that were sung.[59] He found a middle way in the interiorization of sound by means of memory and musical imagination. The true source of music was strategically relocated from the exterior (the voice of the other reaching me through air) to the interior (the a priori of music, the *numeri judiciales* that is always already bestowed upon me).[60] This dislocation of music to the inner sphere is part of the general relocation of the divine with Augustine. In a famous passage from the tenth book in his *Confessions*, he describes how the sensory becomes spiritual and inner:

> But what do I love when I love my God? Not material beauty or beauty of a temporal order; not the brilliance of earthly light, so welcome to our eyes; *not the sweet melody of harmony and song.* . . . It is not these that I love when I love my God. And yet, when I love him, it is true that I love a light of a certain kind, *a voice*, a perfume, a food, an embrace; but they are of the kind that I love in my inner self, when my soul is bathed in light that is not bound by space; *when it listens to sound that never dies away.* . . . This is what I love when I love my God.[61]

With what ear is this timeless sound heard by Augustine? Not the exterior ear, which hears the delightful melodies of harmony and song; not the physical inner ear, which resonates with the skull and registers the heart's beating and the whistle of the brain. Neither is it the "inner ear" of musicians that operates on the basis of previously heard exterior sounds. Augustine's inner ear (*auris interior*) is the ear of the spirit hearing the inner Word.

As Serge Margel argues, this Word is of a different order from the exterior word. It is not a word that simply resounds, but one that resonates through (and even *as*) silence; it is eternal and infinite, without end or beginning.[62] The ear that hears this word is the ear of the heart (*auris cordis*), in the words of Augustine, and is both obedient and capable of turning away from the word: "My soul, you too must listen to the word of God. Do not be foolish; do not let the din of your folly deafen the ears of your heart. For the Word himself calls you to return."[63]

The tenth book reveals that Augustine's path of the inward turn does not lead to a situation where the spiritual senses are purified and opened. Rather, a conversion in the sense of turning inward (and away from the physical-sensory) offers no alternative to the aporetics of a Christian sense-perception that is actively engaged with the world. As Burcht Pranger puts it,

> After his analysis of the profundities of memory Augustine, in the tenth book, turns to the surface of his present life, eleven years after his conversion. What has he achieved so far? Does he live in the permanent presence of the spiritual senses? The result of his self-analysis is quite sobering. There is no denying that he lives the life of a bishop and that his head is full of biblical and devout language. But what about the senses and the sensual? Eating, drinking still tend to be a delightful matter. Sexual thoughts and nocturnal emissions still distract him and hardly give him the impression of being in control.[64]

As was announced with Balthasar's notion of the aporetics of the spiritual senses, Augustine is thrown back upon the world of the senses in his very attempt to evade its temptations. A flight clear and simple from the the hold of the sensory is not possible, and it may not be in order. Pranger shows that for Augustine the turn inward is not so much about the spiritual senses, as "a thinner, spiritualised and disembodied duplication of the senses proper," but rather about a *recycling* motion. The spiritual senses—in so far as they are spiritual at all—do not describe, according to Pranger, a once and for all conversion, but the split-second return (the Augustinian *ictus cordis*) to the "true sound, sight, smell, touch, and taste of Paradise" breaking through the temporalizations (*distentio*) of memory and expectation. Conversion then involves, according to Pranger, an oscillation between rising quickly from a fall and not falling at all (*Confessions*, X, 35), which cannot be described as a moment in linear narrative, but calls for a "vertical poetics" that creates access to breaking through the here and now in an impalpable "flash of eternity," too quick for the pen in the hands the saint.[65] Such a reinterpretation of conversion and of the notion of the spiritual senses offers a point of departure for the movement of return that is described by Messiaen as a breakthrough toward the beyond. With Messiaen, this is a breakthrough that has already, *always already*, taken place, but that remains nevertheless a unique breakthrough "toward the beyond."

In the theological tradition, the awakening of the spiritual senses is subject to a number of conditions. In the words of Jan van Ruusbroec, these are "firstly the light of grace, secondly the act of free will turning toward God, and thirdly a conscience that is purified of all mortal sin."[66] The three conditions hang closely together, as one can turn unconditionally toward God and know Him through the grace of faith only when one is purified of sin. Faith is, in this respect, always a *precondition* for the awakening of the spiritual senses through which God can be known. Only in faith can we speak of "the eyes of faith."[67] For the reception of faith from the perception of the phenomenon as miracle, that is to say, in Marion's words, of the absolute (self-)giving of the phenomenon, the gift of faith is a prerequisite. Although Balthasar pays little attention to this reversal of prerequisites, the problem was already addressed in the New Testament. In the narrative about unbelieving Nazareth, Jesus is accompanied by his disciples when he returns to the place where he was born (Mk 6:1–6). When he teaches in the synagogue, the people are astounded and wonder,

> Is not this the carpenter, the son of Mary, the brother of James, and Joseph, and of Judas, and Simon? And are not his sisters here with us? And they were offended at him. But Jesus said unto them, A prophet is not without honour, but in his own country, and among his own kin, and in his own house. *And he could there do no mighty work*, save that he laid his hands upon a few sick folk, and healed them. And he marvelled because of their unbelief. And he went round about the villages, teaching.[68]

This passage teaches us that there can be no miracle without faith. For Balthasar, who maintains that faith is derived from the object, this means that the Christian relation to the sensory, that is to say, to Incarnation, has reached an aporia. It seems to be impossible to come to faith, if it is to be derived from an object—a phenomenon bestowing faith (that is a miracle)—that at the same time *presupposes* faith. "Then said Jesus unto him, Except ye see signs and wonders, ye will not believe" (Jn 4:48; cf. Jn 11:40). There is an inevitable aporia in the perception of the divine, as in hearing trumpets or the choirs of angels.

When all things are considered, it seems that Messiaen's discourse on breakthrough can neither depart from some "objective evidence" in music, nor from the "subjective evidence" of faith. And yet, faith remains the key word if we trust that in music we find a medium that is aesthetically or religiously meaningful. What, then, is, or might be, faith in music? What does faith in music speculate on?

## FAITH IN MUSIC

The quintessential question on the nature of experiencing art and music in particular, is concerned with the role of faith and belief. Messiaen has indicated that the experience of *éblouissement* leads to faith, and the apparition of such faith is the signal of breakthrough. In general, the experience of a work of art is surrounded with moments of faith and/or belief that interconnect at different moments. Apart from the basic "natural belief" of reason (Hume) and the perceptual faith (Merleau-Ponty's *foi perceptive*) that plays a part in every perception, the experience of art *as art* presupposes a receptivity for belief, for make-believe, that is, for the suspension of disbelief and skepticism. For such suspension the listener, reader, or observer must first of all accept the proffered work and take it for what it is not. The example of painting may clarify this: there is no painting if the observer refuses to accept that the disarray of dots and dashes constitutes a landscape. There must be some willingness to suspend the ontological difference between reality and representation. Referring to poetry, Samuel Taylor Coleridge coined the famous phrase of a "willing suspension of disbelief" to indicate the activity of accepting the material on offer for what it is not.[69]

For Messiaen it is, in this respect, about being prepared to accept the proffered sounds (*sons-couleurs*) as being part of a work of art, just as the glass in stained glass is more than just the glass.[70] Next, the effect of being overwhelmed and dazzled by the effects of that work would have to be accepted as a religious breakthrough (*percée*). There is, in other words, a remarkable chain of events: first the material of chords, colors and dazzlement becomes in and through a *suspension of disbelief* a form of make-believe, a fiction that is *aesthetically* believed in as art. And next this fiction is interpreted as a religious fact, involving a *religious* faith in music that in its totalizing nature erases both the former suspension as well as the former belief.[71] This may have preciously little to do with the divine listening of the spiritual senses. This seems rather about make-believe, at best concerned with the *aesthetic* representation of religious faith. Messiaen, however, does not refer to the representation of faith but to presence and immediacy. This is no immediacy in the regressive sense, as one that precedes reflection (such as in the conscious act of a *willing* suspension) and which implies a regression of listening toward a presymbolic wholeness.[72] Rather, I would contend, this is a case of immediacy *after*, or *through* the (self-)reflection of conscious perception, breaking *through* reflection *toward* what Kierkegaard would describe as a "second immediacy" or "immediacy after reflection."[73]

This immediacy recalls a word that time and again pops up in the discussion of Messiaen's work: naïveté. Whether it is his *langage communicable*, his attempts at representing birdsong in music, the manner in which he set aspects of faith to music, or the blatant vulgarity of some of his works—friend and foe respect, and even admire, Messiaen for his "saintly *naïveté*" (Griffiths).[74] As was seen in Chapter 5, Richard Taruskin advances this quality of Messiaen's music against what he sees as the all too self-conscious attempts of some contemporary composers at putting religion on the map again. It is, to him, an "impressive feat" that Messiaen succeeds in maintaining naïveté in his music even when it borders on kitsch. That is not to say, evidently, that Messiaen was naïve in any sense, nor that his refined and often highly complex music should receive that predicate. Rather, what is at stake here is a probing of the concept of naïveté beyond all childish amazement. Perhaps Kierkegaard's reference to secondariness and return ("*second* immediacy") may contain an indication. Paul Ricoeur wrote in his work on the interpretation of religious symbols about what he called a "second naïveté."[75] This is a hermeneutical experience that comes after the first naivety, the "primitive naïveté," that is characterized by immediacy. According to Ricoeur, it is the expression of "the distress of modernity and a remedy for that distress" that we can believe only by interpreting. "If we can no longer live the great symbolisms of the sacred in accordance with the original belief in them, we can, we modern men, aim at a second naïveté in and through criticism. . . . It is by *interpreting* that we can *hear* again." Ricoeur then sees a possibility that we are aiming for and expect in the return of a naïveté that is nonetheless different from the immediacy of faith that is definitely lost. There is, in other words, a movement of mediation between faith and understanding, and between understanding and having faith anew.

Kierkegaard, in contrast, speaks in terms of an "infinite qualitative difference'" that cannot be mediated dialectically or otherwise. It is all about a leap, the "leap of faith," or the leap of the ear into the *Ur-sprung* (the "ear-igin," so to speak) of listening.[76] In relating to music, the issue is not so much aesthetic enjoyment, Kierkegaard contends, but a specific kind of *acting* (such as leaping is form of acting). The following scene of Kierkegaard in church, pondering the virtues and vices of a hymn strikingly resembles his intellectual forebear Augustine in a similar situation. Inventing his own escape from this typical situation, Kierkegaard writes,

> A hymn, after all, is the production of a poet, and the process no doubt goes something like this: the poet is seized by a mood, and he surrenders to it. Let us now assume that the content of such a hymn is love for his Savior, how the soul loves him, gives up the whole world to have him, etc., and this is set forth in the most glowing expressions. That may be enough. But this hymn is supposed to be sung by the congregation. It always says I in the hymn; consequently, it is I who am singing. Am I able to say such a thing about myself—even in the remotest manner? No; therefore either I must sit without thinking so that I notice nothing at all, or I must be forced into hypocrisy. Generally the law for all religious communication is that it be true. Why? Because religiously there should be a turning in the direction of acting, doing accordingly, and it is precisely this turning which distinguishes the religious from the aesthetic. The aesthetic leads into the wild blue yonder, comes like sneeze and goes like a sneeze. The aesthetic is the moment and is in the moment; religiously, it is precisely the next moment which is decisive, for then I am supposed to act, and if I do not attend to that, I have changed that moment in the church or in the hymn singing into aesthetic enjoyment. Therefore it is very important that everything that is said and sung in church should be true, not that it should be beautiful, great, glorious, ravishing, etc., not that I start to cry while my heart beats violently—no, the question is whether I am primarily related to all this in terms of acting accordingly.[77]

Let us assume that such acting constitutes the leap Kierkegaard thinks is characteristic for faith. How can this leap, this passage, toward a new listening in divine immediacy be carried out? The *Ur-sprung* of faith in music seems to be an impossible task with Messiaen. For faith turned out to be the *conditio sine qua non* such a movement, for breaking through toward the beyond—faith being at the same time the *fruit* and *mark* of such a breakthrough. The aporetics of breaking through and of the transfiguration of the ear appear to indicate a paradoxical doubling of listening, a double entendre. The notion of double listening is exceptionally significant in thinking about Christianity and listening with Messiaen. It appeared above that the circumcision of the ear could be described as a singular transition toward the beyond of listening, in response to the constitutive touch by the outside

(Marion's notion of the flesh). With Messiaen, however, there is *at once* the "having-crossed" the border *and* the "still-facing" it. There is *at once* initiation (circumcision, baptism) *and* affirmation of alienation. Or, speaking in more general theological terms, it is a matter of being *at once* within faith (orthodoxy) *and* outside it (heterodoxy).

*Eblouissement*, then, is Janus-faced, marking on one hand our meeting (and dwelling) with the divine and the eternal life, and on the other hand, our alienation and separation from the divine in the dazzle of our sin. As was pointed out earlier, etymologically this term refers not only to being overwhelmed and blinded but also to weakness, lack, and obscurity, as well as to misdirection and mistake. This double structure of *éblouissement* reveals the subtle aporetics in the figure of breakthrough (*percée*). Breakthrough is not thinkable in a pure sense; it is always already inscribed in the closure (*clôture*) of the frame (the 'fallen' subject with his physical senses). Opening and closure—dazzlement in both senses—are given in *one and the same motion*. It is not possible to have a pure and definitive determination or localization of the boundary between breakthrough and musicolatry, not before, neither at the moment itself, nor in retrospective interpretation. The notion of breakthrough proposed by Messiaen can only be conceived within the aporetic logics of repetition, within the double bind of physical spirituality or spiritual physicality, where a breakthrough that is about to occur has already come about. Hearing the "eternal music of colors" beyond, is, as we have seen, a repetition of the music heard on this side. Repetition, as understood within the logic of iterability, may open a window (the figure or Gestalt) on a completely different view, but it also creates the possibility of denying breaking through toward the "beyond."

In this respect, the position of Messiaen's music is comparable to the ornaments (*parerga*) traditionally framing a painting. In Derrida's famous analysis of the ornamented frame, the ornament—or arabesque, the pejorative term that adequately symbolizes the Kantian contempt for improvised or wordless music—is not subservient to the painting revealed, but constitutes an *intervention* in what is framed, a contamination, both enabling the spectacle as well as demarcating it, dispossessing it and handing it over to the idolatry of the other, the heterodox and impure (as, with Kant, anything that does *not* belong to the purely aesthetic experience).[78] The music of Messiaen is neither the serviceable frame for a pure breakthrough nor a purely idolatrous barrier to a religious passage, but it indicates that "these two apparently contradictory gestures are the very ones—and they are systematically indissociable—of *what* is here deconstructed" (Derrida).[79] As Peter Hill and

Nigel Simeone recount in their biography of Messiaen, many critics in the 1940s were appalled by the language and explicitly stated intentions of this composer. They appealed to the composer to speak only from the staves. Others applauded the Christian surrealism in Messiaen's work. The question, however, remains how we can ever know where, that is, on which side of the line, we are as listeners of this music. We are facing a lack, or more strongly, the very end of all criteria.[80] Messiaen's suggestion of there being a "single reality" to which both sacred and profane music refer is defective in that it vainly posits a third reality in order to mediate the instability of these two musical "realities."[81] As I have tried to show throughout this book, such attempts to predetermine what religious music or the hyperreligious does or means, in fact, obscure or neutralize the great but undecidable gift that sacred music is. This gift, as Augustine was aware, is indispensable but dangerous, and it is by facing this fact that, in spite of his occasional attempts to play down the radical nature of his work, Messiaen was able to create a music that is beyond its name.

# Epilogue: On Affirmation

As Christian Asplund is right to emphasize in an article in which he compares the aesthetics of Cage, Bach, and Messiaen, the music of the last composer does not appeal to a sense of interiority in the way Bach's music does. It seems as though in Messiaen's music the vertical plane of stained-glass windows is answered by a planar experience that leaves all interiority behind. Inspired by Gilles Deleuze, Asplund notes, "Rather than delving or diving into a squalid, striated space of darkness within, Messiaen wants to ascend to a smooth, infinite space of light above, an expanding beyond oneself rather than a retraction within."[1]

Hence, what Gilles Deleuze and Félix Guattari write about music in general seems especially true of Messiaen's: "Music is never tragic, music is joy. But there are times it necessarily gives us a taste for death; not so much happiness as *dying happily, being extinguished*."[2] The music of dazzlement induces a transport along lines of flight that pass through the subject's senses (sound-color) and lead toward a cosmic plane of immanence, an almost tactile texture of transfigured sensibility. Here, death is an event that already seems to have taken place. It returns one's senses to a position that they may have occupied long before the invention of subjectivity. Or it may put them in a new position, among the repetitive deaths of the subject that we have been witnessing and that we shall witness.

As I have argued, this happy dying does not imply a death of the will to affirmation. On the contrary, Messiaen's music, far from exemplifying a Christian music of asceticism or *contemptus mundi*, remains deeply affirmative. In this respect, Messiaen's work is remarkably close to the spirit of Friedrich Nietzsche, who scorned the dark recesses of the German soul and favored the southern qualities of Bizet's *Carmen*. Although Messiaen arguably owes a great deal to Wagner, his affinities seem closer to the sun-stricken lands of the Mediterranean than to the nebulous swamps of the Teutonic imagination. The dialectic of abstinence and redemption that structures *Parsifal* is answered in Messiaen by a joyous Yes-saying. For Messiaen's music is ultimately a music of Yes (*Amen*): it celebrates, it affirms, it surrenders to something (rather than submitting itself).

It is tempting to interpret the music of dazzlement in terms of blackout and negative theology. Such, however, is not the nature of affirmation in Messiaen. As I have tried to argue, his reading of dazzlement is overwhelmingly positive, even in regard to the sensuous aspects of this experience. Rather than involve a leap into blind nothingness, it embraces and affirms a bright and colorful remainder. The summit of dazzlement is, as Messiaen explained while standing in the Saint-Chapelle, an all-violet haze that is clearly perceived despite being overly intense and saturating. Experiencing this, we have not left the world of the senses, and, in Messiaen's account of the continuity between life and death, we presumably never will.

Hence, if there is, as Paul Griffiths suggests, a "saintly naïveté" in Messiaen, it would be that his music affirms an exteriority that cannot be accounted for in terms of spirituality.[3] The sensuous remainder testifies to a materiality that will always remain heterogeneous to the logic of the spirit. To affirm such an exteriority is to say Yes to the materiality of art, and to the uncanny hybrid called religious music. As Jean-Luc Nancy writes in his comment on Hegel's philosophy of art, and particularly on its inability to conceptualize Christian art, "The moment of art in religion cannot remain a moment. Irresistibly it autonomizes itself, and it does so, perhaps, because it is precisely the moment of the thorough autonomy of manifestation—of an autonomy that no longer retains anything of interiority or of spirituality as such."[4] Messiaen courts—again, "the temptation of temptation"—the risk of affirming that which falls outside of the realm of the spirit, and he does so with apparent certainty. Perhaps it is wisdom.

And finally, what about the listener? The relation to an outside, to an element that cannot be incorporated, neither by the intellect nor by the spirit or the emotions—what does all this mean to the ear that is supposed listen? Again we find the motif of affirmation. "The *affirmation*," the Lacanian philosopher Paul Moyaert writes, "that is required of believers is in fact *purely exterior*, that is, it is neither based on adequate intellectual understanding nor on inward feeling. One should not try and understand religious dogmas, one should acknowledge them, even though one may not understand them and may not be able to relate to them emotionally. Here, neither reason is relevant nor the heart."[5] To have faith in Messiaen's music requires no less than that we affirm something that ultimately escapes aesthetic assurances. At a time when choice, meaning and consumer safety are the cornerstones of musical experience, this seems a valuable challenge.

# Notes

## Introduction

1. In June 1991, *La Transfiguration* was performed in this venue under supervision of conductor Reinbert de Leeuw. Messiaen attended this performance, and his wife, the pianist Yvonne Loriod, played. The March 2000 concert performance of the opera *Saint François d'Assise* took place under the same supervision.

2. Longinus, *On the Sublime*, in T. S. Dorsch, *Classical Literary Criticism: Aristotle/Horace/Longinus* (London: Penguin, 1965), 100.

3. See Chapter 4.

4. Peter Hill and Nigel Simeone, *Messiaen* (New Haven: Yale University Press, 2005), 144–168.

5. Throughout the book, the question of *criteria* (such as objective or subjective evidence) is central in order to determine whether or not certain music is religious. The question is prior to its opposite, that is, the question of *who* (rather than *what*) authorize(s) the experience of breakthrough. This more Foucauldian question of the relation between power and knowledge will be the subject of future research.

6. In this respect, I agree with Wilhelm Seidel, who observed that the early romantic religion of art possessed certain qualities that might lead to its rejection as "artificial, false, untrue," but that it also had a core that was totally "unromantic and deserving of respect," making it certainly relevant for the present topic. Wilhelm Seidel, "Absolute Musik und Kunstreligion um 1800," in Helga de la Motte-Haber, ed., *Musik und Religion*, 2nd ed. (Laaber, Germany: Laaber, 2003), 132.

7. See Richard Viladesau, *Theological Aesthetics: God in Imagination, Beauty, and Art* (New York: Oxford University Press, 1999).

8. Cited in Carl Dahlhaus, *The Idea of Absolute Music*, trans. Roger Lustig (Chicago: University of Chicago Press, 1989), 89.

9. Brigitte Massin, *Olivier Messiaen: Une poétique du merveilleux* (Aix-en-Provence: Alinéa, 1989), 178.

10. Olivier Messiaen, *Music and Color: Conversations with Claude Samuel* (Portland, Ore.: Amadeus Press, 1994), 211. The Augustinian influence is clearly manifested in the epigraphs to *Traité de rythme, de couleur, et d'ornithologie* (Paris: Leduc, 1994–2002), vol. 5 (parts I and II). See, for the influence of Augustine's thought on music, Saint Bonaventure, *The Soul's Journey Into God*, trans. Ewert Cousins (Mahwah, N.J.: Paulist Press, 1978), 74, where the Augustinian theology of music is contained within the "journey into God."

11. See Martin Heidegger, "Phenomenology and Theology," in *Pathmarks* (Cambridge: Cambridge University Press, 1998), 43.

12. Jeremy S. Begbie, *Theology, Music and Time* (Cambridge: Cambridge University Press, 2000), 3 n. 2; Jon Michael Spencer, *Theomusicology* (Durham, N.C.: Duke University Press, 1994).

13. Joyce Irwin, ed., *Sacred Sound: Music in Religious Thought and Practice* (Chico, Calif.: Scholars Press, 1983).

14. Albert L. Blackwell, *The Sacred in Music* (Louisville, Ky.: Westminster John Knox Press, 1999).

15. Oskar Söhngen, *Theologie der Musik* (Kassel, Germany: Johannes Stauda Verlag, 1967); de la Motte-Haber, *Musik und Religion*.

16. A copious starting point for such a journey is provided by Hans Seidel, Israel Adler, Reinhard Flender, James McKinnon, and Gustav A. Krieg, "Musik und Religion," in Horst Balz et al., eds., *Theologische Realenzyklopädie* (Berlin: Walter de Gruyter, 1994), 23:441–495.

17. Thomas Clifton, *Music as Heard: A Study in Applied Phenomenology* (New Haven: Yale University Press, 1983); Mikel Dufrenne, *The Phenomenology of Aesthetic Experience*, trans. Edward Casey (Evanston, Ill.: Northwestern University Press, 1973), especially 249–273. Apart from that, my approach differs from these exemplars in that it is far removed from the *empirical* orientation of Clifton as well as from the aesthetic approach of Dufrenne. With the latter, music appears to be reduced to an illustration of the general structure of the aesthetic object he proposes. In using the work of Jean-Luc Marion, I will precisely try to evade reducing music to the "schemes" of aesthetics.

18. "There is no concept or category that leads more directly into what is specific about contemporary theory—or certain aspects of it—than repetition." Samuel Weber, "Repetition: Kierkegaard, Artaud, Pollock and the Theatre of the Image," transcript of a discussion with Terry Smith, Power Institute of Fine Arts, University of Sydney, September 16, 1996.

19. For a survey of this debate, see Phillip Blond, ed., *Post-Secular Philosophy: Between Philosophy and Theology* (New York: Routledge, 1998), and Hent de Vries, *Philosophy and the Turn to Religion* (Baltimore: Johns Hopkins University Press, 1999), 1–39. I will in particular be inspired by thinkers coming forth from the (French) phenomenological tradition and who have explored the aforementioned fault lines, such as Jean-François Lyotard, Jean-Luc Marion, and Jacques Derrida. It is my aim to contribute to this debate by focusing on, and calling attention for the philosophical and theological position vis-à-vis the aural and music, which, in contrast to the position of the visual and of visual arts (cf. Marion), has been rather underexposed in this debate.

## 1.  *It Is a Glistening Music We Seek*

1. Jean-Rodolphe Kars, "Spiritualité de l'oeuvre d'orgue de Messiaen," in *Olivier Messiaen, homme de foi: Regard sur son oeuvre d'orgue* (Paris: Trinité Média, 1995), 75.

2. Olivier Messiaen, *Conférence de Kyoto* (Paris: Leduc, 1988), 1. See also Chapter 5.

3. Olivier Messiaen, *Traité de rythme, de couleur, et d'ornithologie* (Paris: Leduc, 1994–2002), 1:51.

4. Olivier Messiaen, *Music and Color: Conversations with Claude Samuel* (Portland, Ore.: Amadeus Press, 1994), 20–21. In *Conférence de Kyoto* (12), Messiaen does not speak of illuminating faith but of "meditating on" its mysteries.

5. Quoted in Peter Hill and Nigel Simeone, *Messiaen* (New Haven: Yale University Press, 2005), 63.

6. Almut Rössler, *Contributions to the Spiritual World of Olivier Messiaen* (Duisburg, Germany: Gilles & Francke, 1986), 105–106.

7. Olivier Messiaen, *Technique of My Musical Language* (Paris: Leduc, 1956), 1:13.

8. As Marcel Delannoy, one of his fiercest critics in the early 1940s, already noticed, "He seeks to create in his music the power of a personal miracle and then calmly announces that he has succeeded." Quoted in Hill and Simeone, *Messiaen*, 113.

9. Messiaen, *Technique of My Musical Language*, 1:7–8.

10. See, for the association of surrealism and Christianity, Hill and Simone, *Messiaen*, 167–168.

11. Olivier Messiaen, "Reply to 'A Survey,'" *Contrepoints* 3 (March–April 1946): 73–75. Italics in original.

12. As Christian Asplund demonstrates with recourse to Gilles Deleuze, there comes a moment in Messiaen of subjectless religiosity. Christian Asplund, "A Body Without Organs: Three Approaches—Cage, Bach, and Messiaen," *Perspectives of New Music* 35, no. 2 (Summer 1997): 171–187. This insight, and more particularly the special position designated to the senses that it entails, will be more fully explored in Chapters 4 and 6 and in the Epilogue.

13. See Chapters 4 and 5.

14. Rössler, *Contributions*, 96.

15. Messiaen, *Music and Color*, 16.

16. See, for instance, Antoine Goléa, *Rencontres avec Olivier Messiaen* (Paris: Slatkine, 1984), 34; Messiaen, *Music and Color*, 20; *Saint François d'Assise* (Paris: Premières Loges, 1992), 33; *Olivier Messiaen: The Music of Faith* (1986), documentary film directed by Alan Benson (Princeton: Films for the Humanities & Sciences, 2004). His second wife, the pianist Yvonne Loriod, similarly confirms the solidity of Messiaen's faith; see Peter Hill, ed., *The Messiaen Companion* (London: Faber & Faber, 1995), 303. With respect to these iterations, see Chapter 5.

17. See, for instance, Brigitte Massin, *Olivier Messiaen: Une poétique du merveilleux* (Aix-en-Provence: Alinéa, 1989), 25–27; Messiaen, *Music and Color*, 26. Pierre Messiaen also translated the *Fioretti* of Francis of Assisi, which would later play a significant part in the work of his son.

18. Goléa, *Rencontres*, 34.

19. Massin, *Poétique*, 27–28.

20. Goléa, *Rencontres*, 37. The quotation is from John 20:29.

21. Harry Halbreich, *Olivier Messiaen* (Paris: Fayard/Fondation Sacem, 1980), 52–54.

22. Hans Urs von Balthasar, "Bekenntnis zu Mozart," in *Die Entwicklung der musikalischen Idee: Bekenntnis zu Mozart* (Einsiedeln: Johannes Verlag, 1998), 63.

23. Messiaen, *Music and Color*, 213, 241, 244; Rössler, *Contributions*, 52.

24. Halbreich, *Messiaen*, 53–54. The list contains only eight examples of titles (works and parts of works) that refer to suffering and sin. A few can be added, dating from the period after the publication of Halbreich's book: the ninth part ("Les ténèbres") of *Livre du Saint Sacrement*, and especially the seventh tableau ("Les Stigmates") from *Saint François d'Assise*.

25. Rössler, *Contributions*, 52. Loriod confirms this in Hill, *Companion*, 301. She also maintains that Messiaen was someone who "suffered greatly" both as a person and as an artist (ibid., 294).

26. Rössler, *Contributions*, 53.

27. Ibid., 79. Quotations from the Gospel of John and the letters of Paul, however, occur more often in the works of Messiaen than quotations from Revelation. In other words, the weight in content is not wholly balanced by a numerical preponderance. For a table of books from the Bible quoted by Messiaen, see Massin, *Poétique*, 146–149.

28. For correspondences between the works of Messiaen and the liturgical year, see the excellent article by Jean-Rodolphe Kars, "L'oeuvre de Messiaen et l'année liturgique," *La Maison-Dieu* 207 (1996): 95–129.

29. Messiaen, *Conférence de Kyoto*, 12–13. See also Messiaen's speech on receiving the Erasmus Prize in Rössler, *Contributions*, 39–40. For a survey of theological thematics in Messiaen, see Aloyse Michaely, *Die Musik Olivier Messiaens: Untersuchungen zum Gesamtschaffen* (Hamburg: Karl Dieter Wagner, 1988), 31–39.

30. In more than one place, Messiaen expresses the need to defend his convictions against criticism. See *Conférence de Kyoto*, 1, where the most important conflicts are once again recalled. The history of this conflict and of the origin of "the case of Messiaen" is described in Hill and Simeone, *Messiaen*, 52ff.

31. Goléa, *Rencontres*, 37–39.

32. Messiaen, *Music and Color*, 16–17. See Chapter 3 for the latter. A further list of theological works used by Messiaen (till the end of the 1980s) can be found in Michaely, *Die Musik Olivier Messiaens*, 31–39.

33. Rössler, *Contributions*, 91.

34. See, for example, Henry Barraud, "Olivier Messiaen: Compositeur mystique?" *Contrepoints* 1 (January 1946): 101–102.

35. Rössler, *Contributions*, 89.

36. See Hill and Simeone, *Messiaen*, 147.

37. Goléa, *Rencontres*, 38.

38. Igor Stravinsky, *An Autobiography* (London: Calder and Boyars, 1975), 53. Italics in original.

39. Goléa, *Rencontres*, 212.

40. Ibid., 108. See also Alexander Goehr, *Finding the Key: Selected Writings of Alexander Goehr* (London: Faber & Faber, 1998), 46: "For [Messiaen], and this he perpetually emphasised to us, there was no dividing line between the observable world and the microcosm of music."

41. It is, incidentally, remarkable that Messiaen, as far as this expression goes, deems the question less relevant whether feelings and associations evoked in the composer are also musically conveyed to the audience. Goléa, *Rencontres*, 108.

42. Halbreich, *Messiaen*, 13–14.

43. Goléa, *Rencontres*, 107–108.

44. Rössler, *Beiträge*, 93.

45. Massin, *Poétique*, 130. The mosaic of texts on glory and filiation used in *La Transfiguration de Notre-Seigneur Jésus-Christ* constitutes an example of the result of such reading. See the score (Paris: Leduc, 1972), "Textes latins, suivis de leur traduction française." I will say more about this in Chapter 2.

46. Massin, *Poétique*, 122.

47. Rössler, *Contributions*, 28.

48. Messiaen, *Technique of My Musical Language*, 1:7–8.

49. Rössler, *Contributions*, 93. These statements will be discussed more fully in Chapter 5.

50. Messiaen, *Music and Color*, 28. Translation modified.

51. Massin, *Poétique*, 197.

52. Messiaen, *Music and Color*, 46–47.

53. Ibid., 211.

54. Ibid., 231. The conclusion in the last sentence is in line with Messiaen's idea—which can also be found in the work of Balthasar—that the divine is related to the beautiful.

55. Olivier Messiaen, *Lecture at Notre-Dame* (Paris: Leduc, 2001), 4. Translation modified.

56. Ibid., 8.

57. Ibid., 7.

58. Messiaen, *Music and Color*, 29.

59. There can be no misunderstanding about Messiaen's preferences in this respect: "*J'ai horreur de la psychanalyse.*" Messiaen, *Music and Color*, 213.

60. Olivier Messiaen, *Saint François d'Assise: Scènes Franciscaines* (Paris: Leduc, 1990), 89–91.

61. Massin, *Poétique*, 191. Camille Crunelle Hill mentions that Messiaen read the statement by Aquinas in P. Louis Antoine, *Lire François d'Assise: Essai sur sa spiritualité d'après ses écrits* (Paris: Éditions Franciscaines, 1967), 73. Camille Crunelle Hill, "Saint Thomas Aquinas and the Theme of Truth in Messiaen's *Saint François d'Assise*," in Siglind Bruhn, ed., *Messiaen's Language of Mystical Love* (New York: Garland, 1998), 145–146. See also Messiaen, *Music and Color*, 211. The first part of this statement will be addressed later.

62. Saint Thomas Aquinas, *Summa Theologiae* (London: Blackfriars, 1964–80), I–II, q. 101, art. 2, resp. 2.

63. Messiaen, *Music and Color*, 233; see also Halbreich, *Messiaen*, 59.

64. Kars, "Année liturgique," 121.

65. See the way this term is used in Nicolas Boileau-Despréaux, "Traité du sublime ou du merveilleux dans le discours," in *Oeuvres complètes* (Paris: Gallimard, 1966), 338. Chapter 4 contains more on the sublime.

66. These examples are taken from Messiaen, *Music and Color*, 19–37.

67. Messiaen, *Lecture at Notre-Dame*, 5–6.

68. Messiaen, *Music and Color*, 29–30.

69. Ibid., 29.

70. *Méditations sur le Mystère de la Sainte Trinité* counts as an example of the attempt to express divine attributes explicitly (Paris: Leduc, 1973).

71. See Ps 114:4: "The mountains skipped like rams, and the little hills like lambs."

72. The translations used by Messiaen were, first, the French Crampon translation, but later he would also use the Jerusalem Bible, which he appreciated for its poetic qualities. Massin, *Poétique*, 29, and the score of *Éclairs sur l'Au-delà* . . . (Paris: Leduc, 1998).

73. Messiaen, *Traité de rythme*, 1:27–28.

74. See the score of *La Transfiguration*, "Analyse succincte de chaque pièce."

75. See also the quotation from Aquinas used in part XII: "Just as the splendor of Christ's body represented the future splendor of his body, so the splendor of his clothes signified the future splendor of the saints, which will be surpassed by the splendor of Christ, just as the brightness of the snow is surpassed by the brightness of the sun." Aquinas, *Summa*, III, q. 45, art. 2, resp. 3.

76. Messiaen, *Music and Color*, 30–31. Although Messiaen occasionally mentions love as the center or synthesis of his faith (cf. ibid., 37 and 47), it does not play an important part in his sayings. But, as will become clear in the next chapters, love is nevertheless present in his work on a structural level. Sander van Maas, "Forms of Love: Messiaen's Aesthetics of *Éblouissement*," in Robert Sholl, ed., *Messiaen Studies* (Cambridge: Cambridge University Press, 2007).

77. Messiaen, *Music and Color*, 147. Cf. *Avant-scène*, 8, where he describes the effect of *Saint François d'Assise* on himself and, he hopes, on the audience: "It is a wholly interior drama, yet resplendent (*resplendissant*): I hope that the audience will be, just like me, overwhelmed and dazzled (*que le public soit, tout comme moi, ébloui*)."

78. "I'm not a theorist, only a believer, a believer dazzled by the infinity of God!" Messiaen, *Music and Color*, 28.

79. See the score, "Première Note de l'Auteur." Other occurrences in the scores of *Et exspecto resurrectionem mortuorum* (Paris: Leduc, 1966), "Détail des trois premières auditions," on the performance in the Sainte-Chapelle, where music joins the stained glass windows in a "dazzlement of colors," and *Méditations sur le Mystère de la Sainte Trinité*, introduction to Part V, where Messiaen explains his aim to represent the attribute of the Everlasting God as "dazzlement" (*éblouissement*). With respect to the latter, see Messiaen, *Music and Color*, 126: "I treated this notion

like a dazzlement, a glittering flash of color" (*un éblouissement, un scintillement coloré*). Translation modified.

80. The word *éblouissement* is, according to *Le grand Robert* (2nd ed., 1985) derived from the Latin *exblaudire*, formed in turn from the French *blaudi*, meaning "weak." Littré's *Dictionnaire* (1885) suggests a possible double origin: *bleu* (cf. "*faire bleu devant les yeux*") and the High German *blödi*, allegedly meaning "the uncertain, forbidden." The first meaning of *éblouir* in *Robert* is given as "blinding, hurting" (*aveugler, blesser*). Second, *éblouir* means "to strike the eye or spirit with admiration" (*frapper d'admiration* [*la vue ou l'esprit*]); a large group of words is connected to this: *émerveiller* (fill with wonder), *épater* (astonish), *étonner* (amaze), *étourdir* (bewilder), *fasciner* (fascinate), *hypnotiser* (hypnotize), *séduire* (seduce), *surprendre* (surprise), *troubler* (cloud, disturb), and *impressioner* (impress, move). A third meaning of *éblouir* is "to seduce by deception" (*séduire en trompant*)—with the synonyms of abusing and tricking or fooling, meanings that will recur in the discussions of Chapters 3 and 6. *Le grand Robert* defines the noun *éblouissement* as "clouding of the eye provoked by an inner cause (weakness, congestion) or an external cause (shock), generally accompanied by vertigo." Synonyms to *éblouissement* are *berlue* or *hallucination* (distorted view), *syncope* (in the medical sense, faintness), *trouble* (cloudiness), *vertige* (vertigo), and *émerveillement* (wonder), *étonnement* (amazement), and *fascination* and *surprise*.

81. See the score, "Sujet de l'oeuvre et commentaire de chaque mouvement."

82. Rössler, *Contributions*, 43–44; Messiaen, *Music and Color*, 37; Messiaen, *Conférence de Kyoto*, 5–6.

83. *Olivier Messiaen: The Music of Faith.*

84. Messiaen, *Lecture at Notre-Dame*, 13. Translation modified. See also his remarks in *Music and Color*, 63 and 139. Messiaen's account of *éblouissement* is also published on CD; see *Olivier Messiaen: Les couleurs du temps* (INA/Radio France, 2000), CD 2, track 4. Messiaen (in *Music and Color*, 63): "I adore medieval stained glass because, between the lead trefoils, circles, and diamond patterns surrounding the colored figures, there is generally a small area of red crosses against a blue background or of blue crosses against a red background, which combine to give the whole stained-glass window a violet transparency. From a distance, the eye distinguishes neither the figures not the crosses; it sees nothing but an immense violet."

85. Messiaen, *Music and Color*, 37.

86. Ibid. For a general introduction to, and bibliography of, the subject and cultural history of synesthetics, see Nicholas Cook, *Analysing Musical Multimedia* (Oxford: Clarendon Press, 1998), 24–56.

87. Simon Baron-Cohen and John E. Harrison, *Synaesthesia: Classic and Contemporary Readings* (Cambridge, Mass.: Blackwell, 1997), 65–66. In the case of dysesthesia, the person concerned cannot decide conclusively whether she or he has truly heard something that gives a "false" visual stimulation, or whether truly something was seen that also generated a "false" auditory stimulation.

88. Messiaen, *Music and Color*, 40.

89. Rössler, *Contributions*, 43. The exhaustive survey of these sound-colors is to found in Messiaen, *Traité de rythme*, vol. 7.

90. See, respectively, Messiaen, *Music and Color*, 40; Messiaen, *Lecture at Notre-Dame*, 11; Rössler, *Contributions*, 111.

91. Rössler, *Contributions*, 118.

92. Messiaen, *Music and Color*, 146–147. Jonathan Bernard, "Messiaen's Synaesthesia: The Correspondence Between Color and Sound Structure in His Music," in *Music Perception* 4, no. 1 (Fall 1986): 41–42.

93. Messiaen, *Lecture at Notre-Dame*, 4 n. 9ff. He also speaks occasionally of "colored music" (as in ibid., 15).

94. See Chapter 5.

95. Messiaen, *Lecture at Notre-Dame*, 12. Translation modified. Synesthesia therefore has, as such, and regardless of the dazzling effects it can convey when very intense, already a religious potential. It transcends the boundaries of the individual senses, which is one step in the direction of holism of the senses. Messiaen speaks in particular of the relation between sound and color, but he has also attempted, as the title of his work for orchestra *Chronochromie* suggests (which is not about synesthesia but about timbral coloring) to level (or surpass) the barrier between rhythm and color. With respect to the *deçî-tâla* 26b of Sharngadeva ("*mishra varna*," in *Traité de rythme*, 1:278), he speaks, entirely in the spirit of sound-color of a "rainbow of durations." See *Méditations sur le Mystère de la Sainte Trinité*, preface to Part VII: "colors of durations." The term "chromatic durations" is also known: the sequence of consecutive whole numbers (a rhythm, for example, existing of a sequence of 5, 6, 7, 8, and 9 sixteenths).

96. Messiaen says that he also sees colors when listening to music by, for example, Chopin or Debussy. When dazzlement and music is at stake, however, he refers—here and elsewhere—to his own work exclusively.

97. Messiaen, *Lecture at Notre-Dame*, 15.

98. Ibid., 16.

99. Messiaen, *Lecture at Notre-Dame*, 14. Translation modified; italics in original.

100. Ibid., 4. Translation modified.

101. Messiaen, *Music and Color*, 214.

102. Ibid., 246. Messiaen, *Conférence de Kyoto*, 18.

103. *Saint François*, 100.

104. Massin, *Poétique*, 191.

105. Aquinas, *Summa*, I, q. 12, art. 1, resp.

## 2. Five Times Breakthrough

1. Peter Hill and Nigel Simeone, *Messiaen* (New Haven: Yale University Press, 2005), 353.

2. Olivier Messiaen, *Conférence de Kyoto* (Paris: Leduc, 1988), 14–16. The other work is *Saint François d'Assise*, which is referred to in much less detail.

3. For the technical descriptions of these passages, I will often refer to Aloyse Michaely's excellent *Die Musik Olivier Messiaens: Untersuchungen zum Gesamtschaffen*

(Hamburg: Karl Dieter Wagner, 1988). This work, which is remarkably little referred to in the English language, contains so far the only commentary that describes the technique of these passages with ample reference to Messiaen's other works.

4. For the history of its composition, see Hill and Simeone, *Messiaen*, 263–275.

5. Thomas Aquinas, *Summa Theologiae* (London: Blackfriars, 1964–80), Vol. III, q. 45, art. 4, resp. 2.

6. Messiaen, *Conférence de Kyoto*, 14–16. The subsequent sections are each headed by subsequent quotations from this passage.

7. Olivier Messiaen, *Music and Color: Conversations with Claude Samuel* (Portland, Ore.: Amadeus Press, 1994), 57.

8. Olivier Messiaen, *La Transfiguration de Notre-Seigneur Jésus-Christ* (Paris: Leduc, 1972), Part VIII, at fig. 6. See Messiaen's commentary on this part that prefaces the score, "Succinct Analysis of Each Piece."

9. Ibid.

10. Messiaen, *Music and Color*, 149, and *Conférence de Kyoto*, 15. On Messiaen's view of sono-iconographic conventions, see *Music and Color*, 28.

11. See Olivier Messiaen, *Traité de rythme, de couleur, et d'ornithologie* (Paris: Leduc, 1994–2002), 7:277–280 and 165–172. See also Michaely, *Untersuchungen*, 115–22, in particular her comprehensive harmonic analysis at 121.

12. See the passages Messiaen quotes from Parts VIII and XII in particular. The passage from Part IX also involves a grand scale change in texture, but here the new texture builds up more gradually. Obviously, the concept of sudden change does not apply to the chorales that Messiaen mentions (Parts VII and XIV).

13. Aquinas, *Summa*, III, q. 45, art. 4, resp. Translation based on the Latin text as quoted by Messiaen (cf. preface to the score).

14. See the elaborate analysis of Part IX in Michaely, *Untersuchungen*, 611–634. See, with regard to the form of this part, the scheme in ibid., 634. The first half runs from m. 1 to 144 (figs. 1–25), the second from m. 145 to 306 (figs. 26–52). There are more instances of Messiaen's employing musical form as an autonomous matrix, as for instance the passage from Part XII or the work for organ *Méditations sur le Mystère de la Sainte Trinité* (Paris: Leduc, 1973), Parts II, V, and VI.

15. The number three plays a large part in Part IX. Michaely even postulates that the entire part is devoted to this number (Michaely, *Untersuchungen*, 632). It is a line of analysis that is not followed here, in view of Messiaen's suggestion that in this part symbolism—at this level in any case—is erased with the experience of *éblouissement*.

16. With respect to the tam-tam, see the introductions to the recitatives such as Part VIII. Messiaen began to deploy this motif as early as in *Couleurs de la Cité céleste*. See the score (Paris: Leduc, 1966), figs. 30 and 96. It recurs in *Et exspecto resurrectionem mortuorum* (Paris: Leduc, 1966), Part IV, figs. 1, 5, 12, 18, 27 and thrice in the Finale (fig. 36 ff.).

17. For the theme and musical figure of the abyss in Messiaen, see Aloyse Michaely, "L'Abîme: Das Bild des Abgrunds bei Olivier Messiaen," in *Musik-Konzepte* 28 (Munich: Edition text + kritik, 1982), and the earlier mentioned passage from her *Untersuchungen*, especially 629–632.

18. See, for example, Messiaen's commentary on Part II of *La Transfiguration*, prefacing the score; the text of his song-cycle *Harawi*; or the ninth part of *Éclairs sur l'Au-delà*. . . . On the further meaning of birds and bird song in Messiaen, see Sherlaw Johnson, "Birdsong," in Hill, *Companion*, 257–259.

19. Igor Stravinsky, *The Rite of Spring* (London: Boosey and Hawkes, 1947), "Introduction," especially fig. 12, mm. 4–10. There are other instances in *La Transfiguration* that call the *Sacre* to mind. Compare, for example, the orchestral accents in Part XIII, figs. 38–39, to *The Rite of Spring*, "Sacrificial Dance (The Chosen One)," figs. 169 and 170.

20. By "mallets," I mean the family of stick-played idiophones with definite pitch, such as the marimba, the xylophone, the vibraphone, and the xylorimba.

21. The division of these structural layers is as follows: *Bottom level*: gongs, cellos, altos, horns, bass clarinet; *Middle level*: chimes, cellos, second violins, bassoon, clarinets; *Upper level*: Turkish cymbals, first violins, and high woodwinds.

22. Michaely, *Untersuchungen*, 615–616. For a specification of these chords, see Messiaen, *Traité de rythme*, 7:149.

23. Michaely, *Untersuchungen*, 616.

24. Messiaen, *Music and Color*, 48. See the section on this subject in *Technique of My Musical Language* (Paris: Leduc, 1956), 1:13. The use of prime numbers, such as the number three in Part IX, is part of this "charm" too. See *Music and Color*, 79.

25. Messiaen, *Music and Color*, 48.

26. Ibid.

27. See, for example, with respect to the upper layer, the "restart" at fig. 50, m. 8.

28. Michaely, *Untersuchungen*, 619–624. Messiaen found a list of *deçî-tâlas* in an article by Joanny Grosset. The Indian theoretician Sharngadeva included this list in his famous thirteenth-century tract *Samgita-ratnakara*. According to Grosset, the literal meaning of the term *deçî-tâla* is regional or folk (*deçî*) rhythm or composed measure (*tâla*). In ancient Indian theory of music, these popular rhythms are distinguished from classic rhythms (*marga*). Joanny Grosset, "Inde: Histoire de la musique depuis l'origine jusqu'à nos jours," in Albert Lavignac, ed., *Encyclopédie de la musique et dictionnaire du conservatoire* (Paris: Delagrave, 1921), 1:301–304. Messiaen gave an interpretation in his music of a number of the popular rhythms, adapting them to his own rhythmical vocabulary. For Messiaen's version of this list and examples of the way he used these rhythms, see *Traité de rythme*, 1:271–368. In the literature on Messiaen, the names of these *tâlas* are consequently used in French transliteration. This is to highlight Messiaen's speculative usage of Grosset's *deçî-tâlas*, among other things.

29. See the scheme in Michaely, *Untersuchungen*, 620.

30. Ibid., 621–624.

31. For a technical analysis of Part VI, see ibid., 739–743.

32. The same setting is also used for *Et exspecto*, Part I, fig. 5, where in a footnote the reader is warned that "Here, the cry from the abyss!" (*Ici, le cri de l'abîme!*). Cf. Michaely, "L'Abîme," 30–32.

33. *La Transfiguration*, "Analyse succincte."

34. Messiaen, *Traité de rythme*, 7:297. He states that it is here "un blue général, assez léger, clair et translucide, genre blue de Chartres" (a generic blue, but soft, clear, and transparent, a Chartres blue).

35. The E-major triad is an important point of departure and also resting-point in the work, although there is no question of a functional harmonic tonality, in the strict sense, for the work as whole.

36. Messiaen, *Traité de rythme*, 7:122.

37. Footnote to fig. 23 in the score.

38. Michaely, *Untersuchungen*, 745.

39. Messiaen did not publish an analysis of the second appearance of the passage, only of the first. Set a major third lower, it has, according to Messiaen, the following transition: from red (E major) in a context of gold-brown (second mode, second transposition), to an "abyss" in Chartres blue (A-flat major). The contrast then is mostly between red and blue. Messiaen, *Traité de rythme*, 7:296–297.

40. The blue returns quite soon in this sparkle, as the four first color chords of the piano are from the 'blue' second mode (first transposition). The subsequent chord however is again a sparkling chord (in the terminology of Messiaen: a turning chord, first type, 12-B), with a yellow-gold luster (*or jaune éclatant*). See Messiaen, *Traité de rythme*, 7:160.

41. *La Transfiguration*, "Analyse succincte."

42. With Messiaen, the tritone often appears in the closing cadenzas where normally one would have a dominant on the fifth degree.

43. Messiaen, *Music and Color*, 148–149. See also Messiaen, *Traité de rythme*, 7:309–315.

44. Whether Messiaen actually intended the following interpretation is not relevant here.

45. On the connections between color, transposition, and register, see Messiaen, *Lecture at Notre-Dame* (Paris: Leduc, 2001), 11.

46. See Messiaen, *Traité de rythme*, 7:168.

47. In the classic color theories of Goethe and Johannes Itten, green is the complementary contrastive to red. The contrast between red and blue is of a different nature: it is a cold-warm contrast. See Johannes Itten, *The Elements of Color*, ed. Faber Birren, trans. Ernst van Hagen (New York: John Wiley, 1970), 48. Studies of the reaction to color with photosensitive people show that this contrast often causes extreme perceptual reactions, including epileptic fits in extreme cases. See J. Parra et al., "Removal of Epileptogenic Sequences from Video Material: The Role of Color," *Neurology* 64, no. 5 (March 8, 2005): 787–791. In this study, the composition of images, speed alterations, and so on remained constant.

48. When such a saturated primary color appears, one may also expect the appearance of its so-called simultaneous contrast, in this case a green halo around the red. See Messiaen, *Lecture at Notre-Dame*, 10.

49. Naturally, the formal shape of this narrative is too indeterminate to be understood in religious terms exclusively. In the context of a religious interpretation, however, it does shape the kind of religious narrative that can be read in the music. See also Chapter 3.

50. The description and analysis of Part VII has brought forward that it is too risky to postulate a chord's color purely on the basis of the way it fits in a mode or its appearance in other works. Often, the context of the chord turns out to have an unanticipated effect on the eventual result. The major triad on E, for example, properly has the color red, but when it appears in Messiaen's third mode (first and second transposition) it is associated with orange and gray, respectively. What forces reign in this field of associations, and what shade eventually results, only Messiaen can say with any certainty—and even for him it was not always easy to ascertain what he experienced precisely. See his remarks in the documentary for Dutch television *Olivier Messiaen*, dir. Cherry Duyns and Reinbert de Leeuw (VPRO Television, 1994).

51. Michaely, *Untersuchungen*, 165. Her division runs as follows: mm. 1–20; 21–46; 47–76.

52. They do occur in Parts IX and XII.

53. This happens first in m. 5. More saturated passages occur in mm. 25–26, 28–29, 42, 57–58, 61, 63, 71, and 73–74. The majority of these chords can thus be found in the third part, after m. 46.

54. For example, the play of piccolos in m. 40.

55. Messiaen describes the colors of the chords in this formation as descending from "from high to low."

56. This holds only, of course, for absolute pitches, not for registers.

57. Naturally, this also depends on the performance (balance in the orchestra, acoustical circumstances, point of listening, and so on). For this analysis, my reference is Olivier Messiaen, *La Transfiguration de Notre Seigneur Jésus-Christ*, cond. Reinbert de Leeuw (2 CDs, Montaigne Auvidis 782040, 1994).

58. On Messiaen and the sublime, see Chapter 4. The theme of the abyss is, incidentally, concealed in a completely unexpected way in both chorales through the presence of a citation from Alban Berg's opera *Wozzeck* (see Michaely, *Untersuchungen*, 153–156). This concerns a series of three chords from act I, scene 2, where Wozzeck (sensitive to the invisible) meets Andres (totally insensitive to the invisible).

59. Compare the biblical passages where the special is similarly framed, as in the story in Jn 2:1–11 on the wedding at Cana. The matter-of-fact signing off in verse 11 is in striking contrast to the lively descriptions of the miraculous events in the previous verses. In the Gregorian setting of the text, the communio antiphone *Dicit Dominus: Implete hydria* becomes the effect of announcing and signing off (*Dicit Dominus*: respectively "*Hoc signum fecit Iesus primum coram discipulis suis*"); redoubled by the theatrical melody of the middle piece, especially on the groom's exclaiming "*Servasti vinum bonum usque adhuc*" (thou hast kept the good wine until now). This exclamation, which forms a true breakthrough in the piece, is in turn prepared for by a somewhat indeterminate setting (twice *sa*, in chant terminology, and a deceptive rest on *fa*) of the dry statement "*Dicit sponso*" and ends with the transition to "*Hoc fecit.*" This technique has surprisingly much in common with the techniques

used by Messiaen, more than a thousand years hence. See *Graduale Triplex* (Solesmes, France: Abbaye Saint-Pierre de Solesmes & Desclée, 1979), 263.

60. Hill and Simeone, *Messiaen*, 62.

## 3. Balthasar and the Religion of Music

1. Olivier Messiaen, *Music and Color: Conversations with Claude Samuel* (Portland, Ore.: Amadeus Press, 1994), 17, 211; Brigitte Massin, *Olivier Messiaen: Une poétique du merveilleux* (Aix-en-Provence: Alinéa, 1989), 73, 105–106, 151. To my knowledge, Messiaen does not use verbatim quotes of Balthasar in his writings, as he did with Aquinas.

2. Massin, *Olivier Messiaen*, 73; Pascal Ide, "Une rencontre décisive," in *Olivier Messiaen, homme de foi: Regard sur son oeuvre d'orgue* (Paris: Trinité Média Communication, 1995), 76 n. 1.

3. Louis Antoine, *Lire François d'Assise: Essai sur la Spiritualité d'après ses écrits* (Paris: Éditions Franciscaines, 1967), 69 ff. For references to Balthasar in Messiaen, see Peter Hill and Nigel Simeone, *Messiaen* (New Haven: Yale University Press, 2005), 343–344. This refers to the French translation of Hans Urs von Balthasar, "Die Abwesenheiten Jesu," in *Neue Klarstellungen* (Einsiedeln, Switzerland: Johannes Verlag, 1979), 28 ff. See also Hans Urs von Balthasar, *New Elucidations* (San Francisco: Ignatius Press, 1986), 46–60; *Saint François d'Assise* (Paris: Premières Loges, 1992), 33; Cathérine Massip, *Portrait(s) d'Olivier Messiaen* (Paris: Bibliothèque Nationale de France, 1996), 165; Aloyse Michaely, *Die Musik Olivier Messiaens: Untersuchungen zum Gesamtschaffen* (Hamburg: Karl Dieter Wagner, 1988), 742; Pascal Ide, "Olivier Messiaen, musicien de la gloire de Dieu," *Communio* 19, no. 5 (September–October 1994): 97.

4. Alain Michel, "La Transfiguration et la Beauté: d'Olivier Messiaen à Urs von Balthasar," *La recherche artistique*, November–December 1978, 86–89.

5. Michel, "La Transfiguration et la Beauté," 86.

6. There is a certain irony in the fact that Messiaen mentions (in *Music and Color*, 211) Saint Francis while discussing Balthasar.

7. Hans Urs von Balthasar, *The Glory of the Lord: A Theological Aesthetics* (San Francisco: Ignatius Press, 1982), 1:50.

8. Ibid., 38.

9. Ibid.

10. Ibid., 19–20.

11. Ibid., 10.

12. Balthasar, *The Glory of the Lord*, 1:33. According to Balthasar (ibid., 121), this experience should not be understood in a mere psychological sense, but as "the movement of man's whole being away from himself and towards God [*in Gott hinein*] through Christ." Accordingly, *Hingerissenwerden* is understood in terms of *eros* and *agapè*. See also Mario Saint-Pierre, *Beauté, bonté, vérité chez Hans Urs von Balthasar* (Paris: Éditions du Cerf, 1998), 259–263.

13. Balthasar, *The Glory of the Lord*, 1:118.

14. Ibid., 125.

15. See Saint-Pierre, *Beauté, bonté, vérité*, 37–46; Elio Guerriero, *Hans Urs von Balthasar* (Paris: Desclée de Brouwer, 1993), 23–28, 85–86; Hans Urs von Balthasar, "Bekenntnis zu Mozart," in *Die Entwicklung der musikalischen Idee (Versuch einer Synthese der Musik)/Bekenntnis zu Mozart* (Einsiedeln, Switzerland: Johannes Verlag, 1998). For an example of musical metaphorics, see the prologue to *Truth Is Symphonic: Aspects of Christian Pluralism*, trans. Graham Harrison (San Francisco: Ignatius Press, 1987).

16. This genealogy of music seems to imply that in the last stage in history, the most complete information of the divine is conceivable. That, however, would be inconsistent with the idea of "eternally valid answers" of which Gregorian chant, which should be ranged with the second stage, was an example.

17. Saint-Pierre, *Beauté, bonté, vérité*, 64–65.

18. Ibid., 69.

19. Ibid., 78. It should be noted that these comments ignore Nietzsche's questioning of the Apollonian-Dionysian dualism in his later works, notably when he discusses the concepts of *Rausch* and the Grand Style.

20. Ibid., 75, 81. The terminology is derived from Ernst Bloch, *The Spirit of Utopia*. The thematics of clairaudience will be addressed in Chapter 6.

21. Ibid., 79. This may look confusing because Balthasar related melody to the Dionysian. His rejection of the Dionysian only concerns the energetic force of melody when it is admired and elevated in isolation. Balthasar defends melody as form (*Gestalt*), where the vital life force is tied to Apollonian form.

22. As Pascal Ide has shown, the key terms of Balthasar's theological aesthetics (which include, apart from *Gestalt*, *Mysterium*, *Einfaltungen*, *Enthüllung* and *Verhüllung*) go back to Goethe's *Pflanzenmorfologie*. Pascal Ide, *Être et mystère: La philosophie de Hans Urs von Balthasar* (Brussels: Culture et Vérité, 1995), 177–180.

23. Balthasar, *The Glory of the Lord*, 1:513.

24. Balthasar, *Epilogue*, 61.

25. Claude Samuel, *Permanences d'Olivier Messiaen: Dialogues et commentaires* (Arles: Actes Sud, 1999), 51–52.

26. Balthasar, *Die Entwicklung*, 26–27.

27. A similar combination of forces is to be found in rhythm, univocally understood as form by Balthasar (just as in Plato). Pierre Sauvanet, *Le rythme grec d'Héraclite à Aristote* (Paris: Presses Universitaires de France, 1999), 11–21.

28. Balthasar, *Die Entwicklung*, 39–40. A few pages later, Balthasar refers to concentration and expansion as the qualities that connect music to the divine. This can also mean that music concentrates in the subject's inwardness and at once directs the subject to the cosmic grandeur of mystery.

29. Ibid., 40.

30. Ibid., 55.

31. Saint-Pierre, *Beauté, bonté, vérité*, 98–100. There are a number of other passages in Balthasar apart from those mentioned by Saint-Pierre that appear to indicate some influence of the reconciliatory logics of Goethe; see Balthasar, *Die*

*Entwicklung*, 10, 40–41, 48, 51, 56. Most of these moments also indicate a Hegelian strain of thought, despite Saint-Pierre's arguments for Goethe.

32. Saint-Pierre, *Beauté, bonté, vérité*, 98; Balthasar, *Die Entwicklung*, 55.

33. Saint-Pierre, *Beauté, bonté, vérité*, 100. Although Hegel certainly is somewhat one-dimensional, he does speak in the *Lectures on Fine Art* of the soul's being lifted "to the apprehension of a higher sphere." This would come about because music (that is, melody) as "the immediate expression of the inner life" becomes "immediately inner" and imparts to subjectivity "ideality and liberation." Leaving the reduction to absolute knowledge apart, it certainly seems possible to arrive at a Balthasarian notion of form (simultaneous immanence and transcendence) starting from Hegel's description of musical experience. G. W. F. Hegel, *Lectures on Fine Art*, trans. T. M. Knox (Oxford: Clarendon Press, 1988), 2:933.

34. Balthasar, *Die Entwicklung*, 57.

35. Saint-Pierre, *Beauté, bonté, vérité*, 53, 102.

36. Ibid., 103–104.

37. Georg Bichlmair, cited in ibid., 103–104. It can be noticed that Bichlmair speaks of Logos in the same bio-organic terms as Balthasar in his treatise.

38. Balthasar, *Die Entwicklung*, 57.

39. Saint-Pierre, *Beauté, bonté, vérité*, 107.

40. Ibid., 109. The last question that is concerned with the ability to listen will be addressed in Chapter 5, concerning the spiritual senses.

41. Juan de la Cruz, *Canto Espiritual*, Stanza XV.

42. For the theological concept of configuration, see Messiaen, *la Transfiguration*, the words to Part IX as cited in Chapter 2.

43. Saint-Pierre, 110. Music and Logos still are analogous, not the same.

44. Ibid.

45. Rhythm can be understood in terms of an oscillation between the poles of form (*skhéma*) and flow (*rhéo*). Balthasar's image of Logos as "flowing in the world" can, with respect to the latter pole, be viewed as a way of musicalizing the Word. In this interpretation, his text alludes to the ancient representation of Christ as the New Song (cf. Clement of Alexandria), the one and only Orpheus. The passage is, unfortunately, too gnomic to support this interpretation.

46. Balthasar, *Die Entwicklung*, 8, 10.

47. Ibid., 10.

48. Ibid., 56. It is significant to recollect that Balthasar wrote his treatise in 1925, not long after Schoenberg formulated the dodecaphonic method (1923).

49. Ibid.

50. Johann Roten, "Marian Light on Our Human Mystery," in Bede McGregor and Thomas Norris, eds., *The Beauty of Christ: An Introduction to the Theology of Hans Urs von Balthasar* (Edinburgh: T&T Clark, 1994), 126–131.

51. Balthasar, *The Glory of the Lord*, 1:247; Roten, "Marian Light," 127, 130; Saint-Pierre, *Beauté, bonté, vérité*, 262. In Chapter 4 these dynamics will be addressed more fully.

52. The status of language in theology has been the focus of intense philosophical debate in the past decades. Derrida, Lyotard, and Mark C. Taylor, among others, have argued for different reasons that the entire notion of stable language should be seriously doubted. In other words, the appeal on the linguistic sign is not the ideal strategy to check the differentiality of music. For Lyotard's position, see Chapter 5.

53. Ide, "Olivier Messiaen théologien?" in Massip, *Portrait(s) d'Olivier Messiaen*, 40–41. Ide draws on the work of Harry Halbreich, among others.

54. Ibid., 42.

55. Pascal Ide, "Olivier Messiaen, musicien de la gloire de Dieu," 115.

56. Ibid., 116.

57. Ibid., 106. The levels concern common light, the filtered light of stained-glass windows, and eternal light.

58. Ibid., 111–113.

59. Ibid., 112.

60. Saint Thomas Aquinas, *Summa Theologiae* (London: Blackfriars, 1964–80), I, q. 36, art. 4. For the concept of *pondus amoris*, see Saint Augustine, *De civitate Dei*, xi, xvi; *De musica*, 424 (VI, XI, 29); *Confessiones*, XIII, 9, 10. Messiaen also uses the concept of *spiration*; see *Méditations sur le Mystère de la Sainte Trinité* (Paris: Leduc, 1973), Part I, preface.

61. Ide is hesitant in his own conclusions, as if he is aware of the incongruence: "Whatever is the case in this interpretation." Ide, "Olivier Messiaen, musicien de la gloire de Dieu," 112.

62. See the chapter "Song" in Lawrence Kramer, *Music and Poetry: The Nineteenth Century and After* (Berkeley: University of California Press, 1984). The content of musical comment is less important. The concern here is with the reduction involved in letting music speak or ventriloquize in a "propositional" way at all.

63. Messiaen, *Music and Color*, 20.

64. Messiaen, score of *Méditations sur le Mystère de la Sainte Trinité*, 39.

65. Ibid., "Le langage communicable."

66. See, for instance, *Méditations* Part 1 (m. 52 ff), Part 3 (integrally), Part 7 (m. 20 ff).

67. See Andrew Shenton, "Speaking with the Tongues of Men and of Angels: Messiaen's 'langage communicable,'" in Siglind Bruhn, ed., *Messiaen's Language of Mystical Love* (New York: Garland, 1998), 225–245.

68. Emphasis added. The technique of montage in Messiaen provides another example. Cutting up music suggests in this case a form of musical censorship to make way for the intended message. See also *Couleurs de la Cité céleste* (Paris: Leduc, 1966).

69. Messiaen in *Saint François d'Assise*, 14.

70. Messiaen, *Music and Color*, 212–214.

71. Massin, *Poétique*, 208–209.

72. Saint Augustine, *Confessions*, trans. R. S. Pine-Coffin (London: Penguin, 1961), 238 ff. James McKinnon, *Music in Early Christian Literature* (Cambridge: Cambridge University Press, 1999), nos. 351 and 352.

73. The passage makes clear that Augustine cannot always determine whether he is being moved by the beauty of music or by the contents of words. In any case, music adds much to the sense of being religiously moved, so much that it is marked as indispensable. This specific appreciation of music can already be found with Basil the Great and Niceta of Remesiana. McKinnon, *Music in Early Christian Literature*, nos. 130 and 306.

74. Henry Chadwick, "Why Music in Church?" in *Tradition and Exploration: Collected Papers on Theology and the Church* (Norwich: Canterbury Press, 1994), 208.

75. Theologically speaking, the proper experience of *éblouissement* is sinful. See Augustine's *éblouissement* in Book VII of the *Confessions*, 147: "Your light shone upon me in its brilliance, and I thrilled with love and dread alike. And I realized that I was far away from you."

76. McKinnon, *Music in Early Christian Literature*, 352.

77. Balthasar, *Herrlichkeit: Eine theologische Aesthetik* (Einsiedeln, Switzerland: Johannes Verlag, 1988), 2:122.

78. Balthasar, *Die Entwicklung*, 10.

79. There is here an unexpected similarity between his thought and that of Augustine, when in a psalm commentary the latter expresses his confidence in the Christian value of wordless, ecstatic jubilance. It should be noted, however, that Augustine distinguishes between jubilating "in confession," which he also describes as "in justification," and jubilating "in confusion." McKinnon, *Music in Early Christian Literature*, 361.

80. Balthasar, *Die Entwicklung*, 43, emphasis added; see also ibid., 57: "unaussprechlich-überwörtlich."

81. The construct that music is elevated above all the other arts and is not the representation of the divine, but its testimony, seems to derive from Schopenhauer and (via him) Wilhelm Wackenroder and Ludwig Tieck. See Carl Dahlhaus, "Hegel und die Musik seiner Zeit," in Otto Pöggeler and Annemarie Gethmann-Siefert, eds., *Kunsterfahrung und Kulturpolitik im Berlin Hegels* (Bonn: Bouvier Verlag Herbert Grundmann, 1983), 335.

82. Unfortunately, this cardinal point in Balthasar's musical theology is not further elucidated.

83. Balthasar, *Die Entwicklung*, 43, 47.

84. See Immanuel Kant, *Critique of Judgment*, trans. Werner S. Pluhar (Indianapolis: Hackett, 1987), note to §49.

85. Wilhelm Seidel, "Absolute Musik," in *Die Musik in Geschichte und Gegenwart* (Kassel, Germany: Bärenreiter, 1994), 1:15–24.

86. Carl Dahlhaus, *The Idea of Absolute Music*, trans. Roger Lustig (Chicago: University of Chicago Press, 1989), 7.

87. Kant, *Critique of Judgment*, §51; see also §53–§54.

88. Ibid., §53.

89. For a survey of this development, see John Neubauer, *The Emancipation of Music from Language: Departures from Mimesis in Eighteenth-Century Aesthetics* (New Haven: Yale University Press, 1986), especially 193–210, and Wilhelm Seidel,

"Absolute Musik und Kunstreligion um 1800," in Helga de la Motte-Haber, ed., *Musik und Religion* (Laaber, Germany: Laaber, 2003), 135–138.

90. Eduard Hanslick, *On the Musically Beautiful: A Contribution Toward the Revision of the Aesthetics of Music*, trans. Geoffrey Payzant (Indianapolis: Hackett, 1986), 30.

91. Seidel, "Absolute Musik," in Daniel K. L. Chua, *Absolute Music and the Construction of Meaning* (Cambridge: Cambridge University Press, 1999), 168–172.

92. See Chapter 4.

93. E. T. A. Hoffmann, "Alte und neue Kirchenmusik," in David Charlton, ed., *E. T. A. Hoffmann's Musical Writings: Kreisleriana, The Poet and the Composer, Music Criticism*, trans. Martyn Clarke (Cambridge: Cambridge University Press, 1989), 355–356. Hoffmann's approach to history resembles somewhat that of Hegel in *Phenomenology of the Spirit*. His ideas on the essential Christianness in music cannot be reconciled, however, with the Hegelian notion of *Kunstreligion*, which strictly and exclusively refers to the presence of Greek deities in sculpture. This unity of art and religion was never achieved again. Greek *Kunstreligion* was superseded by Christianity, which is not religion of art but revealed religion. This implies that Hoffmann's concept of *Kunstreligion*, where *musical* aesthetic form is melted with *Christian* religious significance, would have been unthinkable to Hegel.

94. Ibid., 355.

95. E. T. A. Hoffmann, "Beethoven's Fifth Symphony," in Charlton, *E. T. A. Hoffmann's Musical Writings*, 238; Dahlhaus, *The Idea of Absolute Music*, 74.

96. When Messiaen claims (Samuel, *Permanences*, 26) to have done something original in bringing with *Trois petites Liturgies* and *La Transfiguration* the Catholic liturgy outside the church, the uniqueness of his acts does not concern the extramural transference (Hoffmann did something similar in his own manner) but resides rather in the fact that the Catholic as such is retained in such a move.

97. Dahlhaus, *The Idea of Absolute Music*, 115.

98. Ibid., 63.

99. Ibid., 103–116. Theodor W. Adorno, "Music and Language: A Fragment," in *Quasi una Fantasia: Essays on Modern Music*, trans. Roy Livingstone (New York: Verso, 2002), 2.

100. As was shown by Lydia Goehr, programmatic music—from which absolute music ostentatiously frees itself—was not all about worldly reference but involved transcendental signification, too. The difference between programmatic and absolute music is therefore less great than often stated. Lydia Goehr, *The Imaginary Museum of Musical Works* (Oxford: Clarendon Press, 1997), 213–214.

101. Balthasar, *Die Entwicklung*, 48.

102. Ibid.

103. Jean-Luc Nancy, *The Muses* (Stanford: Stanford University Press, 1996), 99. Thinking through the relation between music and religion today, would once again involve confronting Hegel with Wagner. Richard Wagner, "Religion and Art," in *Religion and Art*, trans. W. Ashton Ellis (Lincoln: University of Nebraska Press, 1994), 211.

104. Aquinas, *Summa Theologiae*, II–II, q. 91 art. 2 resp. 5.

105. As Marrou, he is known as the author of *Saint Augustin et la fin de la culture antique* (Paris: Boccard, 1983). It is less widely known that he wrote a number of books on music, using the pen name of Henri Davenson. Apart from *Traité de la musique selon l'esprit de Saint Augustin*, these are *Les troubadours* (Paris: Seuil, 1961) and *Le livre des chansons: Ou introduction à la connaissance de la chanson populaire, s'ensuivent cent trent-neuf belles chansons anciennes* (Neuchatel: Éditions de la Baconnière, 1946).

106. Henri Davenson, *Traité de la musique selon l'esprit de Saint Augustin* (Neuchatel: Éditions de la Baconnière, 1942; repr. 1944), 68–71.

107. Ibid., 70.

108. Plotinus, *Enneads*, trans. Stephen MacKenna (London: Penguin, 1991), 411.

109. Davenson, *Traité de la musique*, 26–32.

110. Davenson appears, just as does Balthasar, to be playing down the structural nature of the Augustinian dilemma. First, he strangely suggests that Augustine's not being a musician accounts for his "suspicious and hostile attitude regarding music," and then he posits that Augustine did not differ from the other church fathers in his worries about the pagan association of music and that such worries are not of our age (104). Augustine is not making a generic distinction, however, between theater music and church music. Neither is he concerned with the alleged idolatrous nature of pagan musical practice. Augustine is really concerned with the aporectic nature (indispensable but dangerous) of musical beauty as such. The systematic philosophical and theological problem is not solved by becoming a musician—just the reverse.

111. Philippe Lacoue-Labarthe, *Musica Ficta: Figures of Wagner* (Stanford: Stanford University Press, 1994), 115.

112. Davenson, *Traité de la musique*, 91. Messiaen was aware of Marrou's rejection of his music. Accordingly, he professed little interest to go and read his work. Massin, *Poétique*, 177–178.

113. Massin, *Poétique*, 183, emphasis added; see also 129.


## 4. The Gift of Dazzlement

1. As will be discussed later herein, this reduced musical phenomenon can be referred to in Jean-Luc Marion's terms as both a "poor" and "common" phenomenon.

2. This latter type of saturation also subsumes the sense of repletion that characterizes Messiaen's oeuvre in general: saturation with material, perspectives, variations, and so forth.

3. Pascal Ide, "Olivier Messiaen, musicien de la gloire de Dieu," *Communio* 19, no. 5 (September–October 1994): 111–113.

4. Jean-Luc Marion, *Being Given: Toward a Phenomenology of Givenness*, trans. Jeffrey L. Kosky (Stanford: Stanford University Press, 2002), 195. Translation slightly modified.

5. Ibid.

6. See Marion's trilogy on the theme of givenness: *Reduction and Givenness: Investigations of Husserl, Heidegger, and Phenomenology*, trans. Thomas A. Carlson (Evanston, Ill.: Northwestern University Press, 1998); *Being Given*; and *In Excess: Studies of Saturated Phenomena*, trans. Robyn Horner and Vincent Berraud (New York: Fordham University Press, 2002). The latter elaborates in particular on the four privileged types of the saturated phenomenon that inform this chapter. These four types were already described in *Being Given* (228–233) and are partially based on the phenomenologies of idol and icon discussed in *God Without Being: Hors-Texte*, trans. Thomas A. Carlson (Chicago: University of Chicago Press, 1991), 7–24.

7. Marion, *In Excess*, 31.

8. This is connected to the power of the gaze (thought as the witness or gifted [*adonné*] rather than a constituting onlooker) to resist what is being given. Depending on such resistance, the given becomes visible, and hence the *adonné* itself too, according to Marion, who represents the resistance of the *adonné* as a screen on which the given is splattered. Marion, *In Excess*, 34.

9. Ibid., 31.

10. I understand the term region to refer to Marion's notion of "a regional phenomenality—that of the given phenomenon" (Marion, *Being Given*, 179) and to the distribution, in turn, of this phenomenality in the areas of the poor, the common, and the saturated phenomena; see also 221ff: "Topics of the Phenomenon."

11. Marion, *In Excess*, 34.

12. Marion, *Being Given*, book III (§13–17); Immanuel Kant, *Critique of Pure Reason*, trans. Werner S. Pluhar (Indianapolis: Hackett, 1996), A163 and B204.

13. The example refers to Husserl's famous analysis of appresentation. See Edmund Husserl, *Cartesian Meditations* (The Hague: Nijhoff, 1977), §50. See also Marion, *In Excess*, 62ff and 105, and the related analysis in Marion, *Being Given*, 199–202.

14. Marion, *In Excess*, 35.

15. Ibid, 36; Marion, *Being Given*, 170–173.

16. Ibid., 171.

17. Ibid., 172.

18. Marion, *In Excess*, 41–44.

19. Ibid., 41–42.

20. Ibid., 43.

21. Ibid., 43.

22. Ibid., 43–44.

23. Ibid., 44. Marion emphasizes that, because of this, the origin is not absent because of a lack (in Derridean terms) but because of excess: it does not so much present itself to me but emphatically gives itself, in such abundance that I can never recover from this gift. The process of signification is, in the end, not sealed by me or any other, according to Marion, but by God in the Last Judgment. Only then will the eventual significance of my life be revealed (123). On the terminology and

the role of givenness in the case of saturation with intention, see *Being Given*, 362 n. 37.

24. Marion, *Being Given*, 185–89.

25. Ibid., 186. The quotation refers to Edmund Husserl, *Ideas Pertaining to a Pure Phenomenology and to a Phenomenological Philosophy* (The Hague: Nijhoff, 2004), I, §63.

26. Marion, *Being Given*, 188.

27. Ibid., 199; Marion, *In Excess*, 122.

28. In *Being Given*, the event has a twin function: it is a general definition of the phenomenon in its temporality, and as such a model for the four different types; but it is also the privileged type of saturated phenomenon in terms of the type of quantity (§17 and §23).

29. Ibid., §21–23; Marion, *In Excess*, Chapters 2–5. The type of the flesh (*la chair*) can be connected in the present context to the (auto-)affective ecstasy of the divine touch (cf. Lyotard's reading of Augustine) will guide the discussion on the (auto-)affectiveness of listening in Chapter 6.

30. Marion, *Being Given*, 228, 234.

31. Marion, *God Without Being*, Chapter 1. The idol is not robbed of its religious value and significance, but merely juxtaposed to another and superior possibility. After all, the idol remains "a certain low-water mark of the divine" (14).

32. Marion, *Being Given*, 235. The second requirement follows from Marion's belief that phenomenology cannot (and should not) address factual and concrete revelations. It should be concerned only with the *possibility* of revelation, in which Marion prefers to maintain the distinction between revelation and Revelation. Ibid., 367 n. 90.

33. Ibid., 235.

34. Amply illustrated with quotations, Marion's analysis can be found in *Being Given*, 236–241. Only the main points are rendered in the present text.

35. Ibid. 238–239.

36. Ibid., 244. See also Hans Urs von Balthasar, *The Glory of the Lord: A Theological Aesthetics* (San Francisco: Ignatius Press, 1982), 1:465.

37. Marion, *Being Given*, 215.

38. Ibid.

39. Ibid., 216.

40. Ibid.

41. See Chapter 3.

42. In Chapter 6 this element, which is connected in Marion's thinking to the idea of the flesh (*la chair*), will be discussed more elaborately.

43. Marion, *Being Given*, 152. As we have seen, Marion refers to the appearance of sound before its synthesis and signification, as for example a chord in a rhythmic pattern.

44. Ibid., 131.

45. Ibid., 123.

46. Ibid., 124.

47. Ibid., 350 n. 6. For further comments on Marion and Reznikoff, see my "On Preferring Mozart," *Bijdragen: International Journal in Philosophy and Theology* 65, no. 1 (2004): 97–110.

48. Marion, *Being Given*, 350 n. 5.

49. The philosophical snakes in the grass are deliberately overlooked here, as the notion of anamorphosis mainly serves to prepare the ground for the descriptions of idol and icon that will be considered more laterally for their significance for the analysis of music.

50. Marion, *God Without Being*, 115ff; Marion, *In Excess*, 60–61.

51. Marion, *In Excess*, 63; Marion, *God Without Being*, 9–17.

52. See the preceding section and Husserl, *Cartesian Meditations*, §50.

53. Marion, *In Excess*, 63.

54. Ibid., 68. The quote refers to *Phaidros* 250d, in *Plato: The Collected Dialogues*, ed. E. Hamilton and H. Cairns (Princeton: Princeton University Press, 1996).

55. Marion, *Being Given*, 203.

56. See Plato's allegory of the cave, *Republic* 515c and 517a.

57. Marion, *Being Given*, 230.

58. Marion, *God Without Being*, 203.

59. Ibid., 10.

60. Marion, *In Excess*, 73.

61. See Messiaen's descriptions of color chords quoted in Chapter 2.

62. Olivier Messiaen, *Music and Color: Conversations with Claude Samuel* (Portland, Ore.: Amadeus Press, 1994), 44, 46. It is interesting to note that the solipsistic nature of the experience of dazzlement in Messiaen closely resembles the experience of looking at the saturating paintings of, for instance, Barnett Newman. It could be argued that what Messiaen presents as a "medieval" sense experience (cathedrals, stained glass, and Thomistic sensibility) is in fact a radical reinterpretation of the modernist-formalist "pure" sense experience as a religious experience *in music*.

63. Marion, *In Excess*, 74.

64. Simon Shaw-Miller, *Visible Deeds of Music: Art and Music from Wagner to Cage* (New Haven: Yale University Press, 2002), 158.

65. On the relations between spectral music and the art of Monet and Seurat, see Claudy Malherbe, "Seeing Light as Color; Hearing Sound as Timbre," *Contemporary Music Review* 19, no. 3 (2000): 15–27.

66. Jonathan Harvey, *In Quest of Spirit: Thoughts on Music* (Berkeley: University of California Press, 1999), 42.

67. Yvonne Loriod-Messiaen, "Etude sur l'oeuvre pianistique d'Olivier Messiaen," in Cathérine Massip, ed., *Portrait(s) d'Olivier Messiaen* (Paris: Bibliothèque Nationale de France, 1996), 119; see also Olivier Messiaen, *The Technique of My Musical Language* (Paris: Leduc, 1956), vol. 1, Chapter 14.

68. *Olivier Messiaen: The Music of Faith* (1986), dir. Alan Benson (Princeton: Films for the Humanities & Sciences, 2004). This creed was voiced in more than one place. See for instance *Lecture at Notre-Dame*, 10, and Rössler, *Contributions*, 115.

69. The source for this view appears to be in Jean Marnold's article in *Bulletin de l'Institut Général Psychologique* 2 (1908): 132–133.

70. In the overtone series (starting from the tone *c*) the equal-tempered tritone (600 cents, F-sharp) first appears relative to the fundamental at partial number 11. This partial is an approximation (3 octaves and 551 cents above the fundamental), which can be raised by a skilled trumpet player to a pure F-sharp. In order to legitimate his use of the equal-tempered tritone both as a melodic interval and as a harmonic *ajoutée*, Messiaen refers to this untempered distance C to F-sharp in his *Technique of My Musical Language*, 1:31 and 47; 2: examples 70 and 186). For a slightly better approximation, one would need to climb higher up the overtone series: partial number 23, for instance, is 4 octaves and 628 cents above the fundamental. See Guy Oldham, Murray Campbell, C. Greated, "Harmonics," *Grove Music Online*, www.grovemusic.com.

71. As, for instance, in *Couleurs de la Cité céleste* (Paris: Leduc, 1966). See Harry Halbreich, *Olivier Messiaen* (Paris: Fayard/Fondation Sacem, 1980), 122.

72. Messiaen, *Technique of My Musical Language*, vol. 1, Chapter 14.

73. A crushing aural sensation may be caused by listening to a live performance of *Et exspecto resurrectionem mortuorum*, part 3 (the different crescendos on the tam-tam).

74. Aloyse Michaely, *Die Musik Olivier Messiaens: Untersuchungen zum Gesamt-schaffen* (Hamburg: Karl Dieter Wagner, 1988), 102–106.

75. Harvey, *In Quest of Spirit*, 39.

76. Jonathan Harvey, "The Mirror of Ambiguity," in Simon Emmerson, ed., *The Language of Electroacoustic Music* (London: Macmillan, 1986), 179.

77. Ibid., 178.

78. Ibid., 179.

79. Ibid., 180.

80. Ibid., 181. The bells sounding in *Mortuos Plango, Vivos Voco* for 8-track tape (1980), his first Ircam work, provide another example. The dying sounds seem to represent the gradual withdrawal of the rich spectrum of sounding bells into the fundamental, which Harvey relates to the spiritual notion of turning inward. This would explain the sacrality of (church) bells in many cultures.

81. Ibid., 186–187.

82. Kimmo Korhonen, liner notes to *Meet the Composer: Kaija Saariaho* (2 CDs, Finlandia Records 3984 23407-2, 1999).

83. It follows from the critique on Harvey that it is neither sufficient to adhere to the representational view that the chorale is about "a homecoming into the miraculous," as it was put in the same chapter. The key argument here is that a shift is necessary from such representations and tropes (and the ontology on which they rest) to the structure of musico-religious phenomena.

84. Paul Griffiths, *Olivier Messiaen and the Music of Time* (London: Faber & Faber, 1985), 70.

85. This effect is even more conspicuous in the parallel passage in m. 63. My analysis refers, as before, to the live recording of *La Transfiguration* conducted by Reinbert de Leeuw on June 29, 1991 (CD, Montaigne, MO 782040, 1994).

86. A live experience of this music played on a large romantic organ such as la Cavaillé-Col is irreplaceable. A good approximation is in the recordings of the performance by Hans-Ola Ericsson for the Messiaen Festival (Paris, Eglise de la Trinité, March 8–April 12, 1995) (2 CDs, JADE 30295–2, 1995).

87. The description of the timbral spectacle of this music is hampered by the nature of timbre, which is, as Nancy observes, in a sense the *self* of music that resists the trap of a symbolic language, be it musical notation or words. In this respect it is different from other musical parameters. The analysis of timbre and, moreover, timbre in the non-parametrical sense, therefore remains (necessarily) tentative. Cf. Jean-Luc Nancy, "Être à l'écoute," in Peter Szendy, ed., *Écoute* (Paris: Ircam/L'Harmattan, 2000), 312.

88. Brigitte Massin, *Olivier Messiaen: Une poétique du merveilleux* (Aix-en-Provence: Alinéa, 1989), 170.

89. Balthasar, *The Glory of the Lord,* 1:38.

90. A second reference point would obviously be the intense, metaphysical lyricism that is often present in his music, despite its vertical, sectionalized surface. This aspect—Messiaen's metaphysics of the hypermelodic—will have to be analyzed elsewhere.

91. Messiaen, *Music and Color,* 56. The thought is tempting but dangerous. Christianity has unquestionably appropriated the bell, which was already in use in the prehistory of Christianity, but not without the introduction of a remarkable custom. It appears that in the early stages of Christianity, bells became to be baptized as if they were human (this included the full apparel of names, salt, and oil), which implies that their material shape and their resonance was received in the church. This controversial custom, which, it is said, Charles V prohibited in vain in 789, points in two different directions. On one hand, the bell clearly acquires a special status by becoming part of the body of the Church and partaking in the new life. On the other hand, the bell apparently has to be cleansed from "sinfulness" or from the influence of the satanic. This implies that the sound of the bell may be consecrated, but it is not blessed by itself, even though this is suggested by its unusual treatment in the early history of Christianity. For the music of Messiaen, which occasionally appears to *declare* its "bellness," this constitutes a perilous gesture that, however, may also offer some opportunities. For the theology of the church bell, see Satis N. Coleman, *Bells: Their History, Legends, Making, and Uses* (Westport, Conn.: Greenwood Press, 1971), 84–95.

92. Marion, *In Excess,* 75–81.

93. This is explicitly derived from Levinas. See also *In Excess,* 116–119, and Marion, *Being Given,* 232–233. Balthasar describes the same phenomenon as "flat" imageness. Hans Urs von Balthasar, *Epilogue,* trans. Edward T. Oakes (San Francisco: Ignatius Press, 2004), 62.

94. Marion, *In Excess,* 116–119.

95. Marion, *God Without Being,* 17–18.

96. See Plotinus, *The Enneads,* trans. Stephen MacKenna (London: Penguin, 1991), 442. Similar conversion is described here.

97. Marion, *In Excess*, 80–81.

98. At close consideration, the boundaries between the four types are rather hazy. It is especially difficult to distinguish the event and the icon from one another, because the characteristic reversal involved in anamorphosis, apparently narrowly associated with countenance, is a feature not only of the icon but also of the event, recurring to a certain extent into the chiastic dynamics of the flesh.

99. Marion, *In Excess*, 121–122.

100. Friedrich Schiller, *On the Aesthetic Education of Man* (Oxford: Clarendon Press, 1967), 155.

101. Balthasar, *Epilogue*, 61.

102. Hans Urs von Balthasar, *Die Entwicklung der musikalischen Idee: Versuch einer Synthese der Musik* (Einsiedeln, Switzerland: Johannes Verlag, 1998), 27.

103. Balthasar, *Epilogue*, 66.

104. Edward T. Cone, *The Composer's Voice* (Berkeley: University of California Press, 1974).

105. See Chapter 3.

106. Eduard Hanslick, *On the Musically Beautiful* (Indianapolis: Hackett, 1986), 32; Balthasar, *The Glory of the Lord*, 1:55.

107. Philippe Lacoue-Labarthe, *Typography* (Stanford: Stanford University Press, 1989), 139–207.

108. Messiaen asserts this in Rössler, *Contributions*, 77–78. Nonetheless, he "painted" sunrises and sunsets in his music, as is *Réveil des oiseaux* en *Catalogue d'oiseaux*.

109. This is the case with Lyotard and hypersynthetic/hyposynthetic music, as will be discussed in Chapter 5.

110. Eero Tarasti, *A Theory of Musical Semiotics* (Bloomington: Indiana University Press, 1994), 11 ff. The dissolution, in *Saint François d'Assise*, of the difference between representation and the represented suggested the label of "iconic opera" to Paul Griffiths; see Griffiths, "Saint François d'Assise," in Hill, *The Messiaen Companion*, 504–505.

111. John Tavener, *The Music of Silence: A Composer's Testament* (London: Faber & Faber, 1999), 126.

112. Ibid., 92–93. Modernism and formalism in art, as precisely an exoteric art for its own sake, form a case of idolatry.

113. Ibid., 113.

114. Ibid., 163, 114.

115. Ibid., 129.

116. Ibid., 31.

117. Ibid., 100.

118. It will not have escaped the reader that the "specifically Christian" as what (or who) is being tried to track down in this analysis of Messiaen's alleged Christian music remains an empty notion. The hunt for a specific location will be abandoned at the end of this chapter, so far as it is concerned with a certain quality in the musical phenomenon. In the final chapter, the role of listening will be further

dissected for the effect of dazzlement, as Messiaen called it, in a continuation of the search for what here is dubbed the "specifically Christian" in music or musical experience.

119. Immanuel Kant, _Critique of Judgment_, trans. J. H. Bernard (Amherst, N.Y.: Prometheus, 2000), §§ 23 through 29.

120. See in particular Kiene Brillenburg Wurth, _Musically Sublime_ (New York: Fordham University Press, 2009) and Jan Christiaens, " 'Kunstreligion' en het Absolute in de muziek: Olivier Messiaen's tijdsmetafysica (1949–1951) en het ontstaan van het serialisme (Karlheinz Stockhausen, Karel Goeyvaerts)" (PhD dissertation, Katholieke Universiteit Leuven, 2003).

121. Gerardus van der Leeuw, _Sacred and Profane Beauty: The Holy in Art_ (New York: Holt, Rinehart and Winston, 1963), 231

122. The phallic connotations of "swelling" direct the path toward an analysis of the erotic nature of this music in particular and of music in general. Certain elements hereof will turn up in Chapter 5.

123. Van der Leeuw, _Sacred and Profane Beauty_, 232.

124. See Brillenburg Wurth, _Musically Sublime_. An additional remark about the sublime in Messiaen: it appears from his discourse on breakthrough and dazzlement in _Conférence de Notre-Dame_ that it is not just about a dazzling intensity of experience (the dynamic sublime in Kant) but also about the overwhelming multiplicity of "intentions" and "details."

125. Rudolf Otto, _The Idea of the Holy: An Inquiry Into the Non-rational Factor in the Idea of the Divine and its Relation to the Rational_, trans. John W. Harvey (New York: Oxford University Press, 1958), 5.

126. For examples in Messiaen, see respectively _Des canyons aux étoiles . . ._ (Paris: Leduc, 1989), Part 5; _Apparition de l'Eglise éternelle_ (Paris: Lemoins, 1934); The Holy Spirit in _Messe de la Pentecôte_ (Paris: Leduc, 1951), Part 5; and _Livre d'orgue_ (Paris: Leduc, 1953), Part 5.

127. For example, _Éclairs sur l'Au-delà . . ._ (Paris: Leduc, 1998), Part 3.

128. Otto, _The Idea of the Holy_, 44–45.

129. Ibid., 41, 44. Translation modified.

130. Balthasar, _Herrlichkeit_, 3:817ff, 848–972.

131. Reinhard Hoeps, _Das Gefühl des Erhabenen und die Herrlichkeit Gottes: Studien zur Beziehung von philosophischer und theologischer Aesthetik_ (Würzburg: Echter Verlag, 1989), 230.

132. Ibid., 231–232.

133. Ibid., 231.

134. Ibid., 233.

135. This can be taken to counter Clayton Crockett's view that Balthasar subjects the sublime's negativity to the positiveness of beauty. Clayton Crockett, _A Theology of the Sublime_ (New York: Routledge, 2001), 32.

136. Frederick Christian Bauerschmidt, "The Theological Sublime," in John Milbank, Catherine Pickstock, and Graham Ward, eds., _Radical Orthodoxy: A New Theology_ (New York: Routledge, 1999), 208.

137. Cf. Balthasar, *The Glory of the Lord*, 1:528. The notion of the Christ-form is derived from Gal 4:19.

138. Bauerschmidt, "The Theological Sublime," 209. Bauerschmidt criticizes Balthasar's interpretation of this conventional theological notion in a footnote, but this discussion has no further relevance here.

139. Balthasar, *The Glory of the Lord*, 1:441.

140. Hoeps, *Das Gefühl des Erhabenen und die Herrlichkeit Gottes*, 229–230.

141. Ibid., 251.

142. Marion, *Being Given*, 220.

143. Ibid. Marion's reading of Kant (*Critique of Judgment*, §27) appears to be based, in this respect, on a brief passage in the analysis of the sublime. Elsewhere, as is affirmed by Marion, the experience is governed by the primacy of the ego.

144. The distinction between idol and icon is somewhat sharpened in order to introduce an alternative to the theories of religion in art (*Kunstreligion*).

145. Daniel K. L. Chua, *Absolute Music and the Construction of Meaning* (Cambridge: Cambridge University Press, 1999), 188.

146. T. W. Adorno, "Sacred Fragment: Schoenberg's *Moses und Aron*," in *Quasi una Fantasia: Essays on Modern Music* (New York: Verso, 2002), 242.

147. Philippe Lacoue-Labarthe, *Musica Ficta: Figures of Wagner*, trans. Felicia McCarren (Stanford: Stanford University Press, 1994), 140.

148. Chua, *Absolute Music and the Construction of Meaning*, 189–190. Carl Dahlhaus offers a religious explanation for these dialectics. Such "vacillation between enthusiasm and depression" testifies to the influence of pietism with an "almost manic alternation between trusting faith [*Glaubenszuversicht*] and despairing faith [*Glaubensverzweiflung*]." Dahlhaus, *The Idea of Absolute Music*, trans. Roger Lustig (Chicago: University of Chicago Press, 1989), 91. See also Wilhelm Seidel, "Absolute Musik und Kunstreligion um 1800," in Helga de la Motte-Haber, ed., *Musik und Religion*, 2nd ed. (Laaber, Germany: Laaber, 2003), 146.

149. The apparently simple distinction, in Messiaen's work, between superficial forms of sublimity (*Apparition*) and more transparent forms of glory (*Transfiguration* VIII) should be treated with distrust. The auditive impression of the diaphanous does not guarantee any truthful moment of conversion in which the auditive phenomenon's alterity speaks and sounds. The phenomenology of the idol purported by Marion tells us rather disconcertingly that we can experience "breakthrough" where there is only (according to what criteria?) a case of a reflective idolic moment. Such a fixation is no external threat to the icon, but, according to the logics of iterability, is a precondition for the possibility of iconicity.

150. The question echoes the perhaps most essential question for the Christian believer, namely, how the return of Christ is to be distinguished from the apparition of his double, the feared Antichrist (2 Th 2:5–12). The musical implications of Paul's answer to this question ("they all might be damned who believed not the truth," ibid.) will be discussed in Chapter 6.

## 5. The Technics of Breakthrough

1. Olivier Messiaen, *Conférence de Kyoto* (Paris: Leduc, 1988), 1.

2. Paul Griffiths, *Olivier Messiaen and the Music of Time* (London: Faber & Faber, 1985), 50.

3. Olivier Messiaen, *The Technique of My Musical Language* (Paris: Leduc, 1956), 1:7–8.

4. Almut Rössler, *Contributions to the Spiritual World of Olivier Messiaen* (Duisburg, Germany: Gilles & Francke, 1986), 93.

5. Hanslick speaks in terms of the "construction" and "invention" of music, the perception of which should always include "the ideal content," that is, the musical idea that always already is form. A later, twentieth-century development is to disengage the technical aspect, which is characteristic for the analytical formalism Messiaen was influenced by. Eduard Hanslick, *On the Musically Beautiful* (Indianapolis: Hackett, 1986), 36, 47.

6. Griffiths, *The Music of Time*, 212.

7. Ibid., 50.

8. Ibid., 51.

9. Ibid.

10. That is, by making an appearance or bestowing grace on the listener and granting him or her a glimpse of heaven. See Hans Urs von Balthasar, *The Glory of the Lord: A Theological Aesthetics* (San Francisco: Ignatius Press, 1982), 1:418.

11. Griffiths, *The Music of Time*, 51.

12. See Paul Ricoeur, *Time and Narrative*, trans. Kathleen Blamey and David Pellauer (Chicago: University of Chicago Press, 1990), 3:12–22.

13. Bernard Stiegler, *Technics and Time, I: The Fault of Epimetheus* (Stanford: Stanford University Press, 1998), 210.

14. Jacques Derrida and Bernard Stiegler, *Echographies of Television: Filmed Interviews* (Cambridge: Polity Press, 2002), 41.

15. Chris Doude van Troostwijk, "Phrasing God: Lyotard's Hidden Philosophy of Religion," in Peter Jonkers and Ruud Welten, eds., *God in France: Eight Contemporary French Thinkers on God* (Leuven: Peeters, 2005), 176. See also Lyotard: "The *anima* exists only as affected. . . . This soul is nothing but the awakening of an affectability, and this remains disaffected in the absence of a timbre, a color, a fragrance, in the absence of the sensible event that excites it. This soul does not affect itself, it is only affected by the other, from the outside. . . . The *anima* exists only as forced." Jean-François Lyotard, "Anima Minima," in *Postmodern Fables*, trans. Georges Van Den Abbeele (Minneapolis: University of Minnesota Press, 1997), 242.

16. Jean-François Lyotard, *The Confession of Augustine*, trans. Richard Beardsworth (Stanford: Stanford University Press, 2000), 3.

17. Lyotard, *The Confession of Augustine*, 53.

18. Ibid., 7.

19. Ibid., 49.

20. Ibid., 57.

21. Ibid., 35, 9.

22. Chris Doude van Troostwijk, "Augustinus aan Zee: Absolute Taal en Temporaliteit in Lyotard's Lezing van de *Belijdenissen*," in Jean-François Lyotard, *Augustinus' belijdenis* (Baarn, Netherlands: Kok Agora, 1999), 122–123.

23. Lyotard, *The Confession of Augustine*, 32.

24. Ibid., 3.

25. Ibid., 66–67.

26. Ibid., 67.

27. Doude van Troostwijk, "Augustinus aan Zee," 136.

28. Lyotard, *The Confession of Augustine*, 66.

29. Ibid., 65.

30. Ibid. This tone is perhaps a drone, as it seems to be both single and permanent (required for attuning "my tone").

31. Doude van Troostwijk, "Augustinus aan Zee," 134–135. In this reading, the musico-sacral or sacromusical is not located in the ideal (as, for instance, in Augustine's *De musica*, where it is the *numeri*) but in matter. Lyotard apparently turns Augustine's anthropology inside out. In book 9 and 10 of *De Trinitate*, Augustine divides man into three parts: *mens, animus,* and *anima.* Here, *anima* is ranked at the lowest level of the soul, similar to the "exterior being" of Paul (2 Cor 4:16). The encounter with God is not sought here but at the higher levels, especially in the *mens.* Mary T. Clark, "*De Trinitate*," in Eleonore Stump and Norman Kretzmann, eds., *The Cambridge Companion to Augustine* (Cambridge: Cambridge University Press, 2001), 97.

32. Lyotard, *The Confession of Augustine*, 86. Translation modified.

33. Jean-François Lyotard, "God and the Puppet," in *The Inhuman: Reflections on Time,* trans. Geoffrey Bennington and Rachel Bowlby (Cambridge: Polity Press, 1998), 153–164.

34. Lyotard, "God and the Puppet," 157.

35. Ibid., 153.

36. For clarity's sake: the dimension (dimensionless, except perhaps, as is suggested by Lyotard, in the sense of "*n*-dimensional") of the *anima* is related by Lyotard to the aesthetic. "Anima Minima," 243: "The aesthetic condition is enslavement to the *aistheton,* without which it is anaesthesia."

37. Lyotard, "God and the Puppet," 155.

38. Ibid., 156.

39. Lyotard, "Anima minima," 248.

40. Lyotard, "God and the Puppet," 158.

41. Cicero, for instance, posits that the great noise produced by the spheres has deafened us, but that we can learn to hear this noise again by means of music. "The dream of Scipio," *De re publica* VI:19.

42. An example of such music is, perhaps, in the integral serialism of the early 1950s.

43. Lyotard, "God and the Puppet," 161.

44. Ibid., 162.

45. Ibid., 164. This is reminiscent of certain liminal sounds with Luigi Nono.

46. In order to establish this connection, Lyotard creates a slightly mysterious *glissement* between two contrasting definitions of nuance. On one hand, nuance explodes any synthesis (156–157); on the other hand, this singularity is "condemned to resound and consound" (163). This paradox is not solved. Further, it should be noted that Lyotard's model of hyper- and hyposynthetical music follows more traditional descriptions of music (see Balthasar) as at once most inward (very close) and elusive (grand, strange, remote). However, Lyotard's atomistic view on music is radically different from hylomorphic *Gestalt*. According to the latter perspective, the *anima* cannot be touched by either a single sound wave or white noise, but only by the *Gestalt* of, most ideally, melody.

47. Lyotard, *The Confession of Augustine*, 55.

48. Jacques Derrida, "Of an Apocalyptic Tone Newly Adopted in Philosophy," in Harold Coward and Toby Foshay, eds., *Derrida and Negative Theology* (Albany: State University of New York Press, 1992), 52.

49. Lyotard, *The Confession of Augustine*, 22–25.

50. Ibid., 58: "With a touch, with a fragrance, with his cry, God perhaps (or the devil?) immerses the creature in his presence rather than prizing it therefrom. From the dazed look of daily life, his visit remains hardly discernable."

51. Ibid., 22.

52. Ibid., 86–87.

53. Ibid., 69.

54. Olivier Messiaen, *Lecture at Notre-Dame/Konferenz von Notre-Dame* (Paris: Leduc, 2001), 13.

55. The notion of singularity is differently inflected with Derrida than with Lyotard. Whereas the latter emphasizes the singular as event (syncope, affect, *anima*, etc.), Derrida stresses the "necessary possibility" of the repetition of the singular. Such iterability will be central to the remainder of this chapter and the final chapter as well. See Geoffrey Bennington, "Derrida en Lyotard: Verschillende singulariteiten," in Richard Brons and Harry Kunneman, eds., *Lyotard Lezen: Ethiek, onmenselijkheid en sensibiliteit* (Amsterdam: Boom, 1995), 158–174.

56. Jacques Derrida, "Faith and Knowledge: The Two Sources of 'Religion' at the Limits of Reason Alone," in *Acts of Religion*, ed. Gil Anidjar (New York: Routledge, 2002), 65–66.

57. Emmanuel Mesthene, paraphrased in Jay Newman, *Religion and Technology: A Study in the Philosophy of Culture* (Westport, Conn.: Praeger, 1997), 9.

58. J. Mark Thomas, in Newman, *Religion and Technology*, 14. The snake is an allusion to the biblical serpent implicated in the Fall of Man (Gen 3).

59. Newman, *Religion and Technology*, 110–111.

60. Derrida, "Faith and Knowledge," 100.

61. Hent de Vries, "Horror religiosus," in *Krisis: Tijdschrift voor Empirische Filosofie* 1, no. 4 (2000): 43.

62. See the Vatican website, www.vatican.va, for the rapid expansion in this domain.

63. Newman, *Religion and Technology*, 115–118. Derrida, "Faith and Knowledge," 62 n. 17.

64. In this context, Derrida also mentions the relation between "expropriative and "delocalizing" effects of "tele-technoscience" and the Jewish Diaspora ("Faith and Knowledge," 90–91). On the connections between religion and the media, see Hent de Vries and Samuel Weber, eds., *Religion and Media* (Stanford: Stanford University Press, 2001), especially the passages by de Vries on miracles and special effects, in his contribution "In Media Res: Global Religion, Public Spheres, and the Task of Contemporary Comparative Religious Studies," 23–29.

65. Derrida, "Faith and Knowledge," 79.

66. Jean-Luc Marion, *Being Given: Toward a Phenomenology of Givenness*, trans. Jeffrey L. Kosky (Stanford: Stanford University Press, 2002), 223.

67. Derrida, "Faith and Knowledge," 70, 82.

68. Ibid., 87; see also 82, 98.

69. Richard Taruskin, "Sacred Entertainments," *Cambridge Opera Journal* 15, no. 2 (2003): 109–126. See also Richard Taruskin, *The Oxford History of Western Music* (Oxford: Oxford University Press, 2005), 5:514–528.

70. Taruskin, "Sacred Entertainments," 114.

71. Ibid., 118.

72. Ibid., 119.

73. Ibid.

74. Augustine, *De musica*, in *The Immortality of the Soul*, trans. Robert Catesby Taliaferro (Washington, D.C.: Catholic University of America Press, 1947), Book I, iv, 8; and Book I, vi, 10–11.

75. Ibid., Book I, iv, 7–vi, 12.

76. Derrida, "Faith and Knowledge," 87.

77. Taruskin, "Sacred Entertainments," 118–119.

78. Griffiths, *The Music of Time*, 70.

79. Yvonne Loriod, in Peter Hill, ed., *The Messiaen Companion* (London: Faber & Faber, 1995), 301.

80. See Peter Hill and Nigel Simeone, *Messiaen* (New Haven: Yale University Press, 2005), 342, where reference is made to a toolbox containing color chords and birdsong, which Messiaen apparently used while composing.

81. See, for an analysis of the analogies between the music of Messiaen and the scholastic method, my essay on "The Reception of Aquinas in the music of Olivier Messiaen," in Paul van Geest, Harm Goris, and Carlo Leget, eds., *Aquinas as Authority* (Leuven: Peeters, 2002), 317–331.

82. Rössler, *Contributions*, 67–68.

83. Paul Griffiths, "Messiaen: 'Éclairs sur l'Au-delà,'" liner notes to Olivier Messiaen, *Éclairs sur l'Au-delà* . . . (Deutsche Grammophon CD 439 929–2, 1994).

84. Although Messiaen's music intends to be, in the insightful words of Paul Griffiths, a "Technique for the End of Time," technique with Messiaen is utopian

rather than eschatological. This distinction is introduced by Gabriel Vahanian to accentuate the difference between the kind of technology used to anticipate on the arrival of a new world, and that used to humanize (in the Christian sense) the present world. Gabriel Vahanian, "Religion and Technology," in T. William Hall, ed., *Introduction to the Study of Religion* (San Francisco: Harper & Row, 1978), 241–244.

85. Paul Griffiths, *Modern Music and After: Directions Since 1945* (Oxford: Oxford University Press, 1995), 229. Michael Stegemann speaks in the CD booklet of "a clear, if not transfigured transparance of colours, sounds, and forms." Michael Stegemann, "Die ersehnte Erkenntnis des Unsichtbaren," liner notes to Messiaen, *Éclairs sur l'Au-delà.* . . .

86. Derrida, "Faith and Knowledge," 87.

87. Ibid., 84.

88. Emmanuel Levinas, "The Temptation of Temptation," in *Nine Talmudic Readings*, trans. Annette Aronowicz (Bloomington: Indiana University Press, 1990), 33.

89. Levinas, "The Temptation of Temptation," 33–34.

90. Reginald McGinnis, *La Prostitution sacrée: Essai sur Baudelaire* (Paris: Belin, 1994), 14.

91. G. Guest, "Repetition," in Sylvain Auroux and Jacques Deschamps, eds., *Encyclopédie Philosophique Universelle* (Paris: Presses Universitaires de France, 1990), 2,233.

92. About the latter, see Aloyse Michaely, *Die Musik Olivier Messiaens: Untersuchungen zum Gesamtschaffen* (Hamburg: Karl Dieter Wagner, 1988), 623.

93. The idea of sudden breakthrough then regurgitates an old topos. See Peter Szendy, "L'invention de la surprise: Une conférence sur Haydn et Thomas Mann," in *Musica Practica: Arrangements et phonographies de Monteverdi à James Brown* (Paris: L'Harmattan, 1997), 93–143.

94. Olivier Messiaen, *Traité de rythme, de couleur, et d'ornithologie* (Paris: Leduc, 1994–2002), 1:9.

95. Ibid., 40–43.

96. Olivier Messiaen, *Music and Color: Conversations with Claude Samuel* (Portland, Ore.: Amadeus Press, 1994), 67.

97. Messiaen, *Traité de rythme*, 1:29, 39.

98. It is very much the question whether Messiaen's preference for symmetrical rhythms is exclusively based on the identity logics of symmetry, according to which the middle value of a symmetrical rhythm enjoys sovereign freedom as a symbol of divine transcendence. This leads to the radical immanence of metaphysics where time appears as flux-time, as Buci-Glucksmann calls it. See Christine Buci-Glucksmann, *Esthétique de l'éphémère* (Paris: Galilée, 2003), 29.

99. Messiaen, *Traité de rythme*, 1:42–43.

100. Theodor W. Adorno, *Aesthetic Theory*, trans. Robert Hullot-Kentor (London: Athlone Press, 1999), 219–222. See also Lyotard, "God and the Puppet," 154–155.

101. Augustine, *Confessions*, trans. R. S. Pine-Coffin (Harmondsworth: Penguin, 1961), Book XI.

102. Hent de Vries, *Philosophy and the Turn to Religion* (Baltimore: Johns Hopkins University Press, 1999), 195.

103. As in Paul Griffiths's admirable symbolic interpretation whereby the passage of part XII and its repetition constitute an E-major triad. A subsequent repetition, "perhaps to be imagined as taking place in heaven," would complete the triad. Griffiths, *The Music of Time*, 214.

104. Rokus de Groot, "Affirmation and Restraint: Relationships Between Concepts of Spirituality and Music in the Work of Joep Franssens and Daan Manneke," in *ASCA Brief: Privacies* (Amsterdam: ASCA Press, 2000), 123.

105. Ibid., 126.

106. Ibid.

107. Jean-Luc Nancy, "The Deconstruction of Christianity," in Hent de Vries and Samuel Weber, eds., *Religion and Media* (Stanford: Stanford University Press, 2001), 122–123.

108. Ibid., 123. Translation modified.

109. Ibid., 129–130.

110. See Chapter 2.

111. 2 Th 2:8–12. See also de Vries, *Turn to Religion*, 194.

112. Nancy, "The Deconstruction of Christianity," 119.

113. Ibid., 128.

114. Søren Kierkegaard, *The Sickness Unto Death: A Christian Psychological Exposition for Upbuilding and Awakening*, trans. Howard V. Hong and Edna H. Hong (Princeton: Princeton University Press, 1983), 71–74.

115. See the score (Paris: Leduc, 1990), Act III, seventh Tableau, "Les Stigmates," esp. 111.

116. Søren Kierkegaard, "Crop Rotation," in *Either/Or: A Fragment of Life*, trans. Alastair Hannay (London: Penguin, 1992), 231.

117. See the analysis of liturgical instances of repetition in Jeremy S. Begbie, *Theology, Music and Time* (Cambridge: Cambridge University Press, 2000), 155–175, which also emphasizes the imperative of complexity, interestingness, and a certain religious entertainment.

118. Kierkegaard, *Either/Or*, 75.

119. Kierkegaard, quoted in Edward F. Mooney, "*Repetition*: Getting the World Back," in *The Cambridge Companion to Kierkegaard*, ed. Alastair Hannay and Gordon D. Marino (Cambridge: Cambridge University Press, 1998), 298.

120. "Instead of a timeless universality that somehow condenses itself into particularity, you have a temporal and spatial process of repeating in which the repetition involves not simply the return of the same, but also alteration. What that produces is something which, since Kierkegaard, has more and more been called singularity. It is also somewhat different from the term 'individuality,' which suggests indivisibility and a self-contained quality. The term that Kierkegaard uses in Danish [*Gjentagelsen*] stresses separation, like a cut out. It is singular, and, in contemporary theory,

the notion of singularity is a way of trying to talk about this concretion, this non-absorption of the general in the particular." Samuel Weber, "Repetition: Kierkegaard, Artaud, Pollock and the Theatre of the Image," transcript of a discussion with Terry Smith (Power Institute of Fine Arts, University of Sydney, 1996), 16.

121. Søren Kierkegaard, *Fear and Trembling/Repetition*, trans. Howard V. Hong and Edna H. Hong (Princeton: Princeton University Press, 1983), 149.

122. Mooney compares it to the difference between rehearsing and listening to music: "To picture the contrast between repetition as a task and repetition as a reception, consider the difference between musicians *taking* a repeat (playing a section again with appropriate variation) and the attentive *hearing*, the 'reception,' of that repeat by an awakened audience. Individuals assume, or are placed in, both roles: they are both 'performers' and 'audience' in the music of creation and self development. But as one moves toward the religious or wondrous, one becomes less an actor than an alert receptor. The job of freedom is sustaining receptivity." That is to say, receptivity for God, with whom "all things are possible" (Mt 19:26). "*Repetition:* Getting the World Back," 294.

123. Søren Kierkegaard, *Philosophical Fragments*, trans. Howard V. Hong and Edna H. Hong (Princeton: Princeton University Press, 1987), 61.

124. Mt 19:26; Mk 10:27; 14:36. See also Kierkegaard, *Fear and Trembling*, 46.

125. "The music of Debussy is like water. Water is calm and does not move. When a pebble is thrown in, immediately there are . . . there is a shock and [then] there are waves which circle around that pebble and the water starts to move. And the music of Debussy is like that: there are interruptions and then all of a sudden it starts to move. That interruption has struck me" (La musique de Debussy est comme l'eau. L'eau elle est calme et ne bouge pas. Si vous jetez un caillou dedans, immédiatement il y a des . . . c'est un choc et il y a des ondes qui se tournent autour de ce caillou et l'eau se met a bouger. Et la musique de Debussy est comme ça: il y a des arrêts et puis tout à coup ça bouge. Cet arrêt m'a frappé). In *Olivier Messiaen: The Music of Faith* (1986), dir. Alan Benson (Princeton: Films for the Humanities & Sciences, 2004).

126. Weber, "Repetition," 17–18.

### 6. The Circumcision of the Ear

1. On terminology, see Garry Wills, *Saint Augustine* (New York: Penguin, 1999), xi–xx.

2. See also my "Forms of Love: Messiaen's Aesthetics of Éblouissement," in Robert Sholl, ed., *Messiaen Studies* (Cambridge: Cambridge University Press, 2007).

3. The notions of objective and subjective evidence structure the first part of Hans Urs von Balthasar's main work *The Glory of the Lord: A Theological Aesthetics*, vol. 1, *Seeing the Form* (Edinburgh: T&T Clark, 1989).

4. Olivier Messiaen, *Lecture at Notre-Dame/Konferenz von Notre-Dame* (Paris: Leduc, 2001), 15. Capitals in original.

5. Paul Griffiths, *Modern Music and After: Directions Since 1945* (Oxford: Oxford University Press, 1995), 276.

6. See Andrew Dell'Antonio, ed., *Beyond Structural Listening? Postmodern Modes of Hearing* (Berkeley: University of California Press, 2004).

7. In the comments of William L. Holladay, this passage is compared to circumcising the heart (Jer. 4:4): "If the heart is the seat of the will, the ear is the seat of obedience: the ear of the people is no longer suited for the hearing of Yahweh's word." *A Commentary on the Book of the Prophet Jeremiah Chapters 1–25* (Philadelphia: Fortress Press, 1986), 214.

8. Matthew Henry, *Commentary on the Whole Bible* (1706–1721), vol. 4, www.ccel.org. In this interpretation, "to will" and "to be able to" (the circumcision of the heart and of the ear, respectively) are closely connected: he who does not want to listen shall not be able to listen, either.

9. William McKane, in *A Critical and Exegetical Commentary on Jeremiah* (Edinburg: T&T Clark, 1986), 145. See also Ex 6:12–13.

10. Jacques Derrida, "Shibboleth: For Paul Celan," in *Sovereignties in Question: The Poetics of Paul Celan* (New York: Fordham University Press, 2005), 62–63.

11. Byung-Chul Han, "Derridas Ohr," *Musik & Aesthetik* 1, no. 4 (October 1997): 5–21. See also Jacques Derrida, "Tympan," in *Margins of Philosophy*, trans. Alan Bass (Chicago: University of Chicago Press, 1985), and Christy MacDonald, ed., *The Ear of the Other: Otobiography, Transference, Translation: Texts and Discussions with Jacques Derrida*, trans. Peggy Kamuf and Avital Ronell (Lincoln: University of Nebraska Press, 2006).

12. Plato, *Symposium* 176e, in E. Hamilton and H. Cairns, eds., *Plato: The Collected Dialogues* (Princeton: Princeton University Press, 1996); Han, "Derridas Ohr," 13, 15, 19.

13. Han, "Derridas Ohr," 11.

14. Ibid., 15.

15. Martin Heidegger, quoted in ibid., 14.

16. Peter Szendy, *Listen: A History of Our Ears* (New York: Fordham University Press, 2008), 119–126.

17. Szendy, *Listen*, 120. Italics in original.

18. Quoted in Peter Szendy, "La fabrique de l'oreille moderne: De Wagner à Schoenberg et au-delà," in Peter Szendy, ed., *Écoute* (Paris: L'Harmattan, 2000), 15.

19. Ibid., 19.

20. Theodor W. Adorno, "Types of Musical Conduct," in *Introduction to the Sociology of Music*, trans. E. B. Ashton (New York: Seabury Press, 1976), 5. Translation slightly modified.

21. See Rose Rosengard Subotnik, "Toward a Deconstruction of Structural Listening: A Critique of Schönberg, Adorno, and Stravinsky," in *Deconstructive Variations: Music and Reason in Western Society* (Minneapolis: University of Minnesota Press, 1996), 148–176.

22. Adorno, *Sociology of Music*, 4. Translation slightly modified.

23. Ibid., 3.

24. Ibid.

25. Szendy, *Listen,* 101–102.

26. Adorno, *Sociology of Music*, 17.

27. Pierre Boulez, in Frank Scheffer's documentary *Éclats* (Allegri Film, 1993).

28. He did recognize, by the way, the dangers of fetishizing and totalizing the structural notion of the musical work. But only because such an effect, which involves an extreme subjugation of musical sound material, hinders "the synthesis, the self-production of the work, which reveals the meaning of every Beethoven symphony." Fetishizing music is a phenomenon that he finds precisely with the "adequate" listener. Theodor W. Adorno, "On the Fetish-Character in Music and the Regression of Listening," in Richard Leppert, ed., *Essays on Music* (Berkeley: University of California Press, 2002), 301.

29. Søren Kierkegaard, *The Concept of Irony, with Constant Reference to Socrates*, trans. Lee M. Capel (Bloomington: Indiana University Press, 1971), 264.

30. This distance *is*, in a certain sense, the lack of sense. I will return to this idea in my discussion of Jean-Luc Marion's notion of *chair*.

31. See Camille Bellaigue, "Boredom in Music" (1888), in Harry Haskell, ed., *The Attentive Listener: Three Centuries of Music Criticism* (London: Faber & Faber, 1995), 184–188.

32. Peter Szendy describes under the revealing heading of "*Tout entendre*" the striving of Schoenberg (and his demand, Schoenberg speaks of a moral *duty*) to "hear everything" in a piece of music and to "make the work absolutely transparent to the ear." As I would suggest, this is about striving for a theological perspective in listening, in fact a perspective that in its totality transcends all perspectivity (that is to say, all finitude): the ear of God. See Szendy, "La fabrique de l'oreille moderne," 27–37; see also Szendy, *Listen*, 126–128. See, for the remaining closed of God's "standpoint" and the experience of *vanitas* it is related to, Jean-Luc Marion, *God Without Being: Hors-Texte*, trans. Thomas A. Carlson (Chicago: University of Chicago Press, 1991), 128–129.

33. Kierkegaard, *The Concept of Irony*, 296–297.

34. Ibid., 300: "the ironist [is] the eternal ego."

35. The notion of the demonic is inferred from the sense Kierkegaard attributes to it in *The Sickness Unto Death*: the doubting individual is self-imprisoned and refuses any external goodness. I am especially interested in the tropes of demonic imprisonment, circularity, intensification, totalization, and exclusion. Søren Kierkegaard, *The Sickness Unto Death: A Christian Psychological Exposition for Upbuilding and Awakening*, trans. Howard V. Hong and Edna H. Hong (Princeton: Princeton University Press, 1980), 67–74.

36. Jean-Luc Marion, *Being Given: Toward a Phenomenology of Givenness*, trans. Jeffrey L. Kosky (Stanford: Stanford University Press, 2002), 231–232; Marion, *In Excess: Studies of Saturated Phenomena* (New York: Fordham University Press, 2002), 82–103. For the implications for music of Marion's thought, see my "On Preferring Mozart," *Bijdragen: International Journal in Philosophy and Theology* 65, no. 1 (2004): 97–110.

37. Marion, *In Excess*, 100.

38. Ibid., 87. Emphasis added.

39. Marion, *Being Given*, 231. Although this fleshy unity of feeling and the felt appears to refer overtly to the concept of *chair* with Merleau-Ponty, Marion does not mention his name in this context, but refers to the work of Michel Henry and to Aristotle's *De anima*. See also Marion, *In Excess*, 87 n. 12.

40. Marion, *Being Given*, 231.

41. Ibid.

42. Marion, *In Excess*, 88.

43. Jean-François Lyotard, *The Confession of Augustine* (Stanford: Stanford University Press, 2000), 53.

44. Ibid., 51–56.

45. This reversed perspective creates an opportunity for interpreting spiritual listening as a listening that precedes any constitutive listening in the sense of Adorno, which is, really, a being-listened-to rather than listening in the strict sense. This reversal (or *conversio, anamorphosis*) is closely related to logic of the icon, prayer, and confession in Marion and Derrida.

46. Messiaen, *Lecture at Notre-Dame*, 15.

47. See my earlier "A Transfiguration of the Ear," in Jonneke Bekkenkamp, Sander van Maas, Desirée Majoor, and Markha Valenta, eds., *Missing Links: Arts, Religion and Reality* (Münster, Germany: LIT Verlag, 2000), 157–181.

48. Messiaen, *Lecture at Notre-Dame*, 16.

49. Karl Rahner, "Die geistliche Sinne nach Origenes," in *Schriften zur Theologie* (Zürich: Benziger Verlag, 1975), 12:112. See also Origen, *De oratore*, XIII, 4.

50. Mariette Canévet, "Sens spirituel," in M. Viller, Ferdinand Cavallera, and André Derville, eds., *Dictionnaire de spiritualité ascétique et mystique: Doctrine et histoire* (Paris: Beauchesne, 1990), 14:599. Origen supports his theory with reference to Prov 2:5 and Heb 5:4.

51. Rahner, "Die geistliche Sinne nach Origenes," 115 n. 26.

52. Canévet, "Sens spirituel," 600.

53. Rahner, "Die geistliche Sinne nach Origenes," 118.

54. It remains a question whether there is just a single spiritual sense or a set of five, as with the physical senses. The answer differs according to the author (see Canévet, "Sens Spirituel," 599–600). For Hans Urs von Balthasar it is a matter of principle; he maintains that the adherents of the single sense are too open to mysticism. He therefore prefers authors such as Evagrius Ponticus and pseudo-Macarius, who speak of five senses. See Balthasar, *The Glory of the Lord*, 1:370.

55. Balthasar, *The Glory of the Lord*, 1:367.

56. Ibid., 370–371.

57. Karl Rahner, "Die Lehre von den 'geistlichen Sinnen' im Mittelalter," in *Schriften zur Theologie*, 12:137–172.

58. Saint Bonaventure, "The Soul's Journey Into God," trans. Ewert Cousins, in *Bonaventure* (New York: Paulist Press, 1978), 89.

59. Augustine, *Confessions*, trans. R. S. Pine-Coffin (Harmondsworth: Penguin, 1961), 238–239.

60. Augustine, *De musica*, Book VI, Chapter 4.

61. Augustine, *Confessions*, 211–212. Emphasis added. The turn from music (exterior) to voice (interior) doubtlessly implies a turn from aesthetics to ethics as well, an aspect that will not be further considered here in order to concentrate on the *location*, in thought, of the revelation. Whether celestial music is revealed, or the voice, is less important in this case.

62. Serge Margel, "Un silence de bruit: Les confessions d'une sourde oreille," in Szendy, ed., *Écoute*, 249–251.

63. Augustine, *Confessions*, 81.

64. Burcht Pranger, "Come to Your Senses: Augustine's Conversion," unpublished conference paper, 1999. Among these passages are also those on music cited earlier, which revealed that the inward turn, as conceived by Augustine in *De musica*, of listening as a turning away from the physical-sensory and an opening up of the spiritual ear, is no matter that can easily be decided, and less so once and for all. This insight will guide my thoughts here.

65. Ibid. See also Burcht Pranger, "Time and Narrative in Augustine's *Confessions*," *Journal of Religion* 81, no. 3 (July 2001): 377–393.

66. Cited in Canévet, "Sens spirituel," 613.

67. See Balthasar, *The Glory of the Lord*, 1:24–25, 28–29.

68. My emphasis.

69. Samuel Taylor Coleridge, "Biographia Literaria," in M. H. Abrams, ed., *Norton Anthology of English Literature*, 5th ed. (New York: Norton, 1986), 397–398. This "suspension" later becomes "poetic faith."

70. Leonard Meyer includes "aesthetic belief" in his inventory of a "preparatory set" used by the listener for approaching a musical work of art. Leonard B. Meyer, *Emotion and Meaning in Music* (Chicago: University of Chicago Press, 1961), 73ff. See also Thomas Clifton, *Music as Heard: A Study in Applied Phenomenology* (New Haven: Yale University Press, 1983), 273–276.

71. See the order of experience that Messiaen describes in his *Lecture at Notre-Dame*, 15. First comes art, then dazzlement, then religious faith. This cascade of religious moments helps to understand why Plato may have had misgivings about the truthfulness of the resulting experience.

72. Messiaen speaks of transgression, but his reference to synesthetics might encourage a regressive interpretation. It is suggested by neuropsychological research that synesthesia is a widely spread phenomenon with the newly born and children under four. Synesthetic experiences at a later age are either interpreted as memories of earlier synesthetic perceptions or as the effect of incomplete development and a differentiation of cognition. The difference between transcendental synesthesia—Messiaen—and this regressive synesthesia is marked by faith, which foresees a transfiguration of cognition rather than a regression. I shall be concerned, therefore, with the relevant theological requirements of faith. See Daphne Maurer, "Neonatal Synaesthesia: Implications for the Processing of Speech and Faces [1993]," in Simon Baron-Cohen and John E. Harrison, eds., *Synaesthesia: Classic and Contemporary Readings* (Cambridge, Mass.: Blackwell, 1997), 224–242.

73. For Kierkegaard's notion of second immediacy in and through repetition, see his *Concluding Unscientific Postscript*, trans. Howard V. Hong and Edna H. Hong (Princeton: Princeton University Press, 1992), 111–117.

74. Paul Griffiths, *Olivier Messiaen and the Music of Time* (London: Faber & Faber, 1985), 102.

75. Paul Ricoeur, *The Symbolism of Evil*, trans. Emerson Buchanan (New York: Harper & Row, 1967), 351–352.

76. See Kierkegaard, *Fear and Trembling/Repetition*, 42ff. The leap of faith corresponds to the fideistic belief demanded by Ludwig Tieck of the listener, a parallel that underscores that orthodoxy and the (heterodox) religion of art are structurally entangled and can hardly be distinguished from one another, as here with Messiaen. Tieck, in Wilhelm Heinrich Wackenroder, *Werke und Briefe* (Munich: Carl Hanser, 1984), 349. For the romantic demand of musical faith, see Wilhelm Seidel, "Absolute Musik und Kunstreligion um 1800," in Helga de la Motte-Haber, ed., *Musik und Religion*, 2nd ed. (Laaber, Germany: Laaber, 2003), 145–151.

77. Kierkegaard, "Hypocrisy," in *Journals and Papers*, trans. Howard V. Hong and Edna H. Hong, Vol. I, A:1,379 (XI.2 A 280), in the Past Masters database, http://library.nlx.com. For the Kierkegaardian break between reflection and acting, see ibid., Vol. III L–R: 3,718 (X.1 A 66): "Nothing is more impossible and more self-contradictory than to act (infinitely—decisively) by virtue of reflection. He who claims to have done it merely indicates that he either has no reflection (for the reflection which does not have a counterpossibility for every possibility is not reflection, which is indeed a doubleness) or that he does not know what it is to act."

78. Immanuel Kant, *Critique of Judgment*, trans. Werner S. Pluhar (Indianapolis: Hackett, 1987), par. 16; Jacques Derrida, *The Truth in Painting* (Chicago: University of Chicago Press, 1987), 97.

79. Derrida, *The Truth in Painting*, 73. Emphasis in original: "de *ce qui* se déconstruit ici."

80. See Hans Urs von Balthasar, "Criteria," in *Elucidations* (San Francisco: Ignatius Press, 1998), 20–33.

81. Antoine Goléa, *Rencontres avec Olivier Messiaen* (Paris: Slatkine, 1984), 41. For further comments on this phrase, see my "Sacred Music in Theory," in Rokus de Groot and Albert van der Schoot, ed., *Redefining Musical Identities: Reorientations at the Waning of Modernism* (Rotterdam: ArtEZ Press/Veenman, 2007), 67–75.

*Epilogue: On Affirmation*

1. Christian Asplund, "A Body Without Organs: Three Approaches—Cage, Bach, and Messiaen," in *Perspectives of New Music* 35, no. 2 (Summer 1997): 184.

2. Gilles Deleuze and Félix Guattari, *A Thousand Plateaus: Capitalism and Schizophrenia*, trans. Brian Massumi (Minneapolis: University of Minnesota Press, 2002), 299. My emphasis.

3. Paul Griffiths, *Olivier Messiaen and the Music of Time* (London: Faber & Faber, 1985), 102.

4. Jean-Luc Nancy, *The Muses* (Stanford: Stanford University Press, 1996), 51.

5. Paul Moyaert, *Ethiek en Sublimatie: Over* De Ethiek van de Psychoanalyse *van Jacques Lacan* (Nijmegen: Sun, 1994), 53.

# Bibliography

Abrams, M. H., ed. *The Norton Anthology of English Literature.* 5th ed. New York: Norton, 1986.

Adorno, Theodor W. *Aesthetic Theory.* Trans. Robert Hullot-Kentor. London: Athlone Press, 1999.

———. *Essays on Music.* Ed. Richard Leppert. Berkeley: University of California Press, 2002.

———. *Introduction to the Sociology of Music.* Trans. E. B. Ashton. New York: Seabury Press, 1976.

———. *Quasi una Fantasia: Essays on Modern Music.* Trans. Roy Livingstone. London: Verso, 2002.

Antoine, Louis. *Lire François d'Assise: Essai sur sa spiritualité d'après ses écrits.* Paris: Éditions Franciscaines, 1967.

Asplund, Christian. "A Body Without Organs: Three Approaches—Cage, Bach, and Messiaen." *Perspectives of New Music* 35, no. 2 (Summer 1997): 171–187.

Augustine. *Confessions.* Trans. R. S. Pine-Coffin. London: Penguin, 1961.

———. *The Immortality of the Soul.* Trans. Robert Catesby Taliaferro. Washington, D.C.: Catholic University of America Press, 1947.

Auroux, Sylvain, and Jacques Deschamps, eds. *Encyclopédie Philosophique Universelle.* Paris: Presses Universitaires de France, 1989–98.

Balthasar, Hans Urs von. *Elucidations.* San Francisco: Ignatius Press, 1998.

———. *Die Entwicklung der musikalischen Idee/Bekenntnis zu Mozart.* Einsiedeln, Switzerland: Johannes Verlag, 1998.

———. *Epilogue.* San Francisco: Ignatius Press, 2004.

———. *The Glory of the Lord: A Theological Aesthetics.* 7 vols. San Francisco: Ignatius Press, 1982.

———. *New Elucidations.* Trans. Mary Theresilde Skerry. San Francisco: Ignatius Press, 1986.

———. *Truth Is Symphonic: Aspects of Christian Pluralism.* Trans. Graham Harrison. San Francisco: Ignatius Press, 1987.

Baron-Cohen, Simon, and John E. Harrison, *Synaesthesia: Classic and Contemporary Readings.* Cambridge, Mass.: Blackwell, 1997.

Barraud, Henry. "Olivier Messiaen: Compositeur mystique?" *Contrepoints* 1 (January 1946): 101–102.

Begbie, Jeremy S. *Theology, Music and Time*. Cambridge: Cambridge University Press, 2000.

Bekkenkamp, Jonneke, Sander van Maas, Desirée Majoor, and Markha Valenta, eds. *Missing Links: Arts, Religion and Reality*. Münster, Germany: LIT Verlag, 2000.

Bernard, Jonathan. "Messiaen's Synaesthesia: The Correspondence Between Color and Sound Structure in His Music." *Music Perception* 4, no. 1 (Fall 1986): 41–68.

Blackwell, Albert L. *The Sacred in Music*. Louisville, Ky.: Westminster John Knox Press, 1999.

Blond, Phillip, ed. *Post-Secular Philosophy: Between Philosophy and Theology*. New York: Routledge, 1998.

Boileau-Despréaux, Nicolas. *Oeuvres complètes*. Paris: Gallimard, 1966.

Bonaventure, Saint. *The Soul's Journey Into God/The Tree of Life/The Life of St. Francis*. Trans. Ewert Cousins. Mahwah, N.J.: Paulist Press, 1978.

Brillenburg Wurth, Kiene. *Musically Sublime*. New York: Fordham University Press, 2009.

Brons, Richard, and Harry Kunneman, eds. *Lyotard Lezen: Ethiek, onmenselijkheid en sensibiliteit*. Amsterdam: Boom, 1995.

Bruhn, Siglind, ed. *Messiaen's Language of Mystical Love*. New York: Garland, 1998.

Buci-Glucksmann, Christine. *Esthétique de l'éphémère*. Paris: Galilée, 2003.

Chadwick, Henry. *Tradition and Exploration: Collected Papers on Theology and the Church*. Norwich: Canterbury Press, 1994.

Charlton, David, ed. *E. T. A. Hoffmann's Musical Writings: Kreisleriana, The Poet and the Composer, Music Criticism*. Trans. Martyn Clarke. Cambridge: Cambridge University Press, 1989.

Christiaens, Jan. " 'Kunstreligion' en het Absolute in de muziek: Olivier Messiaen's tijdsmetafysica (1949–1951) en het ontstaan van het serialisme (Karlheinz Stockhausen, Karel Goeyvaerts)." PhD dissertation, Katholieke Universiteit Leuven, 2003.

Chua, Daniel K. L. *Absolute Music and the Construction of Meaning*. Cambridge: Cambridge University Press, 1999.

Clifton, Thomas. *Music as Heard: A Study in Applied Phenomenology*. New Haven: Yale University Press, 1983.

Coleman, Satis N. *Bells: Their History, Legends, Making, and Uses*. Westport, Conn.: Greenwood, 1971.

Cook, Nicholas. *Analysing Musical Multimedia*. Oxford: Clarendon Press, 1998.

Coward, Harold, and Toby Foshay, eds. *Derrida and Negative Theology*. Albany: State University of New York Press, 1992.

Crockett, Clayton. *A Theology of the Sublime*. New York: Routledge, 2001.

Dahlhaus, Carl. *The Idea of Absolute Music*. Trans. Roger Lustig. Chicago: University of Chicago Press, 1989.

Davenson, Henri. *Traité de la musique selon l'esprit de Saint Augustin*. Neuchatel: Éditions de la Baconnière, 1942; reprint 1944.

De la Motte-Haber, Helga, ed. *Musik und Religion*. Laaber, Germany: Laaber, 1995.

Dell'Antonio, Andrew, ed. *Beyond Structural Listening? Postmodern Modes of Hearing*. Berkeley: University of California Press, 2004.

Derrida, Jacques. *Acts of Religion*. Ed. Gil Anidjar. New York: Routledge, 2002.

———. *Sovereignties in Question: The Poetics of Paul Celan*. New York: Fordham University Press, 2005.

———. *The Truth in Painting*. Chicago: University of Chicago Press, 1987.

Derrida, Jacques, and Bernard Stiegler. *Echographies of Television: Filmed Interviews*. Cambridge: Polity Press, 2002.

Dorsch, T. S. *Classical Literary Criticism: Aristotle/Horace/Longinus*. London: Penguin, 1965.

Doude van Troostwijk, Chris. "Augustinus aan Zee: Absolute Taal en Temporaliteit in Lyotards Lezing van de *Belijdenissen*." In Jean-François Lyotard, *Augustinus' belijdenis*, 101–138. Baarn, Netherlands: Kok Agora, 1999.

Dufrenne, Mikel. *The Phenomenology of Aesthetic Experience*. Trans. Edward Casey. Evanston, Ill.: Northwestern University Press, 1973.

Emmerson, Simon, ed. *The Language of Electroacoustic Music*. London: Macmillan, 1986.

Finscher, Ludwig, ed. *Die Musik in Geschichte und Gegenwart: Allgemeine Enzyklopädie der Musik*. Kassel: Bärenreiter, 1994.

Goehr, Alexander. *Finding the Key: Selected Writings of Alexander Goehr*. London: Faber & Faber, 1998.

Goehr, Lydia. *The Imaginary Museum of Musical Works*. Oxford: Clarendon Press, 1997.

Goléa, Antoine. *Rencontres avec Olivier Messiaen*. Paris: Slatkine, 1984.

*Graduale Triplex*. Solesmes, France: Abbaye Saint-Pierre de Solesmes & Desclée, 1979.

Griffiths, Paul. "Messiaen: 'Éclairs sur l'au-delà.'" Liner notes to Olivier Messiaen, *Éclairs sur l'Au delà*. Deutsche Grammophon CD, 1994.

———. *Modern Music and After: Directions Since 1945*. Oxford: Oxford University Press, 1995.

———. *Olivier Messiaen and the Music of Time*. London: Faber & Faber, 1985.

Groot, Rokus de. "Affirmation and Restraint: Relationships Between Concepts of Spirituality and Music in the Work of Joep Franssens and Daan Manneke." In *ASCA Brief: Privacies*, 107–129. Amsterdam: ASCA Press, 2000.

Groot, Rokus de, and Albert van der Schoot, eds. *Redefining Musical Identities: Reorientations at the Waning of Modernism*. Rotterdam: ArtEZ Press/Veenman, 2007.

Guerriero, Elio. *Hans Urs von Balthasar*. Paris: Desclée de Brouwer, 1993.

Halbreich, Harry. *Olivier Messiaen*. Paris: Fayard/Fondation Sacem, 1980.

Hall, T. William, ed. *Introduction to the Study of Religion*. San Francisco: Harper & Row, 1978.

Hamilton, E., and H. Cairns, eds. *Plato: The Collected Dialogues*. Princeton: Princeton University Press, 1996.

Han, Byung-Chul. "Derridas Ohr." *Musik & Aesthetik* 1, no. 4 (October 1997): 5–21.

Hannay, Alastair, and Gordon D. Marino. *The Cambridge Companion to Kierkegaard*. Cambridge: Cambridge University Press, 1998.

Hanslick, Eduard. *On the Musically Beautiful: A Contribution Towards the Revision of the Aesthetics of Music.* Trans. Geoffrey Payzant. Indianapolis: Hackett, 1986.

Harvey, Jonathan. *In Quest of Spirit: Thoughts on Music.* Berkeley: University of California Press, 1999.

Haskell, Harry, ed. *The Attentive Listener: Three Centuries of Music Criticism.* London: Faber & Faber, 1995.

Hegel, G. W. F. *Lectures on Fine Art*, vol. 2. Trans. T. M. Knox. Oxford: Clarendon Press, 1988.

Heidegger, Martin. *Pathmarks.* Cambridge: Cambridge University Press, 1998.

Hill, Peter, ed. *The Messiaen Companion.* London: Faber & Faber, 1995.

Hill, Peter, and Nigel Simeone. *Messiaen.* New Haven: Yale University Press, 2005.

Hoeps, Reinhard. *Das Gefühl des Erhabenen und die Herrlichkeit Gottes: Studien zur Beziehung von philosophischer und theologischer Aesthetik.* Würzburg, Germany: Echter Verlag, 1989.

Holladay, William L. *A Commentary on the Book of the Prophet Jeremiah Chapters 1–25.* Philadelphia: Fortress Press, 1986.

Husserl, Edmund. *Cartesian Meditations.* The Hague: Nijhoff, 1977.

———. *Ideas Pertaining to a Pure Phenomenology and to a Phenomenological Philosophy.* The Hague: Nijhoff, 2004.

Ide, Pascal. *Être et mystère: La philosophie de Hans Urs von Balthasar.* Brussels: Culture et Vérité, 1995.

———. "Olivier Messiaen, musicien de la gloire de Dieu." *Communio* 19, no. 5 (September–October 1994): 94–117.

Irwin, Joyce, ed. *Sacred Sound: Music in Religious Thought and Practice.* Chico, Calif.: Scholars Press, 1983.

Jonkers, Peter, and Ruud Welten, eds. *God in France: Eight Contemporary French Thinkers on God.* Leuven: Peeters, 2005.

Kant, Immanuel. *Critique of Judgment.* Trans. Werner S. Pluhar. Indianapolis: Hackett, 1987.

———. *Critique of Pure Reason.* Trans. Werner S. Pluhar. Indianapolis: Hackett, 1996.

Kars, Jean-Rodolphe. "L'oeuvre de Messiaen et l'année liturgique." *La Maison-Dieu* 207 (1996): 95–129.

Kierkegaard, Søren. *The Concept of Irony, with Constant Reference to Socrates.* Trans. Lee M. Capel. Bloomington: Indiana University Press, 1971.

———. *Concluding Unscientific Postscript.* Trans. Howard V. Hong and Edna H. Hong. Princeton: Princeton University Press, 1992.

———. *Either/Or: A Fragment of Life.* Trans. Alastair Hannay. London: Penguin, 1992.

———. *Fear and Trembling/Repetition.* Trans. Howard V. Hong and Edna H. Hong. Princeton: Princeton University Press, 1983.

———. *Philosophical Fragments.* Trans. Howard V. Hong and Edna H. Hong. Princeton: Princeton University Press, 1987.

————. *The Sickness Unto Death: A Christian Psychological Exposition for Upbuilding and Awakening.* Trans. Howard V. Hong and Edna H. Hong. Princeton: Princeton University Press, 1983.

Kramer, Lawrence. *Music and Poetry: The Nineteenth Century and After.* Berkeley: University of California Press, 1984.

Lacoue-Labarthe, Philippe. *Musica Ficta: Figures of Wagner.* Stanford: Stanford University Press, 1994.

————. *Typography.* Stanford: Stanford University Press, 1989.

Lavignac, Albert, ed. *Encyclopédie de la musique et dictionnaire du conservatoire.* Paris: Delagrave, 1921.

Levinas, Emmanuel. *Nine Talmudic Readings.* Trans. Annette Aronowicz. Bloomington: Indiana University Press, 1990.

Lyotard, Jean-François. *The Confession of Augustine.* Trans. Richard Beardsworth. Stanford: Stanford University Press, 2000.

————. *The Inhuman: Reflections on Time.* Trans. Geoffrey Bennington and Rachel Bowlby. Cambridge: Polity Press, 1998.

————. *Postmodern Fables.* Trans. Georges van den Abbeele. Minneapolis: University of Minnesota Press, 1997.

Malherbe, Claudy. "Seeing Light as Color; Hearing Sound as Timbre." *Contemporary Music Review* 19, no. 3 (2000): 15–27.

Marion, Jean-Luc. *Being Given: Toward a Phenomenology of Givenness.* Trans. Jeffrey L. Kosky. Stanford: Stanford University Press, 2002.

————. *God Without Being: Hors-Texte.* Trans. Thomas A. Carlson. Chicago: University of Chicago Press, 1991.

————. *In Excess: Studies of Saturated Phenomena.* Trans. Robyn Horner and Vincent Berraud. New York: Fordham University Press, 2002.

Marnold, Jean. "Contribution to Discussion." *Bulletin de l'Institut Général Psychologique* 2 (1908): 132–133.

Massin, Brigitte. *Olivier Messiaen: Une poétique du merveilleux.* Aix-en-Provence: Alinéa, 1989.

Massip, Cathérine. *Portrait(s) d'Olivier Messiaen.* Paris: Bibliothèque Nationale de France, 1996.

McGinnis, Reginald. *La Prostitution sacrée: Essai sur Baudelaire.* Paris: Belin, 1994.

McGregor, Bede, and Thomas Norris, eds. *The Beauty of Christ: An Introduction to the Theology of Hans Urs von Balthasar.* Edinburgh: T&T Clark, 1994.

McKane, William. *A Critical and Exegetical Commentary on Jeremiah.* Edinburgh: T&T Clark, 1986.

McKinnon, James. *Music in Early Christian Literature.* Cambridge: Cambridge University Press, 1999.

Messiaen, Olivier. *Conférence de Kyoto.* Paris: Leduc, 1988.

————. *Lecture at Notre-Dame / Konferenz von Notre-Dame.* Paris: Leduc, 2001.

————. *Music and Color: Conversations with Claude Samuel.* Portland, Ore.: Amadeus Press, 1994.

————. "Reply to 'A Survey.'" *Contrepoints* 3 (March–April 1946): 73–75.

————. *Technique of My Musical Language*. 2 vols. Paris: Leduc, 1956.

————. *Traité de rythme, de couleur, et d'ornithologie*. 7 vols. Paris: Leduc, 1994–2002.

Meyer, Leonard B. *Emotion and Meaning in Music*. Chicago: University of Chicago Press, 1961.

Michaely, Aloyse. "L'Abîme: Das Bild des Abgrunds bei Olivier Messiaen." In *Musik-Konzepte* 28, 7–55. Munich: Edition text + kritik, 1982.

————. *Die Musik Olivier Messiaens: Untersuchungen zum Gesamtschaffen*. Hamburg: Karl Dieter Wagner, 1988.

Michel, Alain. "La Transfiguration et la Beauté: d'Olivier Messiaen à Urs von Balthasar." *La Recherche Artistique*, September–October 1978, 86–89.

Milbank, John, Catherine Pickstock, and Graham Ward, eds. *Radical Orthodoxy: A New Theology*. London: Routledge, 1999.

Nancy, Jean-Luc. *The Muses*. Stanford: Stanford University Press, 1996.

Neubauer, John. *The Emancipation of Music from Language: Departures from Mimesis in Eighteenth-Century Aesthetics*. New Haven: Yale University Press, 1986.

Newman, Jay. *Religion and Technology: A Study in the Philosophy of Culture*. Westport, Conn.: Praeger, 1997.

*Olivier Messiaen, homme de foi: Regard sur son oeuvre d'orgue*. Paris: Trinité Média Communication, 1995.

Otto, Rudolf. *The Idea of the Holy: An Inquiry Into the Non-rational Factor in the Idea of the Divine and Its Relation to the Rational*. Trans. John W. Harvey. New York: Oxford University Press, 1958.

Parra, J., et al. "Removal of Epileptogenic Sequences from Video Material: The Role of Color." *Neurology* 64, no. 5 (March 8, 2005): 787–791.

Plotinus, *Enneads*. Trans. Stephen MacKenna. London: Penguin, 1991.

Pöggeler, Otto, and Annemarie Gethmann-Siefert, eds. *Kunsterfahrung und Kulturpolitik im Berlin Hegels*. Bonn: Bouvier Verlag Herbert Grundmann, 1983.

Pranger, Burcht. "Come to Your Senses: Augustine's Conversion." Unpublished conference paper, 1999.

————. "Time and Narrative in Augustine's *Confessions*." *Journal of Religion* 81, no. 3 (July 2001): 377–393.

Rahner, Karl. *Schriften zur Theologie*. Zürich: Benziger Verlag, 1975.

Ricoeur, Paul. *The Symbolism of Evil*. Trans. Emerson Buchanan. New York: Harper & Row, 1967.

————. *Time and Narrative*, vol. 3. Trans. Kathleen Blamey and David Pellauer. Chicago: University of Chicago Press, 1990.

Robert, Paul, and Alain Rey, eds. *Le grand Robert de la langue française: Dictionnaire alphabétique et analogique de la langue française*. 2nd ed. Paris: Dictionnaires Le Robert, 1985.

Rössler, Almut. *Contributions to the Spiritual World of Olivier Messiaen*. Duisburg, Germany: Gilles & Francke, 1986.

*Saint François d'Assise*. L'Avant-scène opéra 4. Paris: Premières Loges, 1992.

Saint-Pierre, Mario. *Beauté, bonté, vérité chez Hans Urs von Balthasar*. Paris: Éditions du Cerf, 1998.

Sauvanet, Pierre. *Le rythme grec d'Héraclite à Aristote.* Paris: Presses Universitaires de France, 1999.

Schiller, Friedrich. *On the Aesthetic Education of Man.* Oxford: Clarendon Press, 1967.

Seidel, Hans, Israel Adler, Reinhard Flender, James McKinnon, and Gustav A. Krieg. "Musik und Religion." In Horst Balz et al., eds., *Theologische Realenzyklopädie,* 23:441–495. Berlin: Walter de Gruyter, 1994.

Seidel, Wilhelm. *Die Musik in Geschichte und Gegenwart.* Kassel, Germany: Bärenreiter, 1994.

Shaw-Miller, Simon. *Visible Deeds of Music: Art and Music from Wagner to Cage.* New Haven: Yale University Press, 2002.

Sholl, Robert, ed. *Messiaen Studies.* Cambridge: Cambridge University Press, 2007.

Söhngen, Oskar. *Theologie der Musik.* Kassel, Germany: Johannes Stauda Verlag, 1967.

Spencer, Jon Michael. *Theomusicology.* Durham, N.C.: Duke University Press, 1994.

Stegemann, Michael. "Die ersehnte Erkenntnis des Unsichtbaren." Liner notes to Olivier Messiaen, *Éclairs sur l'Au-delà. . . .* Deutsche Grammophon CD, 1994.

Stiegler, Bernard. *Technics and Time, I: The Fault of Epimetheus.* Stanford: Stanford University Press, 1998.

Stravinsky, Igor. *An Autobiography.* London: Calder and Boyars, 1975.

Stump, Eleonore, and Norman Kretzmann, eds. *The Cambridge Companion to Augustine.* Cambridge: Cambridge University Press, 2001.

Subotnik, Rose Rosengard. *Deconstructive Variations: Music and Reason in Western Society.* Minneapolis: University of Minnesota Press, 1996.

Szendy, Peter, ed. *Écoute.* Paris: Ircam/L'Harmattan, 2000.

———. *Listen: A History of Our Ears.* New York: Fordham University Press, 2008.

———. *Musica Practica: Arrangements et phonographies de Monteverdi à James Brown.* Paris: L'Harmattan, 1997.

Tarasti, Eero. *A Theory of Musical Semiotics.* Bloomington: Indiana University Press, 1994.

Taruskin, Richard. *The Oxford History of Western Music.* 6 vols. Oxford: Oxford University Press, 2005.

———. "Sacred Entertainments." *Cambridge Opera Journal* 15, no. 2 (2003): 109–126.

Tavener, John. *The Music of Silence: A Composer's Testament.* Ed. Brian Keeble. London: Faber & Faber, 1999.

Thomas Aquinas, Saint. *Summa Theologiae.* London: Blackfriars, 1964–80.

Van der Leeuw, Gerardus. *Sacred and Profane Beauty: The Holy in Art.* New York: Holt, Rinehart and Winston, 1963.

Van Geest, Paul, Harm Goris, and Carlo Leget, eds. *Aquinas as Authority.* Leuven: Peeters, 2002.

Van Maas, Sander. "On Preferring Mozart." *Bijdragen: International Journal in Philosophy and Theology* 65, no. 1 (2004): 97–110.

Viller, Marcel, Ferdinand Cavallera, and André Derville, eds. *Dictionnaire de spiritu-alité ascétique et mystique: Doctrine et histoire*. Paris: Beauchesne, 1990.

Vries, Hent de. "Horror religiosus." *Krisis: Tijdschrift voor Empirische Filosofie* 1, no. 4 (2000): 41–53.

———. *Philosophy and the Turn to Religion*. Baltimore: Johns Hopkins University Press, 1999.

Vries, Hent de, and Samuel Weber, eds. *Religion and Media*. Stanford: Stanford University Press, 2001.

Wackenroder, Wilhelm Heinrich. *Werke und Briefe*. Munich: Carl Hanser, 1984.

Wagner, Richard. *Religion and Art*. Trans. W. Ashton Ellis. Lincoln: University of Nebraska Press, 1994.

Weber, Samuel. "Repetition: Kierkegaard, Artaud, Pollock and the Theatre of the Image." Transcript of a discussion with Terry Smith, Power Institute of Fine Arts, University of Sydney, September 16, 1996.

Wills, Garry. *Saint Augustine*. New York: Penguin, 1999.


*Films*

*Éclats*. Dir. Frank Scheffer. Amsterdam: Allegri Film, 1993.

*Olivier Messiaen*. Dir. Cherry Duyns and Reinbert de Leeuw. The Hague: VPRO Television, 1994.

*Olivier Messiaen: The Music of Faith* (1986). Dir. Alan Benson. Princeton: Films for the Humanities & Sciences, 2004.


*Recordings*

Messiaen, Olivier. *Livre du Saint Sacrement*. Performed by Hans-Ola Ericsson. Éditions Jade, 1995.

———. *La Transfiguration de Notre Seigneur Jésus-Christ*. Cond. Reinbert de Leeuw. Montaigne Auvidis, 1994.

*Olivier Messiaen: Les couleurs du temps. Trente ans d'entretiens avec Claude Samuel*. Radio France, 2000.

Saariaho, Kaija. *Meet the Composer: Kaija Saariaho*. Finlandia Records, 1999.


*Musical Scores*

Messiaen, Olivier. *Apparition de l'Église éternelle*. Paris: Lemoine, 1934.

———. *Couleurs de la Cité céleste*. Paris: Leduc, 1966.

———. *Des canyons aux étoiles . . .* Paris: Leduc, 1989.

———. *Éclairs sur l'Au-delà. . . .* Paris: Leduc, 1998.

———. *Et exspecto resurrectionem mortuorum*. Paris: Leduc, 1966.

———. *Livre d'orgue*. Paris: Leduc, 1953.

———. *Méditations sur le Mystère de la Sainte Trinité*. Paris: Leduc, 1973.

————. *Messe de la Pentecôte*. Paris: Leduc, 1951.

————. *Saint François d'Assise: Scènes Franciscaines*. Paris: Leduc, 1990.

————. *La Transfiguration de Notre-Seigneur Jésus-Christ*. Paris: Leduc, 1972.

Stravinsky, Igor. *The Rite of Spring*. London: Boosey and Hawkes, 1947.